# Play as Engagement and Communication

## ONE WEEK LOAN

)

UNIVERSITY PRESS OF AMERICA,® INC.
Lanham • Boulder • New York • Toronto • Plymouth, UK

**Copyright © 2010 by**
**University Press of America,® Inc.**
4501 Forbes Boulevard
Suite 200
Lanham, Maryland 20706
UPA Acquisitions Department (301) 459-3366

Estover Road
Plymouth PL6 7PY
United Kingdom

Library of Congress Control Number: 2010920645
ISBN: 978-0-7618-5083-0 (paperback : alk. paper)
eISBN: 978-0-7618-5084-7

In memory of Eunice Gilbert, the aunt who knew all about play — from story-telling and magic cupboards to sandcastle building and British pantomimes

# Previous Titles in Play & Culture Studies

Series Editors:
**Stuart Reifel, Jaipaul L. Roopnarine, and James Johnson,**

# Contents

## III. TEACHER SUPPORT FOR PLAY IN EDUCATIONAL SETTINGS

## IV. REFLECTIONS ON THE NATURE OF PLAY

# Foreword

I am honored to write a brief foreword to this new volume of the *Play & Culture Studies* series, *Play as engagement and communication* edited by Eva E. Nwokah. This volume is the tenth in this series and the fourth volume under my series editorship. I have enjoyed this position very much. All the books in the series are wonderful contributions to the literature on play; the chapters in each book are stimulating and informative and reveal a panoply of topics attracting attention in the field of play research and scholarship.

As Brian Sutton-Smith noted in the preface to his masterful *The Ambiguities of Play,* it is hard to get at play directly and attempts to comprehend its complexity in all its fullness demand multiple disciplines. These disciplines bring along with them different subject matter, methods, theories, and jargon, or in Brian's words, "rhetorical baggage". The Association for the Study of Play (TASP), founded in 1974, is a multi-disciplinary group of academicians and independent intellectuals who accept this challenge. *Play & Culture Studies* is the main publication of TASP.

The mission of *Play & Culture Studies* and TASP is to further play scholarship. We aspire to contribute to making the 21st century 'The Play Century' when play manifestations, values, uses, and the science behind this, become more fully realized and understood. During the first decade of this century, play research, theory generation, and theory modification have been 'playing out' very well. We are off to a good start. But clearly we are far from being 'played out'. After all, fortunately, our focus and intellectual passion is centered on play—a phenomena of tremendous range and profound depth. We are confident our curiosity cannot ever be fully satisfied—and that our intellectual play, that the spirit of "Researcher The Player" will go on forever. Now let us play together and enjoy *Play as engagement and communication.*

Jim Johnson, Penn State
Play & Culture Studies, Series Editor

# Introduction

## Eva E. Nwokah

Children benefit from forming positive relationships with others including adults and animals and such contexts for play provide rich opportunities to expand on children's imaginative and symbolic thinking. Adults also benefit from many types of play and playful interactions. Most play is social or occurs in the presence of others. Key components of play may include sharing, physical exchanges, negotiation, and intellectual and creative collaboration through emotion, action, signs, gestures or words. This involves both engagement with another and communication through verbal or nonverbal means. This theme is the thread that links the chapters in this volume, through investigation and discussion on dyadic and group interaction that is multi-ethnic, cross-species, child-child, and adult-child in many different contexts and settings. This volume is multidisciplinary with authors from the fields of education, early childhood education, second language learning (ESL), child/human development and family studies, psychology, biology, and sociology.

Section 1, *Child Play with Adults and with Animals*, focuses on how children connect and communicate with non-peers, animals, and adults through the medium of play. In the first chapter *Michael Patte* reports on a participatory research project that examined the perceived therapeutic benefits of student interactions and play episodes on hospitalized children and their families. Results from the research project included that the undergraduate students found their interactions and play episodes to be beneficial to the hospitalized children and their family members and that undergraduate students believed that the experience better prepared them to work with children and families on a variety of levels in the future. The second chapter by *Gail Melson* recognizes the unique relationships that emerge from the human-animal connection and the depth of emotional engagement that often binds both species through vocal, gestural and intuitive channels of communication. She gives an in-depth review of the current knowledge and understanding of this topic that has impacted so many lives over the centuries. *Hui-Chin Hsu and Jihyun Sung* focus on dyadic interaction between mothers and infants. They present the results of a longitudinal study that analyzed different styles of mother-infant play, didactic (directing infant's attention towards an object) and social-oriented (directing infant's attention to the mother), and the relationship between their behaviors at infant age three months and six months.

Section 2, *The Complexities of Child-Child Play in Different Contexts*, covers several areas of research related to children's play with each other. Peer relationships provide a foundation for the use of language and action in the sharing of play experiences throughout the lifespan. *Rachana Karnik and Jonathan Tudge* used ethnographic observations to study preschool children's everyday activities including pretend play. They found that children engaged in pretend play in more than half of their observations and that the types of play varied by ethnicity, social class, and gender. *Sandra Chang-Kredl and Nina Howe* also examine pretend play and report on an investigation of verbal and physical communication in children playing with popular media-based character toys compared to generic toys and the differences in the quality of play impacted by toy type. Cognitive aspects of play between children and their impact on engagement are explored in the next two papers. *Robyn Holmes* investigated emotions related to the experience of cheating during peer play in game playing, whether this was their own cheating behavior or a response to cheating by others. She contrasts the differences in reported responses between preschool and kindergarten children and also exposes possible conflict in children between the desire to win at games and the need for peer friendships. Understanding and responding to others also is the theme of *Hui-Chin Hsu and Patricia Janes*'s chapter. They apply the concept of Theory of Mind (understanding the minds/perspectives of others) to the context of pretend play. They examine the relationship between of two aspects of pretend play, enactment and meta-play, in dyads who are matched and mismatched in their Theory of Mind abilities.

Section 3, *Teacher Support for Play in Educational Settings*, consists of two papers that explore concepts of play in educational settings. *Michelle Tannock* reviews the literature on rough and tumble play and the range of current views by educators on this type of play. She provides ideas for both play assessment and the promotion of change in negative perspectives by early childhood personnel. *Mira Berkley and Kate Mahoney* describe their observations of socio dramatic play in an early childhood setting and provide suggestions for ways that preschool staff could support such play opportunities.

In Section 4, *Reflections on the Nature of Play*, *Thomas Henricks* expands his previous work on play that provides in-depth sociological and philosophical perspectives on what we mean by the multi-dimensional concept of play and its application in many contexts. He presents four types of play as manipulation, rebellion, dialogue, and exploration and discusses how these are dynamically linked to the different patterns of relationship in various play situations involving the player, objects and other persons.

As shown by the range of contributions in this volume, play is a dynamic and complex phenomena that is an integral part of life experiences. How play helps us connect and communicate with others and our surroundings remains an interdisciplinary field open to continued insights and discoveries.

The work of editing this volume would not have been possible without the extensive efforts of two assistant editors, Joanne Naylor, M.S., East Carolina University and Alycia Fulton, B.S. University of North Carolina at Greensboro. All the reviewers who agreed to provide blind reviews for the numerous submissions also are thanked for their thoughtful and timely contributions and assistance. Finally, the support and work of the series editor, Jim Johnson, is enthusiastically acknowledged and appreciated.

## BIBLIOGRAPHY

Baptiste, N. (1995). Adults need to play too. *Early Childhood Education Journal*, *23*(1), 33–35.

Brown, S. & Vaughan, C. (2009). *Play: How it shapes the brain, opens the imagination and invigorates the soul.* New York: Avery.

Ginsburg, K. (2007). The importance of play in promoting healthy child development and maintaining strong parent-child bonds. *Pediatrics, 119*(1), 182–191.

Pellegrini, A. D. & Smith, P. K. (2004). *The nature of play: Great apes and humans.* New York: The Guilford Press.

# Part I

# CHILD PLAY WITH ADULTS AND WITH ANIMALS

*Chapter One*

# The Therapeutic Benefits of Play for Hospitalized Children

## Michael Patte

The benefits of play in the lives of children are varied and well documented. For example, active, physical, and cognitively stimulating play has been shown to have a positive impact on brain growth and development (Zwillich, 2001); aerobic endurance, muscle strength, motor coordination, and attentiveness (Clements and Jarrett, 2000); and a wide range of social/emotional competencies including respect for rules, coping skills, self-discipline, leadership skills, aggression control, conflict resolution, and an appreciation for the culture and beliefs of others (Jarrett & Maxwell, 2000).

While these benefits are vital to the overall well-being of all children, they are especially important to the healing process of sick and hospitalized children. Health care professionals find that play provides a vital coping mechanism for sick children that allows them to deal with illness, hospitalization, procedures, surgery, and various treatments. Play also fosters self-expression which allows sick children to openly and freely express a full range of feelings. Such openness allows medical professionals to better understand a child's feelings and fears about a wide range of illnesses. Some common forms of therapeutic play to help children cope in hospitalized settings include:

- *Distraction Play*—which is based on the premise that the more young patients are absorbed in play and distracted from a medical procedure, the less their experience of pain.
- *Expressive Play*—enables young patients to express complex feelings associated with illness or hospitalization.
- *Developmental-Support Play*—supports normal childhood development that may otherwise be disrupted as a result of hospitalization and treatment.

Examples include peer group activities that allow the young patients to
learn social skills.
* *Medical Play*—prepares young patients mentally for painful or invasive
  procedures through familiarization of the medical equipment and process,
  and rehearsals of helpful coping behavior.

While attending the Association for the Study of Play's Annual Conference
in St. Catharines, Ontario, in the spring of 2006, I attended several sessions
dealing with medical play and the therapeutic benefits of play for hospitalized
children. These sessions served as a catalyst for developing an interest in the
field of Child Life and creating a relationship with a children's hospital in my
community. Through this relationship several child life specialists and I conceptualized a twenty hour field experience for undergraduate early childhood
students that blended the complimentary fields of play and Child Life.

One of the requirements in my undergraduate early childhood courses is
fieldwork. Students typically spend time in a variety of educational and community settings to learn about services and programs offered to children and
families. When a representative from the hospital came to class to describe
her experience as a child life specialist and about the possibility of playing
and interacting with hospitalized children, the undergraduate students expressed a high level of interest. In fact, 35 out of 37 undergraduate students
enrolled in my class requested the children's hospital as their first choice for
the fieldwork site.

As a result of these experiences, I conceptualized a student participatory
research project for 35 undergraduate early childhood education students to
carry out in a children's hospital located in Pennsylvania. The students spent
twenty hours during the fall 2006 semester interacting and playing with children and families admitted to the children's hospital. All students participating in the research project spent six hours training to be a volunteer at the
children's hospital under the guidance of a registered child life specialist. Part
of the training involved professional ethics and the importance of maintaining
strict confidentiality. Therefore, student participating in the research project
were considered to be official volunteers of the children's hospital.

Throughout the research project students kept a daily journal detaining (a)
the date and time of each visit, (b) a summary of the activities completed,
and (c) a reflective component addressing how the experience related to our
class reading and discussions. Students then used the data gleaned from the
experience to write a final report documenting the perceived benefits of their
interactions and play episodes on the overall well-being of the hospitalized
children and their families and describing how participating as a volunteer in
the children's hospital better prepared them to effectively work with children

and families in the future. The data from the student final reports are shared in this research article. Research questions guiding this project included:

1. What is the field of Child Life about and what opportunities does the child life specialist certification offer?
2. What are the perceived benefits associated with my interactions and play episodes to the overall well-being of hospitalized children and their families?
3. How has the volunteer field experience at the children's hospital better prepared me to work with children and families in the future?

Why is this information important? Information gleaned from this research project can provide undergraduate early childhood majors with additional career options in the form of Child Life Specialist certification through blending their interest in child growth and development with play. The additional certification would provide a wider menu of employment opportunities for students. Further, this research project may provide students with a greater level of compassion and empathy for the circumstances faced by hospitalized children and their families through prolonged exposure in an institutionalized setting. Such an outlook may transcend to relationships the students form with all of the children and families they encounter in their future career as a teacher or child life specialist.

## CHILD LIFE DEFINED

### Child Life Programs

Child life specialists alleviate stress and anxiety faced by many children in a variety of healthcare settings. Presently there are more than 400 Child Life programs found throughout the United States and Canada (Directory of Child Life Programs, 2003). Child Life services are offered in a variety of health care settings including hospitals, pediatric physician and dental offices, outpatient clinics, counseling clinics, and other environments including a pediatric population (Brown, 2001). Services offered through child life help children to cope with the psychosocial trauma often experienced during and after these experiences. Child Life programs may decrease the stress experienced by children and families and improve their abilities to cope effectively with traumatic situations. According to the American Academy of Pediatrics (2003) child life professionals espouse a philosophy of family centered care in health care facilities.

There are three components in the credentialing process of a child life specialist which include a minimum of a bachelor's degree in child life, child development, human development, or a related field; the fulfillment of a 480–600 hour child life internship under the supervision of a certified child life specialist; and a passing score on the standardized certification assessment. Theories of child development, play, stress and coping, family systems, developmental assessments, and collaborative teamwork abilities are the foundation for child life professional practice. In addition, child life specialists develop specializations complementary to the patients they serve such as infants, toddlers, elementary school age children, adolescence, critically ill children, etc.

Effective child life programs provide developmentally appropriate play, reassuring psychological preparation for various procedures, and assistance in the planning and rehearsing of coping skills (Thompson, 1989). Child life specialists serve as an integral part of a multidisciplinary and family-oriented model of care. Collaboration between the family, physicians, and other members of the health care team is essential in the development of a plan of care (American Academy of Pediatrics, 2003).

## The Role of Play

Due to its familiar and reassuring nature for children, play is the primary modality of a child life program. Research suggests that play can make traumatic experiences less frightening and more comfortable for children (Thompson, 1995). There are plenty of venues for play in child life programs including medical and surgical areas, clinics, emergency rooms, waiting areas, and sibling care centers. Play opportunities are differentiated for various developmental levels including socio-dramatic play for toddlers and games with rules for school age children and adolescents (Berk, 2004). Further, a variety of auxiliary programs like animal therapy, therapeutic clowning, music therapy and art therapy offer additional supportive activities spanning the gamut of ages of pediatric patients (Kaminski, Pellino, & Wish, 2002).

Medical play is a popular activity used by child life specialists to help children cope with their feelings. This type of active play allows children to gain control over their experiences and may offer insights into a variety of medical procedures (McGrath & Huff, 2001). There are many examples of child directed medical play including exploration of medical equipment, socio-dramatic play, games depicting medical procedures or themes, and creating artwork using medical materials. All of these activities allow children to tackle a frightening situation with greater familiarity which will build a foundation for dealing with difficult experiences in the future (Fortunato, 2000).

## Psychological Preparation

A second important element of a child life program is preparing children for hospitalization, surgeries, doctor visits, and procedures. The process of psychological preparation involves sharing accurate and developmentally appropriate information concerning stressors and strategies for coping with those stressors (Fortunato, 2000). Such preparation programs that familiarize children and families with the circumstances and procedures they will face are now common in most hospitals. According to McDonald (2001), programs such as these drastically reduce emotional anxiety in hospitalized children. For example, two studies with children in a hospital setting indicated that preparation programs before surgery lowered children's anxiety levels and improved their comfort levels (Zahr, 1998).

In preparing children and families for procedures, child life specialists provide accurate descriptions of the procedures and help children to express what they think will happen (Fortunato, 2000). According to Gaynard, Goldberger, & Laidley (1991) during psychological preparation before a procedure takes place, child life specialists use plain body outline dolls and other dolls as helpful tools to qualm children's fears. Further, child life specialists allow children to examine medical equipment and provide developmentally appropriate explanations about their use (McGee, 2003). Hataya, Olsson, & Lagerkranser (2000) found such information and opportunities to handle equipment help to make the uncertain events more manageable, reduce anxiety, and allow children to plan and employ coping strategies. Some popular strategies employed include relaxation, visualization, guided imagery, and a variety of pain management techniques.

## Family Support

Family support and education is the third important element of child life services. Family involvement is encouraged in patient care due to the positive impact the family plays in the adjustment of children to the health care experience (Johnson, Jeppson, & Redburn, 1992). Due to the fact that anxiety experienced by family members can be transmitted to the children receiving services, child life specialists help family members understand their child's response to treatment and promote parent/child play sessions for comforting their children during various procedures (Solnit, 1984). Further, child life services extend to well siblings through developmentally appropriate teaching strategies aimed at making sense of their brother or sister's illness. In addition, specifically trained child life specialists may offer grief support activities for family members in the case of critical injury or even death. Any health care experience can be difficult for families on a variety of levels.

Child life specialists help to diffuse the adverse effects of various health care experiences for children and families.

## METHODS

The research project was conducted during the fall 2006 semester by undergraduate early childhood education students enrolled in the Seminar in Learning Experiences (62.322) class. Three guiding questions created by the researcher were used to generate data about the field of child life, the perceived benefits of interactions and play episodes with hospitalized children and families, and how a twenty hour field experience at a children's hospital may have better prepared the undergraduate students to serve children and families in the future.

### Participants of the Study

Participants of the research project included thirty-five undergraduate early childhood education majors and thirty children and their families who were admitted to a children's hospital located in Pennsylvania. The undergraduate students served as the researchers in the project and were selected due to the fact that they enrolled in the Seminar in Learning Experiences (62.322) class. Conducting the research project was a course requirement for all students. Students not comfortable volunteering in the children's hospital chose an alternate site to conduct their fieldwork. The children and families admitted to the children's hospital volunteered to participate in the study and informed consent was granted by the parents/guardians of each child. In addition, parents/guardians also signed informed consent forms on behalf of their children as a requirement of participating in the project.

### Participant Observation

Observations are a primary source of generating data in qualitative research. Participant observation requires the researcher to immerse her-himself in the subject under study. It is presumed that the researcher can obtain a deeper understanding of the subject using participant observation as compared to questionnaire items. Reasons to employ this method include reliance on first-hand information, strong face validity of data, and reliance on straightforward methods. Some limitations of participant observation as a data generating technique include increased threat to objectivity on the part of the researcher, unsystematic data generating techniques, reliance on subjective measurement, and possible observer effects.

In this research project, undergraduate students became participant observers. The students collected data from the children's hospital for twenty hours during the fall 2006 semester. Undergraduate students collected data on the three guiding questions mentioned above using the elements suggested by Taylor & Bogdan (1984), including:

1. The setting: What is the physical environment like?
2. The participants: Describe who is in the scene, how many people, and their roles.
3. Activities and interactions: What is going on? How do the people interact with the activity and with one another?
4. Frequency and duration: When did the situation begin? How long did it last? What are the occasions that give rise to it?
5. Subtle factors: Including informal and unplanned activities and nonverbal communication.

Such an immersion allowed the undergraduate students to hear, see, and begin to experience reality as the participants do. Participant observation encouraged the undergraduate students to expand their knowledge and develop a sense of what was important. The students realized the challenge of combining participation and observation in order to become capable of understanding the guiding questions as an insider while describing them as an outsider.

## Data Analysis

Student reflective journals and final reports were used to generate data concerning the field of child life, the perceived benefits of interactions and play episodes with hospitalized children and families, and how a twenty hour field experience at a children's hospital may have better prepared the undergraduate students to serve children and families in the future. Data analysis proceeded in four phases: (1) initial reading; (2) second and third readings to begin to extract themes and patterns; (3) creation of meaningful categories and subcategories; and (4) reporting of initial findings.

At the completion of the analysis phase, an outline was developed by the author to frame the study in an effort to create a clear picture of student responses and reactions to the three guiding questions. The outline was expanded to include excerpts from the student journals and final reports. Quotations which were representative of the themes contained in the outline were chosen from the original data set. The quotations which provided the richest illustration of the themes were included in the results.


# RESULTS

Undergraduate student ideas and responses to the project's three guiding questions have been synthesized here into categories denoted by subheadings which introduce each section.

## Responsibilities of Child Life Specialists

All the undergraduate researchers were familiar with the field of Child Life and the job description and responsibilities of child life specialists after participating in the research study. This knowledge was obtained through readings and discussions throughout the semester in the class, coupled with immersion in a twenty-hour field experience in a children's hospital. The four major components of the Child Life field identified by the undergraduate researchers included medical play, preparation, patient support, and family support.

Medical play was defined as play which allows the patients to interact with some of the common medical equipment and to express their feelings about the experience of being admitted to a hospital. One student researcher described the medical play process in action. "Usually they will go step by step through a practice run of a medical procedure and they will use a doll and medical equipment to let the child practice on the doll to understand what their role in the procedure will be when it is actually happening. It helps children to adjust to unfamiliar and strange situations and work through their emotions."

Child life specialists also used preparation as a vital strategy to instruct patients and family members on the procedures they may experience during their stay in the hospital. A student witnessing the process in action stated "To demonstrate the procedure of hooking up an intravenous drip, the child life specialists use large dolls and allowed the children to insert needles just like in the real procedure. This process helps the children cope with the scary thought of having a needle in their body during their stay in the hospital." An additional program offered to prepared children for a stay in the hospital was called a "Gurney Journey" which provided a personalized child's eye view tour of the hospital.

Supporting patients before, during, and after a medical procedure was a third component of the field of Child Life identified by the undergraduate researchers. "Tender Paws" was a unique animal therapy program offered for children admitted to the hospital which was extremely beneficial to the patients, especially those who were missing the comfort of a family pet. The hospital also provided an on-site teacher to work with children who were missing school. In addition, upon being admitted to the hospital, the children receive a blanket and a special box of developmentally appropriate toys and activities to help ease the transition from home to hospital. The staff also ran a variety of events for children including trick-or-treating during Halloween and a variety of other enjoyable shows to entertain the children.

Creating a safe haven of support and care for the family of hospitalized children was identified by the undergraduate researchers as the fourth component in the field of Child Life. One student described the process this way,

> For the parents, the hospital offers supportive intervention to strengthen the family bond, education about their child's developmental milestones, information about the effects of hospitalization on children and families, and opportunities for experiencing hospitalization through the eyes of a child.

## Benefits of Interaction and Play

All together 100 percent of the undergraduate students believed their interactions and play episodes with children and families admitted to the children's hospital were beneficial to both groups on a variety of levels. The benefits for the children and families identified by the student researchers are summarized below.

*Benefits for children.* Students participating in the children's hospital field placement identified several benefits of the play episodes and interactions offered for the hospitalized children. One such benefit was providing opportunities for the children to remain physically and mentally active. Depending on the age, condition, and individual interest of each child, the university students provided a variety of activities to actively engage the children. One student described her role in this process with, "The patients' physical development was an integral part of my duties as a volunteer. I was able to get the children up out of bed and moving around." In a similar vein, a second student explained "throughout my interactions with the children during my time at the hospital I saw first-hand how play positively impacted them on a variety of levels. For example, play helped children, especially those who just had surgery to strengthen their fine and large muscle development."

Many of the university students believed that playing and interacting with the children offered a sense of normalcy during a somewhat stressful stay in the hospital. One student articulated this notion by sharing,

Outside of dramatic play, when would a three year old give someone a needle? For that matter, when is a three year old in control of anything? Everyday, all day, people are entering Paige's room at all times of the day and night and doing things she does not like. Because Gilbert is imaginary, Paige alone completely controls his every action. Play can be such a powerful mode of response to a new and perhaps scary experience where the content and meaning are ambiguous and the outcome is uncertain. This defines Paige's existence within the hospital and likely her experience with cancer. I was especially intrigued during my second visit when she changed roles. I would be very interested in knowing what had occurred to make the role of consoler more powerful to her than being the inflictor of needles. Perhaps it was a nurse who held her hand and helped her through a difficult time. At other times play offers normalcy for Paige. To simply play with her dolls where there is a mommy, daddy, and little girl eating dinner together provides a glimpse into everyday normal life.

University students observed that the hospitalized children often appeared frightened and homesick, and that engaging in play allowed the children to focus on the game rather than their condition. One student described this distraction effect with "the play experiences had a range of positive effects on the children. For some children it helped to pass the time and offered a distraction. It also helped to reduce anxiety and elevate the spirits of the children." Another student concurred, "One of the children I interacted with exhibited signs of feeling better both physically and emotionally. This child was able to engage in play which took his mind off of everything else going around and made it possible for him to sleep." A third student shared, "I feel that playing helped them because they were able to forget about being stuck in a hospital and focus on having fun and being a kid again."

According to the university students, many of the hospitalized children sought reassurance in the absence of their parents. After consistently spending time with the children, the university students gained their trust and earned the title of friend. One student described the process this way, "Another way I helped to enhance the well-being of the children was through being a friend. The children came to realize that I was not there to hurt them, but rather to just be a friend." An additional student shared, "The babies I worked with were too young to engage in any complicated or imaginary play situations, so instead I held them, rocked them to sleep, or simply talked to them as I patted their backs. In my studies I have learned that simple, yet meaningful, physical connections with young children can make a world of difference in regard to their comfort level and overall happiness." A third student recounted, "One experience that truly remains in my mind was when I was able to put an exhausted and hurting three-week-old baby to sleep by simply adjusting him to lie on my shoulder a certain way so that he could breathe easily. Knowing that

I gave the baby boy the comforting touch and attention he wanted and needed was an incredible feeling."

Socializing with people not affiliated with the hospital was viewed by the student researchers as an important benefit for the hospitalized children. Some children admitted to the hospital had parents that worked during the day in order to keep their medical benefits. For these children, the majority of their interactions during the day were with hospital personnel. University students participating in the field experience were viewed by students as "outsiders" in a good way. One student described the importance of social interactions in the lives of the children with, "Many of the children I came in contact with were desperate for some type of stimulation. I often brought them crafts to work with and books to read." A second student further shared, "By playing games with her the time passed by more quickly and she was able to build up her social skills with me."

These social interactions also provided opportunities for the children to express their feelings. One student explained this process, "Socially, the play episodes helped children to work and cooperate with others and to verbalize their thoughts about what they were feeling."

The university students also believed that playing with the hospitalized children offered a much needed support system. To highlight this benefit one student shared, "The play episodes I offered helped the children not to worry about all of the negative things that were happening in their daily lives and to focus on the positive and fun things. I just love that in a way I can take the pain away from a child even for a little while when I focus on what the child likes to do." An additional student summarized how this support system transformed one little girl right before her eyes.

One of the most remarkable children I had the opportunity to work with was a three year old girl with cancer. The first time I ever say her perfect little face was when she was lying in bed looking perfectly miserable. As I entered her room I wondered if my interactions could help to cheer her up. I decided to try and warmed her up by asking questions about her Shrek doll and engaging in imaginary play. Not only did my interactions make a difference, they brought out a whole new side of the little girl that I had no idea existed. She was transformed from a sad little girl to a talkative, energetic, and creative child right before my eyes. After the first day, I engaged in play sessions with her several times over the course of the following months. Each time we played I was more amazed by her vivid imagination and spunky attitude. Until I met her I never realized that children with an illness do not feel bad for themselves, nor do they want people around them to feel bad for them. Children inflicted with an illness just want to be treated like children. Their medical conditions get enough attention from the doctors and nurses. All the other wonderful little bits that make up who they are need attention from the other people in their lives.

*Benefits for families.* The university student researchers also believed the field experience at the children's hospital benefited families on a variety of levels. The first of these benefits identified included learning how to be a good listener. In their interactions with families, the university students often mentioned that the parents just wanted someone to listen to their life story. One student explained the process this way,

> I did not really have the chance to interact with parents all of the time but on the days I did it was nice. They talked with me as if I was part of their lives. We talked about their home lives and other children they had. Most of the time they would tell me how hard it was to work, take care of things around the house, and be at the hospital as much as they could. I felt supportive of the families. I was there if they needed a break and I was there to just listen. I think that is the most important part of being a child life volunteer.

Another university student agreed,

> I personally saw that parents and families are much more willing to open up to the volunteers. For many families it was such a relief to interact with someone other than a doctor or a nurse. Having someone to converse with other than medical staff was an important part of my volunteer efforts.

A second major benefit of the field experience for families was that it provided the parents with a much appreciated break to take a walk, get some fresh air, or grab a bite to eat. One student explained, "It was also great to give the parents a rest, even if it was for only fifteen minutes. I can't imagine the stress and emotions running through their heads daily wondering when they will be going home and if their child would ever recover." Yet another student shared, "I was able to give many parents half hour breaks so they could have some time to themselves and possibly get something to eat. It is very stressful and emotionally draining for the parents to see their children suffer and to encounter multiple doctors and nurses throughout the day." A third student agreed, "Another child I interacted with was an eight week old boy. I sat with him for half an hour one day while his mother took a brief break for lunch. I feel I positively impacted the mother by sitting there with her child and providing her some down time."

The notion of providing a support system for families was a third major benefit identified by the university student researchers. One student framed the support system benefit with,

> Even though at first I thought I was being a nuisance to many of the families in the hospital, I now realize that some of the families appreciated and needed my help. When I came into contact with some of the families their first ques-

tion was, "What college do you go to and why are you here?" After telling them, they enjoyed telling me stories about their college days, and for those ten minutes, it seemed as if they had let go of the problems they were facing to reminisce about easier days.

A second student shared a similar notion,

> One aspect of the Child Life program that could be improved would be paying more attention to the emotional well being of the families. The attitude and well being of the family is a vital component in the healing process of the child. We have witnessed first-hand on several occasions how the child's mental state is attuned with that of the parents. I believe the hospital staff should provide in-house support groups for parents to discuss their thoughts and feelings with other parents.

Finally, a third student believed "The greatest way my time at the children's hospital impacted families was by showing that they do not have to go through this rough time alone and that there are people to help them through it."

## Future Preparation

One hundred percent of the undergraduate students found the 20-hour field experience beneficial in preparation to work with children and families in the future. Their responses were organized into categories which are summarized below.

*Benefits for University students.* University student researchers found the field experience at the children's hospital better prepared them to work with children and families in the future in many ways. Building confidence in collaborating with families was one such benefit of the field experience. One student shared,

> This experience built my self-esteem in terms of working collaboratively with families. On several occasions during the experience I provided families much needed breaks to grab a bite to eat or to spend some time alone. Knowing that the families trusted me to care for their children for a few minutes really boosted my confidence. I plan to draw confidence from this experience when developing trusting relationships with families in the future.

Another student agreed, "The whole experience made me feel much more comfortable working with families and children from a variety of different backgrounds and cultures."

A second way the field experience benefited the university students was through helping them overcome their fears about working with sick children.

Many of the students were surprised with their ability to look beyond the illness and focus on the positive aspects each child had to offer. One student described the process this way, "The experience allowed me to build confidence in finding a way to help children feel better, while gaining insight on how children persevere through difficult times. It also challenged me to overcome my fear of hospitals by knowing I was there to help children and families in need."

Developing a heightened sense of compassion and empathy was a third benefit identified by many university students associated with the field experience. One student focusing on compassion shared, "Volunteering at the hospital has taught me to be compassionate. At first glance you do not know where these children come from and what type of life they lead at home. In the end, is does not really matter because compassion transcends all of these variables." A second student reflected about an increased sense of empathy, "The field placement helped me to develop a sense of sincere empathy as I witnessed firsthand the difficulties many families face."

University students also found the field experience improved their ability to be a good listener, an important quality for new teachers to hone. One student expressed this quality with, "For the first time in my life, I feel that I honestly made a difference in the lives of other people. Not only did I provide an outlet for the children to express themselves and have fun while at the hospital, but I served as a sounding board for parents who needed to tell their personal stories." A second student shared similar sentiments, "I exhibited the courage to talk with parents about problems they were having, even thought I was a complete stranger to them. These parents opened up to me and it taught me that it doesn't hurt to listen to someone else's problems."

Advocacy is a quality foreign to many undergraduate students. Sometimes it takes a life changing personal experience that hits close to home for someone to become a true advocate for a cause. For some of the undergraduate students, volunteering at the children's hospital was just such an experience. One student described her advocacy efforts on behalf of children at the hospital with,

After this experience I will never look at the children in my care the same way again. Having held a child who died a few days later had a huge impact on me. If I had known he was going to die I'm sure I would have held him longer, sang with more passion, and stroked his hair one more time. My job requires me to constantly be looking at the long-term goals of the children, to analyze and guide their every area of development. I am not used to looking at only today because there may not be a tomorrow. When I think of Mason I will think of how fragile children are. When I think of Paige, she will remind me of how strong children are. It has been a month since I've been at the hospital and I can still see Mason's blue eyes and I can hear Paige's little voice calling for Gilbert. I hope I can remember them as clearly a year from now. Children need to be guided and their development encouraged, but the visits to the hospital impacted upon me that children need also to be celebrated and allowed to enjoy every day of their childhood. As adults we need to remember that childhood is short and delicate. Life is fragile with no guarantees of tomorrow. My experiences at the hospital helped me remember that play helps children cope and that childhood is precious.

Participating in the field experience was an eye-opening experience for all of the undergraduate students. Interacting with hospitalized children provided a new perspective for many of the students; a perspective of not sweating the small stuff that happens in life and to be grateful for all of their blessings. One student explained the transformation with,

> This experience was eye-opening to me because I feel that I sometimes take for granted the little things such as my health, which is the most important thing to be thankful for. Without good health, life is a huge struggle, and it made me so thankful for my life. Overall I felt my time in the hospital was a rewarding experience and helped me to see that there are people that have bigger problems than me and to not sweat the little things in life.

Another student concurred, "This experience was one way to get back in touch with reality and how important it is to appreciate the simple things that many people take for granted."

Although students often discuss the importance of play in the lives of children, these discussions often focus on the academic or physical benefits. The therapeutic benefits of play are often overlooked. However, through participating in the field experience, the students gained keen insights into the therapeutic benefits of play. One student highlighted this notion with, "The far reaching implications for the power of play in the lives of children are eloquently articulated by the father of kindergarten, Friedrich Froebel, 'Play is the highest expression of human development in childhood, for it alone is the free expression of what is in a child's soul." An additional student expressed similar sentiments, "When the children and I were engaged in play I witnessed their stress levels drop tremendously. Playing allowed them moments in time to relieve feelings of constant worry. Through play, the children were able to express what was troubling them without using words. It provided chances for the children to feel normal in an environment that was anything but that." A third student shared a valuable life lesson taken from the experience, "This experience has changed the way I look at children. When you look at a child who is ill, don't look at the illness, look beyond and you will see that the child wants to run and play just like any other child. As a future teacher, this is one of the most important things I can ever learn."

A basic tenant of teacher preparation programs is to differentiate instruction based upon the individual needs of the children in your care. Some of the undergraduate students found the field placement helped to hone this valuable teaching competency. One student described the process this way, "The children's hospital experience required me to consider each child on an individual basis, in terms of the child's distinctive personality, stage of development, and needs, which had to be addressed before determining what activities to introduce. I will need this fundamental skill as a future teacher, as I must decide what each child currently needs and prioritize my instruction according to those needs."

An additional benefit of participating in the field experience for some of the students was expanding their career options. Several of the students were intrigued by the field of Child Life and continued volunteering at the hospital after their required hours were fulfilled. These students expressed a strong interest in becoming a child life specialist. One student shared, "This experience opened my eyes to the possibility of enhancing my degree in early childhood education by obtaining child life certification."

A second student agreed, "I now realize that this is something I would love to continue doing in the future." While a third student shared a goal for the future, "I feel that this field experience has provided me with a new professional goal for the future."

Having a positive impact on the hospitalized children and their families was a benefit of participating in the field experience mentioned by most of the undergraduate students. One student described this impact with, "I especially enjoyed seeing the children's faces light up when I came into their room, and I loved the way they acted when they wanted to show me something that they had done. I loved hearing them talk with me each day and how they never wanted me to leave them." A second student addressed the positive impact of the experience on families, "I also feel that I helped the parents of children admitted to the hospital because they could find comfort in knowing that volunteers like me were looking after their children's needs that extended beyond the physical aspect of their treatments and recoveries." A third student became more open minded and less judgmental of families through the experience, "I think the experience taught me how to be more understanding and open-minded when it comes to working with families. I learned that I cannot always judge families based upon what I see due to many underlying variables."

A final benefit of participating in the field experience highlighted by students was a heightened awareness of working in a collaborative team to best meet the needs of all children. One student addressing this benefit shared, "By working with the child life staff I learned what it's like to be part of a team working together for a specific purpose. In the future I will be able to draw upon this experience to help other colleagues who have children with serious illnesses in their care."

## IMPLICATIONS

Emerging from this research project are several implications for pre-service early childhood teachers and schools of education preparing such candidates to work with diverse student and parent populations.

### Harness the Benefits of Play to Enrich the Lives of Children on a Variety of Levels

Play has been a staple in the lives of children for generations. The colors, sights, and sounds experienced during play etched lasting memories and impressions still vivid today. Such experiences offered a break from the rigors of the day and provided the physical, cognitive, and social rejuvenation that our developing bodies and minds longed for. But are these experiences available for children today, or are they no more than a faded memory from the nostalgic past?

While fond memories of play abound for grown-ups, many children today have much different experiences. Attitudes towards play as being frivolous, impractical, and unproductive are pervasive in the present-day climate of increased teacher and school accountability to meet proficiency on academic standards mandated by NCLB. Many schools across the country are altering, reducing or eliminating time devoted to play. This trend is not new. Doris Sponseller in *Play as a Learning Medium* (1974) espoused similar concerns over thirty years ago:

> When early learning is defined as being only academic learning, play is often taken out of the curriculum to achieve these goals. The elementary school years have traditionally valued work in the classroom and have relegated play to recess time only. Kindergarten teachers are reporting that with increasing emphasis on accountability for reaching early academic objectives, there is now less time for play in their classrooms. And often the movement toward educational content in the preschools is interpreted in ways which cause downgrading or even abandonment of play time in preschools as well.

With life becoming more stressful, structured, and complicated for many children, it is vital that play remains part of daily landscape. And while the many benefits associated with play including brain growth and development, aerobic endurance, muscle strength, motor coordination, respect for rules, self-discipline, leadership skills, aggression control, conflict resolution, and an appreciation for the culture and beliefs of others are important, we must also highlight and endorse the therapeutic benefits of play which provide a vital coping mechanism for children that allows them to deal with traumatic events and to openly and freely express a full range of feelings.

## Encourage Fieldwork in a Variety of Settings that Encourage Growth and Reflection

Each of the undergraduate and graduate courses I teach requires fieldwork to provide opportunities to apply the content offered in class, to develop relationships with school and community agency personnel, and to develop the skills and competencies necessary to become a reflective professional educator. In the past, many of the field sites I selected were in daycare centers, preschools, or primary school classrooms. I have since realized the importance of expanding the field sites to include a variety of community agencies that support children and families. Since this specific research project examined the therapeutic benefits of play, a children's hospital seemed to be the most appropriate venue. Imagine how different the results of the project may have been if the students conducted the research in a public school classroom.

The field experience offered at the children's hospital accomplished all of the goals for fieldwork mentioned above. In terms of applying content explored in class, the field experience allowed students to expand upon lectures, readings, and conversations about the therapeutic benefits of play and observe them actualized in real-time. Student journals and final reports were rich with descriptions detailing the dramatic changes observable in the hospitalized children's attitudes, dispositions, and actions when they were engaged in play.

Further, the students were able to form professional relationships with the child life specialists and learn about the career possibilities the field of Child Life has to offer. The students also developed relationships with the parents of the hospitalized children that provided much needed confidence in establishing and maintaining interpersonal relationships. In addition, the students learned the importance of teamwork, individualizing their activities based upon specific student needs, and the therapeutic benefits of play for children in crisis. Therefore it is vital to provide undergraduate students with the opportunity to conduct fieldwork in a variety of settings to encourage professional growth and reflection.

## Broaden Certification Options for Early Childhood Majors

One of the goals of the field experience was to provide students with a glimpse into the world of Child Life and to expand their future career opportunities. While the majority of students who participated in the study did not express an interest in obtaining child life specialist certification, many of the students were intrigued by the possibility. Based upon their interest I researched colleges and universities across the country that offer child life certification programs at both the undergraduate and graduate levels and the possibility of creating a child life certification track for students enrolled in my university. Based upon my research, I developed a proposal to offer the child life specialist certification at my university that is presently under review. If approved by the university curriculum committee, undergraduate and graduate students will soon have the ability to be trained as a certified child life specialist and to pursue their professional calling to support children and families, be it in a classroom or hospital setting.

## REFERENCES

American Academy of Pediatrics, Committee on Hospital Care. (2003). Family-centered care and the pediatrician's role. *Pediatrics, 112*, 691–697.

American Academy of Pediatrics, Committee on Hospital Care. (2003). Physician's roles in coordinating care of hospitalized children. *Pediatrics, 111*, 707–709.

Berk, L.E. (2004). *Infants, children, and adolescents.* Boston, MA: Allyn and Bacon.

Brown, C.D. (2001). Therapeutic play and creative arts: Helping children cope with illness, death, and grief. In A. Armstrong-Dailey & S. Zarbock (Eds.), *Hospice care for children* (pp. 250–283). New York, NY: Oxford University Press.

Child Life Council. (2003). *Directory of child life programs.* Rockville, MD: Child Life Council.

Clements, R. & Jarrett, O.S. (2000). Elementary school recess: Then and now. *National Association of Elementary School Principals, 18*(4), 1–4.

Fortunato, G. (2000). Preparing your child for urologic surgery. *Family Urology, 1*, 18–21.

Gaynard, L., Goldberger, J., & Laidley, L.N. (1991). The use of stuffed, body-outline dolls with hospitalized children and adolescents. *Child Health Care, 20*, 216–224.

Hatava, P., Olsson, G., & Lagerkranser, M. (2000). Preoperative psychological preparation for children undergoing ENT operations: A comparison of two methods. *Pediatric Anaesthia, 10*, 477–486.

Jarrett, O.S. & Maxwell, D.M. (2000). What research says about the need for recess. In R. Clements (Ed.), *Elementary school recess: Selected readings, games, and activities for teachers and parents* (pp. 12–23). Lake Charles, LA: American Press.

Johnson, B.H., Jeppson, E.S., & Redburn, L. (1992). *Caring for children and families. Guidelines for hospitals.* Bethesda, MD: Association for the Care of Children's Health.

Kaminski, M., Pellino, T., & Wish, J. (2002). Play and pets: The physical and emotional impact of child life and pet therapy on hospitalized children. *Child Health Care, 31,* 321–335.

McDonald, C. (2001). Ask the doctor: meet the professional child life specialists—making the tough times a little easier. *Exceptional Parent Magazine, 84,* 80–82.

McGee, K. (2003). The role of a child life specialist in a pediatric radiology department. *Pediatric Radiology, 33,* 467–474.

McGrath, P., & Huff, N. (2001). What is it?: Findings on preschoolers' response to play with medical equipment. *Child Care Health Development, 27,* 451–462.

Solnit, A. J. (1984) Preparing. *Psychoanalytic Study of the Child, 7,* 613–632.

Sponseller, D. (Ed). (1974). *Play as a learning medium.* Washington D.C.: National Association for the Education of Young Children.

Taylor, S.J., & Bogdan, R. (1984). *Introduction to qualitative research.* New York: Wiley.

Thompson, R.H. (1995). Documenting the value of play for hospitalized children: The challenge of playing the game. *ACCH Advocate, 2,* 11–19.

Thompson, R.H. (1989). Child life programs in pediatric settings. *Infants and Young Children, 2,* 75–82.

Zahr, L.K. (1998). Therapeutic play for hospitalized preschoolers in Lebanon. *Pediatric Nursing, 23,* 449–454.

Zwillich, T. (2001). Brain scan technology poised to play policy. Retrieved http://www.loni.ucla.edu/~thompson/MEDIA/RH/rh.html.

## Chapter Two

# Play between Children and Domestic Animals

## Gail F. Melson

Play is the activity most emblematic of childhood. Children across cultures devote considerable time to play. Since the 1930's, theory (Erikson, 1977; Piaget, 1962; Vygotsky, 1967) and research have explored the significance of play for children's development. Social play, in particular, has been linked to reciprocity, empathy, perspective taking, social skills, moral reasoning, and cognitive growth (Johnson, Christie, & Wardle, 2005). Yet fundamental questions about play persist. Definitional issues remain contested (Smith, et al., 1985). Developmental effects, once seen as far ranging, are now in question (Power, 2000).

Our understanding of play has been impeded further by an overly narrow focus on selected contexts of and participants in children's play. Most attention continues to focus on peer play, that is, play between children of roughly the same age and developmental stage, with limited study of the features and developmental impact of play between children of differing ages, including siblings (Farver, & Wimbarti, 1995; Howe, Fiorentino, & Gariepy, 2003), or between parent (caregiver) and child (Fogel, 1993). Thus, both theory and research need to expand their focus to include multiple play partners and play contexts for children.

Especially missing from scholarly attention is children's play with non-human animals (hereafter, referred to as *animals*). As with many other areas of development, what I have called an anthrocentric bias (Melson, 2001) has restricted scholarly inquiry to children's interactions only with other humans. This bias obscures an important aspect of children's experiences. More broadly, attention to children's experiences across, not just within species, can aid understanding of developmental phenomena, such as play. In considering child-animal play, we can shed light on unresolved issues such as the definition of play, the features of play, and the developmental significance of play.

In this chapter, I explore children's play with animals, particularly with those most commonly kept as pets—dogs and cats. Five major questions guide this inquiry: (1) how might child-animal play be conceptualized? (2) What are the features of play between children and pets? (3) How is this play similar to and different from social play that children engage in with other humans? (4) What are some sources of variation in child-animal play? (5) What might be the developmental significance of children's play with non-human play partners such as animals? Because empirical support relevant to these questions is limited at present, my focus will be on setting out a conceptual framework and research agenda to guide future work.

## THE IMPORTANCE OF PETS AND OTHER ANIMALS IN CHILDREN'S LIVES

The relative neglect in the research literature of the topic of children's play with animals is surprising, given the pervasive presence of pets as part of the ecology of childhood, particularly in North America and Western Europe. For example, in the U.S., over 75% of households report at least one resident animal. It is estimated that over half of all households in the European Union have at least one pet (Serpell, 1996). In both the U.S. and the E.U., households with children under 18 years of age are most likely, compared to other household types, to have animals (Humane Society of the United States, 2006). Even in countries like Japan and China, where pet ownership rates historically have been lower than in North America and Western Europe, keeping animals is rapidly rising, particularly among families with children. In sum, the demographic data on animal presence within the home environments of children suggests that pets are an important component within the ecology of child development. At minimum, pets are available at home, every day, as *potential* play partners.

Beyond the home environment, animals are found within other microsystems (Bronfenbrenner, 1979) or family and community settings that form the fabric of children's lives. For example, seven and ten-year-olds included pets in their neighborhood along with those in their own homes as among the ten most important individuals to them and as among their "special friends" (Bryant, 1985). Classrooms, particularly in preschools, day care centers, and elementary schools, often have resident or visitor animals. In a survey of 37 Northern California elementary school teachers in 30 schools, 59% reported having animals in the classroom, most commonly small 'pocket pets,' such as hamsters, gerbils, and guinea pigs, or small reptiles, such as iguanas, snakes and lizards, and fish (Zasloff, Hart, & DeArmond, 1999). Rud and Beck (2003) report survey results that about half of the Indiana elementary school teachers had or wanted to have classroom pets. More broadly, places to observe and interact with animals are popular with families with children. Nature parks, zoos, and aquariums draw millions of children and their families annually, more than to any professional sports event (Melson, 2001).

There is accumulating evidence that pets are not merely present in children's home, neighborhood, and school environments, but they also play important roles for both adults and children. Parental estimates of children's time spent with pets in care and play indicate that on average, children devote as much time to their animals as to younger siblings, if present. Moreover, children without younger siblings spend more time playing and caring for pets than do pet-owning children who have younger siblings (Melson & Fogel, 1996). These findings suggest the possibility that pets may function as outlets for play and nurture in some of the ways that younger siblings do.

Such a possibility is strengthened by findings that pet owners overwhelmingly consider their pets to be family members. For example, in a random sample of households in Providence, Rhode Island, 80% of pet owners identified their pet as a "very important" member of their household (Albert & Bulcroft, 1986). Children also identify their resident animals as family members and generally report high attachment (in the sense of feeling a close emotional bond) to their pets (Poresky, et al, 1988).

In surveys, parents say they acquired an animal principally "for the children," although other motivations also are cited (Melson, 2001). This view is strongest among adults who had pets during childhood (Serpell, 1981). Children report that their pets provide important, intimate, and rewarding relationships. Studies of social support that include questions about animals (or about "individuals," thereby avoiding an anthropocentric bias) show that children identify support functions that pets provide. For example, Furman (1989) found that elementary school age children chose ties to pets over those to friends or parents as most likely to last "no matter what" and "even if you get mad at each other." Similarly, in a study of five year olds with pets at home, 42% spontaneously mentioned their animal when asked: "Who would you turn to if you felt sad, angry, happy, or need to tell a secret?" (Melson, & Schwarz, 1994). On average, ten-year-olds named nearly two pets ($M = 1.89$) as "special friends" and included one pet among the ten individuals most important in their lives (Bryant, 1985).

Children not only view pets as providing social support but also as providing sources of wellbeing, in effect making children feel good. When children aged eight to twelve were asked to take photographs reflecting their own sources of wellbeing, the children included pictures of pets more frequently than did parents or teachers reporting on the children's sources of wellbeing (Sixsmith, et al, 2007). Thus, the emotional, affective, and social roles that pets play for children make it likely that these animals would be part of children's play.

Research on the contexts most likely to elicit children's play directs further attention to animals. Rubin, et al., (1983) identify the features of play-friendly contexts: availability of play partners or engaging materials, child-directed choices, and a secure environment where basic needs are met. Pets are not only present in the majority of children's environments, as discussed above, but they are readily available. Children's interactions with pets, once basic safety concerns are met, are generally not structured by adults but are child-directed. Finally, there is evidence that children may derive a sense of security from pet presence and attention (Melson, 2001).

Children's involvement with pets takes place within the context of attentiveness to animals in general. The *biophilia hypothesis* (Wilson, 1984; Kellert & Wilson, 1993; Kellert, 1997) posits that because humans coevolved with other life forms, humans have an innate predisposition to attend to living things. There is accumulating evidence in support of this hypothesis. Infants, toddlers, and preschoolers respond with heightened interest to unfamiliar live animals as compared to unfamiliar adults (Ricard & Allard, 1992), or novel toy animals (Kidd & Kidd, 1987; Nielsen & Delude, 1989). This differential attentiveness means that animals, when present, are likely to be salient aspects of a child's environment.

## DEFINING CHILD-ANIMAL PLAY

Children's play with other humans has been notoriously difficult to define, but often easy for observers to recognize (Smith, Takhvar, Gore, & Vollstedt, 1985). Nonetheless, there is general consensus (Rubin, et al., 1983; Spodek & Saracho, 1987) that common characteristics of play include: intrinsic motivation (satisfaction in the activity itself), child versus external control, flexibility and creativity, active engagement by the child, and a quality of "playfulness," i.e., physical, social, and cognitive spontaneity. Others, from Parten (1932) to Elkind (2007), have conceptualized play in terms of a typology of categories. This typology generally distinguishes among manipulative or exploratory play (with toys or other objects), practice play, and social play of varying degrees of coordination, symbolization, and organization (Pellegrini, & Bjorklund, 2004; Smilansky, 1968). Definitions of play among animals—the young of many non-human species spend considerable time in play—show many similarities with those proposed for child-human play (Power, 2000).

As Bekoff and Byers (1998) note, inter-species play, like play among con-specifics (individuals/organisms of the same species), also is easy to recognize but difficult to characterize. Two approaches may be distinguished: (1) an *ethological* approach that defines play behaviors based on close observation of human-animal interaction; and (2) a *social constructivist* approach emphasizing human creation of meaning. In the first approach, certain observed behaviors occurring between child and animal are labeled 'play.' In the second approach, the child's intentions, understandings, and 'creation of meaning' (e.g., we are now "playing") are most important (Samuelson & Johansson, 2006).

From the ethological approach, Horowitz and Bekoff (2007) provide a useful definition of human-animal play, "Voluntary, coordinated behavior, which often follows 'routines' or games containing identified play behaviors that last for two or more turns by each participant." They derive this definition from observations of adult human play with dogs in which examples of *routines* include object retrieval games (fetch), object possession games (tug-of-war), feigning games (wrestling, growling), and parallel behavior (running alongside one another) (Horowitz and Bekoff, 2007).

The second, social constructivist, approach considers participants' intentions and meanings as crucial in defining an interaction as play. Many animal species use specific behaviors as play signals of the intent to play (e.g., the dog's play 'bow') or intent to stop playing (Power, 2000). Similarly, children employ behavioral, affective, and cognitive signals that frame an interaction as play. Thus, the two approaches—ethological and social constructivist—are complementary rather than opposing. Specific behaviors, such as play signals, can reliably portray internal states of intention and emotion.

Definitions of child-animal social play may be compared to definitions of child-human social play. The features characteristic of the child-human social play—creative, releasing, reciprocal, symbolic, communicative, unpredictable, joyous, and with an 'as if' quality (Samuelson & Johansson, 2006)—overlap considerably with both the ethological and social constructivist approaches to defining child-animal play.

However, because play signals and other play behaviors evolved within species for play between con-specifics, there are particular challenges in defining and understanding interspecies play. Children must 'read' the intentions and affect of an animal from its behaviors and vocalizations, and vice versa. When children accurately do so, one might define the interaction from the perspective of both participants as play. However, children also may impose a play frame on interactions with a pet. (Of course, inaccurate 'reading' of the play intentions of another human also occurs.)

The tendency to impose a play frame on interactions with pets may stem from several sources. One reason is the well-documented human inclination toward *anthropomorphism*, whereby nonhuman behavior is characterized in terms of human feelings, thoughts, and actions (Guthrie, 1997). Thus, a parrot tilts its head and its owner believes this is evidence of puzzlement. A dog licks its owner's hand and its owner is sure it is a sign of affection.

Although humans tend to anthropomorphize broadly, attributing intentions and feelings to computers, machines, cars, and even abstract blobs, pets and domestic animals have features that especially elicit anthropomorphic attributions. Those species more similar to humans—mammals, for example, in contrast to invertebrates—are more likely to be anthropomorphized in Western cultures (Eddy, Gallup, & Povinelli, 1993; Horowitz & Bekoff, 2007). Moreover, attributions of human characteristics are likely to be directed toward species that show *neoteny*, or the persistence of juvenile features, such as large round eyes and a disproportionately large head relative to torso. Apart from physical cues, behaviors such as autonomous, goal-oriented, and adaptive movement reliably elicit biological and psychological attributions. Even videos of two-dimensional shapes (Scholl & Tremoulet, 2000) or abstract blobs (Rakison & Poulin-Dubois, 2001) that appear to move in smooth trajectories toward an apparent goal lead children and adults to interpret the shapes as intentional agents with personality and emotions.

Both the physical and behavioral characteristics of pets and domestic animals make them prime candidates for anthropomorphism. Indeed, children (and adults) overwhelmingly attribute psychological states (e.g., intentions), emotions, and personality to pets (Melson, et al, 2009). While this is true across species commonly kept as pets, dogs and cats are particularly likely to be seen as full social partners, at least potentially. From the social constructivist perspective, these anthropomorphizing attributions mean that children can and often do construct the meaning of interactions with animals as social play, even when the animal is not engaging in play behaviors. Just as children attribute a variety of intentions and emotions to animals, children also are likely to project specific *play* intentions, emotions, and behaviors onto the animal, thus casting the animal as a social play partner.

A second reason that children may impose a play frame on interactions with pets stems from the cultural and social roles that companion animals play in human society. For many pet owners, pets are a source of amusement, pleasure, diversion, leisure activity, and fun. They are, among other things, *play objects*. Historically, the role of animals as play objects has become more salient as some of the other reasons for keeping animals—work, transportation, hunting, and food production—have waned (Grier, 2006). Hence, both children and adults frequently approach pets within a play frame.

From the social constructivist perspective, child-animal social play may be defined as: *Any interaction with an animal which the child constructs or defines as social play.* A child's play with a pet might be seen as analogous to a mother's scaffolding of social interactions with her infant (Kaye & Charney, 1981). As an example, a mother engages in 'conversation' with her infant, by supplying, on behalf of the infant, appropriate verbal and nonverbal responses to her social bids. In the case of a child with a gerbil, the child might rub the animal's fur, pause, observe the animal's behavior, and then say, "Oh, so you like that? You want another rub?" The child may then pause again and answer "OK." In this way, the child 'scaffolds' or provides both sides of an interactive routine.

The more limited interactive repertoire of animals (with respect to play with humans) and the dependent status of pets within human families may make scaffolded play interactions more likely with pets than with human peers or adults. In addition, the status of pets as inherently dependent upon human care is likely to affect play interactions in other ways. For example, there may not be a clear distinction between play behaviors and care-giving behaviors. Thus, in observations of children aged seven to fifteen interacting with an unfamiliar, friendly dog, petting and stroking the dog occurred frequently along with play routines such as 'fetch' with a ball (Melson, et al, 2009). Similarly, research observations of adults with their own dogs showed that the pet owners engaged in care and comfort giving behaviors, similar to those usually directed at human young. Along with play behaviors, such observations led the researchers to characterize the behavior of adult pet owners as "interspecific parental behavior." (Prato-Previde et al, 2006).

## CHARACTERISTICS OF CHILD-ANIMAL PLAY

From the ethological perspective, Horowitz and Bekoff (2007) have identified key features of human play with dogs: (1) regular and reliable mutual responsiveness, including coordinated joint attention; (2) behaviors signaling intent to play or to stop playing; (3) mutuality, in which each play partner reacts dynamically to the actions of the other; and (4) contingent activity, in which each partner reacts to what the other has just done. However, these features may not provide a full taxonomy of human social play with dogs, since the observations were of adults, not children, interacting with their own dogs in outdoor spaces such as dog parks. Laboratory observations of children during a short 'free play' time with an unfamiliar but friendly dog observed 'tummy rub' routines of dog inviting petting by rolling on its back, and the child rubbing the dog's proffered stomach and petting the dog while scaffolding a conversation (Melson, et al, 2009). Different contexts may elicit different play routines with dogs.

Species differences also are important. Dogs, compared to other species including primates, are particularly skilled in interpreting human social signals because dogs have co-evolved in human environments (Hare & Tomasello, 1999; Miklosi, Topal, & Csanyi, 2004). Thus, the observed coordinated, responsive, mutual, and contingent routines are unlikely to occur when children play with pets such as cats, rabbits, hamsters, gerbils, lizards, etc. In the case of these species, we might expect children more frequently to exhibit scaffolded play routines, in which the child provides, usually in a pretend fashion, the responses of the play partner.

The existence of such anthropomorphism and scaffolding should not lead us to assume that child-animal play is equivalent to children's play with stuffed animals or toys. From infancy, children perceive and respond to animals as other subjectivities or persons. As Myers (2007) notes: "Crucially, animals are social others not as if they were simply behaving inanimates, but rather because they display the hallmarks of being truly subjective others" (p.10). Myers' (2007) observations of preschool children responding to various species underscored children's attentiveness to and fascination with an animal's distinctive repertoire of behaviors—the snake's slither or the turtle's crawl—and children's use of these behaviors as the basis of interactions with the animal.

## TYPES OF CHILD-ANIMAL PLAY

Existing typologies of play, derived from observations of child-child interactions, are helpful frameworks for hypothesizing about categories of child-animal play. Again, there is a paucity of empirical research on this topic.

### Manipulative, Exploratory Play with Animals

Parten's (1932) typology identifies solitary, independent play with objects as the first "stage" of play. Others have defined this type of play as "sensori-motor," "exploratory," or "mastery" (Elkind, 2007). It is now clear that such play is developmental and remains a type of play activity present alongside later 'stages' of play. Do children treat living animals as toys or novel objects, engaging in exploratory, sensori-motor play with them? Existing evidence, while limited, suggests that generally, the answer is: "No." Even children under one year of age differentiate their behavior toward living things from toys or other inanimate objects (Nielsen & Delude, 1989). Exploratory, manipulative behavior is higher with objects than with unfamiliar living animals. Detailed classroom observations of preschool children with animals find that the children treat the animals as other subjectivities, with intentions, feelings, and autonomous behaviors, rather than as objects (Myers, 2007). Comparison of seven to fifteen-year-old children's unstructured "play time" with robotic dogs (objects designed to emulate living animals) and unfamiliar living dogs shows that manipulative, exploratory behavior is relatively high with the robotic dog, but is almost non-existent with the living dog (Melson, et al, 2009). There is little evidence that children interact with living animals in ways that parallel exploratory, manipulative behavior with toys or other objects. The default response to an animal is as a social other.

Some instances of exploratory play with animals, treated as novel objects, can occur with young children. Without adult supervision, young children may respond to an animal in ways that endanger the animal's welfare, for example, pulling on a cat's tail, or dumping fish out of a fishbowl "to see what happens." Such behaviors should be distinguished from cruelty toward animals, which is defined by indifference or pleasure at the suffering of an animal (Ascione, 1998).

## Social Play with Animals

Since children engage animals, both familiar and novel, as other subjectivities, most child-animal play is inherently social. As noted above, dogs can and do participate as social partners in routines such as "fetch" and "catch." Dogs are more adept, even than other primates, in maintaining joint attention with a human, signaling play intentions and behaviors and coordinating play interchanges. Other animal species are less finely attuned to human behaviors.

Most child-animal interaction differs from human interaction in specific ways that may be expected to influence child-animal play: (1) the animal is experienced as a distinct subjectivity (given qualities such as feeling, beliefs and desires created in the mind of the child) different from other humans, other living things (e.g. plants), or objects, both natural and constructed; (2) the animal's contribution to interaction is nonverbal; (3) individual species of animals have distinct repertoires of movement and interaction, what Myers (2007) calls "characteristic vitality" (p.11); (4) because animals, with the possible exception of dogs (see 'routines' above), cannot participate fully as social partners, children play an active role in structuring and constructing social play encounters; (5) because pets are dependent on human care, interactions with them often draw on the repertoire of parental care-giving behaviors, making play with and care of an animal less clearly distinguished (Prato-Previde, Fallani, & Valsecchi, 2006).

Illustrations of social play with animals, observed in young children (Myers, 2007), may help to convey the unique features of this type of play. One example is *animal-embodiment*, whereby a child pretends to be an animal and plays with the animal as with a con-specific. This can also occur in the absence of the living animal, when several children take on animal identities in *animal pretend* play. Another is *play with objects*, such as dangling a string for a cat to swat, or offering a ball to a dog. A fourth might be called *animal conversation*, as described in an example of scaffolding above, in which the child talks with the animal, supplying both halves of the conversation.

## SOURCES OF VARIATION IN CHILD-ANIMAL PLAY

At least four classes of variation can be distinguished: child characteristics, animal characteristics, relationship characteristics, and situational characteristics.

### Child Characteristics

Developmental stage, as indexed by age, has been related to children's understanding of and behavior toward animals (Melson, 2001). Research on the development of naïve biology, or conceptions about animates versus inanimates, indicates that preschoolers view self-initiated movement as part of the essence of animals but not machines (Gelman & Gottfried, 1996) and attribute the causal mechanism of such movement to 'vital energy' or life force (Inagaki, 1997). According to Inagaki and Hatano (1996), children generally construct a vitalist biology by ages 5–6 and an intuitive particulate theory of inanimate matter between 8 and 12 years old. These underlying understandings lead children with increasing age to become more aware of the distinct behavioral repertoires of individual animals and to adapt their behaviors accordingly. Emerging conceptions of naïve biology, naïve psychology, and naïve physics influence children to treat living animals as autonomous, self-directed beings with intentions, emotions, and thoughts.

In addition to a child's developmental stage, behaviors with an animal may reflect the individual child's temperament, experience, and adaptive behaviors. There is limited evidence at present to support this hypothesis, however. For example, attachment to one's pet predicted some differences in seven to fifteen-year-olds' behaviors toward and cognitions about an unfamiliar but friendly dog during a short play session (Melson, Kahn, Beck, & Friedman, 2009). Specifically, children who were more strongly attached to their pets directed more verbalizations including greetings, commands, and questions toward the unfamiliar dog. Pet attachment was associated with children's attributions of mental states and moral standing. Children with higher pet attachment (as compared with pet owning children with lower attachment) were more likely to describe the unfamiliar dog as having intentions and feelings (mental states), and the children judged the dog as more deserving to be treated fairly and justly and kept from harm (moral standing).

Children with specific disabilities respond with recognizable patterns of interaction to a therapy dog. In observations of children and adolescents with anorexia, bulimia, anxiety disorder, or autism with a therapy dog, distinct patterns of interaction allowed observers, blind to the child's diagnosis, to correctly assign 77.5% of the children to their diagnostic group (Prothmann, et al, 2005). Children with autism engaged in many brief interaction episodes while children with anxiety disorder interacted less often but for longer periods.

## Animal Characteristics

Little is known about how animal characteristics—species differences and individual differences within species—might affect children's behaviors, including play behaviors with animals. Naturalistic observations of preschool children with various species of classroom animals showed that the children were sensitive to the varying behavioral repertoires of the species present—turtles, snakes, gerbils, etc. (Myers, 2007). Parents, in their choice of companion animals, place emphasis on the right 'match' between the animal and the child's needs (Melson, 2001), indicating a broad belief that children respond differently to animal characteristics. Case studies of children's responsiveness to therapy animals are replete with examples of children who differ in their reactions to different species and to individual members of the same species (Melson, 2001).

## Relationship Characteristics

Although supporting research is currently lacking, it can be hypothesized that as with any relationship, over time a child and his or her pet would develop a distinct pattern of mutual responsiveness. The play routines of dog and dog owner observed by Horowitz and Bekoff (2007) imply that over time and experience, the two play partners have coordinated and integrated their behaviors into mutually satisfying 'games' such as 'catch' and 'fetch.' To properly document the dynamic relationship patterns of humans and animals in play, there is need for longitudinal research, particularly during the early stages of the relationship.

## Situational Characteristics

The context of interaction is likely to be influential in a number of ways. Some situations are framed as "play," and when both participants enter that frame, they would be expected to engage in play behaviors. Second, as noted earlier, there are specific cultural and social contexts that encourage human-animal play responses. Consider a pet owner taking his or her dog to a dog park "to play" and then taking the same dog to the veterinarian for shots. Finally, some animals are viewed by their owners as primarily objects of play and companionship, while other animals have working roles, such as hunting dog, sheep-herding dog, therapy dog, barnyard mouser cat, or race horse. While play behaviors occur between humans and those animals who 'work' for them, it is likely that both the frequency and quality of play may differ depending on the context of the human-animal relationship. Again, the paucity of research leaves us with speculation on this point.

## THE DEVELOPMENTAL SIGNIFICANCE OF CHILD-ANIMAL PLAY

The contributions of play to children's development continue to be explored and remain subject to debate. As Power (2000) notes, "play is not *essential* for normative development, but instead has evolved as one pathway through which individuals can learn about their environment, establish relationships with others, and practice and refine skills that facilitate their survival or otherwise increase their reproductive success . . . its effects on development may be general and/or specific" (p.8).

Building on Power's (2000) conceptualization of play as one among many pathways in development, a number of questions about child-animal play in relation to children's development can be posed: (1) Are play experiences with animals compensatory, additive, reflective, or unrelated to play experiences with other humans, especially other children? The theoretical rationale behind much animal-assisted therapy with children is that guided therapeutic play experiences with animals can *compensate* for dysfunctional or abusive experiences with humans (Fine, 2006). However, the *additive* hypothesis should also be considered. Perhaps play experiences with animals provide certain unique enrichment not readily available in human-human interactions. For example, play with animals relies on the non-verbal channel (at least from animal to human) and requires 'reading' the behavioral signals of a different species, thereby perhaps contributing to perspective-taking and empathy development (Daly & Morton, 2006). Similarly, children may have opportunities to engage in specific types of play, such as rough and tumble play, with certain animals. Alternately, the *reflective* hypothesis is also tenable. Specifically, the child-animal play experience may reflect or be a consequence of the child's development in other areas. Thus, a child who is already more skilled in perspective-taking and empathy may thereby be more able to "read" an animal's play signals. Finally, the *unrelated* hypothesis suggests child-animal play may be unrelated to other types of play and also unrelated to developmental outcomes of interest.

(2) Is child-animal play associated with simultaneous or delayed outcomes? Katcher and Wilkins (2000) have suggested that animal assisted therapeutic interventions generally result in symptom reduction and other beneficial outcomes only when the animals are present. They caution that developmental effects may not persist in the absence of animal. Until longitudinal evaluations demonstrate delayed or long term changes in children's development as a result of involvement with pets or other animals, this point must be taken seriously.

(3) Can child-animal play be isolated, even theoretically, from other aspects of interaction between child and animal and from the entire context? Attributing developmental outcomes to child-animal play alone may not be possible. Katcher and Beck (2006) note that children's experiences with animals, particularly educational or therapeutic experiences, almost always take place in situations with adults, perhaps teachers and therapists, and often in natural settings, such as parks. It is not possible to separate effects due to the other humans and to the setting from the experiences with the animal itself.

## LIMITATIONS AND CAUTIONS

Despite the importance of animals in children's lives, the study of child-animal relationships remains in its infancy. Basic descriptive studies are lacking. The range of play experiences that children have with pets is far from clear. There is virtually no longitudinal research to describe play within the context of child-animal relationships over time.

As scholars address these gaps in evidence-based knowledge, there are some guidelines to consider: (1) the focus on developmental effects on children should not obscure attention to animal welfare issues. We need to know more about ways that children play with animals that may harm, neglect, or not properly optimize care for the animal's wellbeing. Such findings can then aid in designing humane education efforts to support public knowledge and nurturance of animals. (2) Studies of child-animal play should adopt a dynamic systems perspective, recognizing the complexity of contextual effects (Melson, 2008). (3) Cultural, historical, and social diversity in children's relationships with animals mandate that these sources of variation be examined more closely in the study of child-animal play. (4) Children's interactions with animals should be studied not in isolation but rather in relation to children's relationships with other humans, with artifacts, such as computers and robotic pets, and with broader involvement with the natural world. Only by doing so, can we identify the unique contributions of involvement with animals to children's development.

## REFERENCES

Albert, A., & Bulcroft, K. (1986). Pets and urban life. *Anthrozoos, 1*, 9–23.

Ascione, F. R. (1998). Children who are cruel to animals: A review of research and implications for developmental psychopathology. In R. Lockwood, & F. R. Ascione, (Eds.), *Cruelty to animals and interpersonal violence: Readings in research and application* (pp. 83–104). West Lafayette, IN: Purdue University Press.

Bekoff, M., & Byers, J. (Eds.). (1998). *Animal play: Evolutionary, comparative and ecological perspectives.* Cambridge: Cambridge University Press.

Bronfenbrenner, U. (1979). *The ecology of human development.* Cambridge, MA: Harvard University Press.

Bryant, B. (1985). The neighborhood walk: Sources of support in middle childhood. *Monographs of the Society for Research in Child Development*, Serial No. 210, 50, No. 3.

Daly, B., & Morton, L. L. (2006). An investigation of human-animal interaction and empathy as related to pet preference, ownership, attachment, and attitudes in children. *Anthrozoos, 19*, 113–127.

Eddy, T. J., Gallup, G. G., Jr., & Povinelli, D. J. (1993). Attribution of cognitive states to animals: Anthropomorphism in comparative perspective. *Journal of Social Issues, 49*, 87–101.

Elkind, D. (2007). *The power of play: How spontaneous, imaginative activities lead to happier and healthier children.* Cambridge, MA: DaCapo Press.

Erikson, E. (1977). *Toys and reasons.* NY: Norton.

Farver, J. A., & Wimbarti, S. (1995). Indonesian children's play with their mothers and siblings. *Child Development, 66*, 1493–1503.

Fine, A. H. (2006). (Ed.). *Handbook of Animal-Assisted Therapy.* 2nd ed. San Diego: Elsevier.

Fogel, A. (1993). *Developing through relationships.* Chicago: University of Chicago Press.

Furman, W. (1989). The development of children's social networks. In D. Belle (Ed.), *Children's social networks and social supports* (pp. 151–172). New York: Wiley.

Gelman, S. A., & Gottfried, G. M. (1996). Children's causal explanations for animate and inanimate motion. *Child Development, 67,* 1970–1987.

Grier, K. C. (2006). *Pets in America: A history.* Chapel Hill, NC: University of North Carolina Press.

Guthrie, S. E. (1997). Anthropomorphism: A definition and a theory. In R. W. Mitchell, N. S. Thompson, & H. L. Miles (Eds.), *Anthropomorphism, anecdotes and animals* (pp. 50–58). Albany, NY: SUNY Press.

Hare, B., & Tomasello, M. (1999). Domestic dogs (Canis familiaris) use human and conspecific social cues to locate hidden food. *Journal of Comparative Psychology, 113,* 173–177.

Horowitz, A. C., & Bekoff, M. (2007). Naturalizing anthropomorphism: Behavioral prompts to our humanizing of animals. *Anthrozoos, 20,* 23–35.

Howe, N., Fiorentino, L. M., & Gariepy, N. (2003). Sibling conflict in middle childhood: Influence of maternal context and mother-sibling interaction over four years. *Merrill-Palmer Quarterly, 49,* 183–208.

Humane Society of the United States. U. S. pet ownership statistics (2006). Retrieved http://www.hsus.org/pets/issues_affecting_our_pets/pet_overpopulation_and _ownership_statistics/us_pet_ownership_statistics.html.

Inagaki, K. (1997). Emerging distinctions between naïve biology and naïve psychology. In H. M. Wellman & K. Inagaki (Eds.), *The emergence of core domains of thought: Children's reasoning about physical, psychological and biological phenomena. New Directions for Child Development,* Vol. 75 (pp. 27–44). San Francisco: Jossey-Bass.

Inagaki, K., & Hatano, G. (1996). Young children's recognition of commonalities between animals and plants. *Child Development, 67,* 2823–2840.

Johnson, J. E., Christie, J. F., & Wardle, F. (2005). *Play, development, and early education.* Boston: Pearson.

Katcher, A. H., & Beck, A. M. (2006). New and old perspectives on the therapeutic effects of animals and nature. In A. H. Fine (Ed.), *Handbook of animal-assisted therapy: Theoretical foundations and guidelines for practice.* 2nd ed. (pp. 39–48). New York: Academic Press.

Katcher, A. H., & Wilkins, G. G. (2000). The Centaur's lessons: Therapeutic education through care of animals and nature study. In A. H. Fine (Ed.), *Handbook of animal-assisted therapy: Theoretical foundations and guidelines for practice* (pp. 153–177). New York: Academic Press.

Kaye, K., & Charney, R. (1981). Conversational asymmetry between mothers and children. *Journal of Child Language, 8,* 35–50.

Kellert, S. R. (1997). Kinship to mastery: *Biophilia in human evolution and development.* Washington, D.C.: Island Press.

Kellert, S. R., & Wilson, E. O. (Eds.) (1993). *The biophilia hypothesis.* Washington, D. C.:Island Press.

Kidd, A. H., & Kidd, R. M. (1987). Reactions of infants and toddlers to live and toy animals. *Psychological Reports, 61,* 455–464.

Melson, G. F. (2001). *Why the wild things are: Animals in the lives of children*. Cambridge, MA: Harvard University Press.

Melson, G. F. (2008). Children in the living world: Why animals matter for children's development. In A. Fogel, B. King, & S. G. Shanker, (Eds.), Human development in the twenty-first century: Visionary ideas from systems scientists (pp. 147–154) New York: Cambridge University Press.

Melson, G. F., Kahn, P. H. Jr., Beck, A., & Friedman, B. (2009). Robot pets in human lives: Implications for the human-animal bond and for human relationships with personified technologies. *Journal of Social Issues, 65,* 545–567.

Melson, G. F., Kahn, P. H. Jr., Beck, A., Friedman, B., Roberts, T., & Garrett, E. (2009). Children's behavior toward and understanding of robotic and living dogs. *Journal of Applied Developmental Psychology. 30,* 92–102.

Melson, G. F., & Schwarz, R. (1994). *Pets as social supports for families with young children*. Paper presented to the annual meeting of the Delta Society. New York, Oct.

Miklosi, A., Topal, J., & Csanyi, V. (2004). Comparative social cognition: What can dogs teach us? *Animal Behavior, 67,* 995–1004.

Myers, G. (2007). *The significance of children and animals*. West Lafayette, IN: Purdue University Press.

Nielsen, J. A., & Delude, L. A. (1989). Behavior of young children in the presence of different kinds of animals. *Anthrozoos, 3,* 119–129.

Parten, M. (1932). Social participation among preschool children. *Journal of Abnormal Psychology, 27,* 243–269.

Pellegrini, A. D., & Bjorklund, D. F. (2004). The ontogeny and phylogeny of children's object and fantasy play. *Human Nature, 15,* 23–43.

Piaget, J. (1962). *Play, dreams and imagination in childhood*. NY: Norton.

Poresky, R. H., Hendrix, C., Mosier, J. E., & Samuelson, M. L. (1988). Young children's companion animal bonding and adults' pet attitudes: A retrospective study. *Psychological Reports, 62,* 419–428.

Power, T. G. (2000). *Play and exploration in children and animals*. Mahwah, NJ: Erlbaum.

Prato-Previde, E., Fallani, G., & Valsecchi, P. (2006). Gender differences in owners interacting with pet dogs: An observational study. *Ethology, 112,* 64–73.

Prothmann, A., Albrecht, K., Dietrich, S., Hornfeck, U., Stieber, S., & Ettrich, C. (2005). Analysis of child-dog play behavior in child psychiatry. *Anthrozoos, 18,* 43–58.

Ricard, M., & Allard, L. (1992). The reaction of 9–10-month old infants to an unfamiliar animal. *Journal of Genetic Psychology, 154,* 14.

Rubin, K. H., Fein, G. G., & Vandenberg, B. (1983). Play. In P. H. Mussen, & E. M. Hetherington (Eds.), *Handbook of child psychology,* Vol. 4 (pp. 693–774). NY: Wiley.

Rud, A. J., & Beck, A. M. (2003). Companion animals in Indiana elementary schools. *Anthrozoos, 7,* 242–252.

Samuelson, I. P., & Johansson, E. (2006). Play and learning—inseparable dimensions in preschool practice. *Early Child Development and Care, 176,* 47–65.

Scholl, B. J., & Tremoulet, P. D. (2000). Perceptual causality and animacy. *Trends in Cognitive Science, 4*, 299–309.

Serpell, J. (1981). Childhood pets and their influences on adult attitudes. *Psychological Reports, 49*, 651–654.

Serpell, J. (1996). *In the company of animals: A study of human-animal relationships.* (London: Cambridge University Press).

Sixsmith, J., Gabhainn, S. N., Fleming, C., & O'Higgins, S. (2007). Children's, parents', and teachers' perceptions of child wellbeing. *Health Education, 107*, 511–523.

Smilansky, S. (1968). *The effects of socio-dramatic play on disadvantaged preschool children.* Oxford, England: John Wiley & Sons.

Smith, P.K., Takhvar, M., Gore, N., & Vollstedt, R. (1985). Play in young children: Problems of definition, categorization and measurement. *Early Child Development and Care, 19*, 25–41.

Vygotsky, L. S. (1967). Play and its role in the mental development of the child. *Soviet Psychology, 12*, 62–76.

Wilson, E. O. (1984). *Biophilia.* Cambridge, MA: Harvard University Press.

Zasloff, R. L., Hart, L. A., & DeArmond, H. (1999). Animals in elementary school education in California. *Journal of Applied Animal Welfare Science, 2*, 347–357.

## Chapter Three

# Mothers' Social and Didactic Actions during Play: Contributions of Infant Affect

## Hui-Chin Hsu and Jihyun Sung

In addition to nurturing behavior, parents engage in two primary modes of actions in early infancy: social and didactic (Bornstein, 2002; Bornstein & Tamis-LeMonda, 1990). *Social actions* are those that parents use to express feelings toward their infants and to engage them in dyadic emotional exchanges. By contrast, *didactic actions* are physical or verbal strategies that parents utilize to encourage their infants to attend to objects or events external to the parent-infant dyad. When directing infant attention to objects or events in the immediate surroundings, parents provide opportunities for their infants to observe, explore, and learn about the external world.

Research suggests that maternal didactic and social actions directly and indirectly contribute to the development of infant play, cognition, language, and concepts of self (Belsky, Goode, & Most, 1980; Bornstein, 1988; Bornstein & Tamis-LeMonda, 1997; Keller, Yovsi, Borke, Kartner, Jensen et al., 2004). Despite their developmental significance, relatively little is known about the frequency and temporal characteristics of these maternal actions during play in early infancy. It is also unknown whether mothers employ distinctive action styles during play. This study investigated the characteristics and style of mothers' actions during social and didactic play. In addition, mothers' actions are coherently structured with their infants' activities: maternal engagement in social actions is related to the social interest in infants, whereas maternal didactic actions are related to the visual and tactile explorations of infants (Bornstein, Tamis-LeMonda, Pecheux, & Rahn, 1991). In this study, we further examined the contribution of infant affect to the characteristics and style of maternal actions during different interactive contexts of play.

# CHARACTERISTICS OF MATERNAL ACTIONS DURING PLAY

Although mothers' beliefs about parenting are not correlated with observed or self-reported social or didactic actions (Bornstein, Cote, & Venuti, 2001), their self-reported didactic, not social, actions are positively correlated with observed maternal sensitivity and child responsiveness during mothers' play with their toddlers (Bornstein, Hendricks, Haynes, & Painter, 2007). Early studies indicate that maternal preference for social or didactic actions is influenced by the cultural value system (e.g., Bornstein, Tamis-LeMonda, Tal, Ludemann, Toda et al., 1992; Keller, Lohaus, Kuensemueller, Abels, Yovsi et al., 2004; Keller, Yovsi, Borke, Kartner, Jensen et al., 2004). For example, compared to French and Japanese mothers, American mothers tend to show a preference for didactic actions, rather than social actions (Bornstein et al., 1991; Bornstein et al., 1992; Bornstein, Tal, & Tamis-LeMonda, 1991; Bornstein, Tamis-LeMonda, Pascual, Haynes, Painter et al., 1996). Despite cross-cultural differences, as infants mature, mothers demonstrate a universal pattern in decreasing social actions and increasing didactic actions. When their infants are about six months old, mothers engage in more didactic than social actions in mother-infant play (Bornstein, & Tamis-LeMonda, 1990; Bornstein, Tamis-LeMonda, Tal, et al., 1992; Bornstein, Cote, & Venuti, 2001) and show individual preferences in styles of interaction (e.g., Bornstein et al., 1992). The transactional approach proposed by Sameroff (Sameroff & Chandler, 1975; Sameroff & Mackenzie, 2003) suggests that development is a process of continuous dynamic interactions between the individual and the experience provided by the social context. Taking this approach, mothers' play behaviors can be conceptualized as developmental outcomes of transactions in the mother-infant interaction.

Furthermore, the frequency of social and didactic actions in mothers of toddlers has been found to be uncorrelated (Vibbert & Bornstein, 1989), indicating little concordance between the two types of maternal actions. It appears that maternal social and didactic actions are distinctively different. During play, maternal actions change from one moment to the next. Individual differences have been found in the temporal sequencing of maternal actions. For example, mothers and their first-born infants are more likely to continue the same pattern of communication than mothers and their later-born infants (Hsu & Fogel, 2003). The temporal dynamics of mothers' actions in transitioning in and out of social and didactic actions are not known. Thus, in addition to replicating previous findings on the frequency characteristics of maternal actions, this study examined the temporal characteristics of maternal social and didactic actions during play.

# INFANT AFFECT IN CONTEXTS

Infant fussing and crying reach their peak at around the second month of age and decline steadily thereafter (Barr, 1990). After this two-month shift, infants spend more time in an alert active state (Wolff, 1987), maintain visual attention for a longer time (Haith, Bergman, & Moore, 1977), and begin social smiling (Wolff, 1987). This developmental transition in infant affect marks a qualitative change in mothers' social play with their infants. For example, mothers show an increased contingent response to infant smiling and positive affective signals during the first three months of life (Lavelli & Fogel, 2005; Symons & Moran, 1994). Given this developmental transition, the present study focused on three-month-olds' affect and its contribution to later maternal-infant play behaviors.

The functionalist perspective of infant affective displays has theorized that positive and negative affect not only reflect infants' internal states of feeling but also serve social functions in regulating others' responses (cf. Horstmann, 2003; Shiota, Campos, Keltner, & Hertenstein, 2004). By three months of age, infants' positive affect is likely to occur during social engagement with their parents (e.g., Kaye & Fogel, 1980; Messinger, Fogel, & Dickson, 2001). Mothers react to their infants' smiles with social actions such as talking, smiling, and touching in an attempt to elicit further positive affective exchanges (e.g., Kaye & Fogel, 1980). Regardless of the interactive context, infant positive affect is consistently related to maternal positive affect (Miller, McDonough, Rosenblum, & Sameroff, 2002). By contrast, when responding to infant negative affect, mothers tend to use social-focused and didactic-focused responses. A social-focused response is characterized by soothing the infant with vocalization, rhythmical touch, and care-taking (Jahromi, Putnam, & Stifter, 2004; Keller & Scholmerich, 1987); a didactic-focused response is characterized by engaging and/or shifting infant attention to objects or external events (Crockenberg & Leerkes, 2004; Jahromi et al., 2004). Mothers are more likely to use didactic-focused responses to distract their infants who have cried for extended periods of time (Jahromi et al., 2004). Mothers also exercise differential responsiveness by deliberately ignoring some cry signals (cf. Hubbard & van Ijzendoorn, 1991; van Ijzendoorn & Hubbard, 2000). The context in which infant distress occurs appears to alter maternal actions (cf. Wood & Gustafson, 2001).

Infants' positive and negative affect are highly sensitive to the interactive context. The volatile and transient nature of infant affect makes it difficult to study in the natural home environment. Mild perturbations introduced experimentally can effectively alter infants' affective expressions. The use of the maternal "still-face," in which a mother intentionally ceases all interactive activities and looks at the infant with a neutral expression, has been reported to change the affect of an infant. Infants as young as two months of age demonstrate decreased positive affect as well as increased negative affect in response to the challenge of maternal "still face" (e.g., Moore, Cohn, & Campbell, 2001; Tronick, Als, Adamson, Wise, & Brazelton, 1978; Weinberg & Tronick, 1994, 1996).

Evidence suggests that the known correlations between infant affect and maternal response are not affected by the "still-face" challenge whereas infant positive affect is associated with increased maternal overall involvement and positive affect, and infant negative affect is correlated with decreased maternal sensitivity and positive affect (Miller et al., 2002; Rosenblum, McDonough, Muzik, Miller, & Sameroff, 2002). However, little is known about the association of infant affect observed before and after the "still-face" challenge at any early age with maternal social and didactic actions several months later.

## THE PRESENT STUDY

Because of rapid developmental changes during the first months of life, this study examined the contribution of three-month-olds' facial affect in play to their mothers' social and didactic play actions when the infant was six months of age. The first goal of this study was to replicate and extend previous investigations of the frequency and temporal characteristics of mothers' actions and to identify distinctive styles in their actions during play. The difference and concordance between maternal social and didactic actions in terms of frequency and temporal characteristics were examined. The second goal of this study was to examine the longitudinal association of infant affect with the frequency and temporal characteristics of maternal social and didactic actions during play. Specifically, this study examined the possible relationship between infant affect observed before and after the still-face challenge at three months and the mothers' social and didactic actions observed during play at six months. Consistent with the functionalist account of interpersonal functions of infant affect, we hypothesized that infant positive and negative affect would be differentially linked to the frequency and temporal characteristics of maternal-infant actions three months later. It was expected that infant positive affect would predict frequent maternal social actions and a decreased likelihood for terminating such actions. In contrast, it was expected that infant negative affect would predict mothers' frequent didactic actions and an increased likelihood for initiating such actions. Furthermore, given the known effect of contextual influences, it was expected that infant negative affect observed after the still-face challenge would show a stronger association with maternal actions than those observed before the challenge. Guided by the transactional model, our final goal was to investigate the relationship between early infant positive and negative affect and the mothers' stylistic preferences for types of action (social v. didactic) at the six month observation. Based on the theoretical and empirical work on the moderation effect of context, we hypothesized that infants' decreased positive affect and increased negative affect observed after the "still-face" challenge would be significantly associated with mothers' stylistic preference for didactic actions, whereas infants' increased positive affect and decreased negative affect would be significantly associated with mothers' stylistic preference for social actions.

## METHOD

### Participants

Thirty-two mothers and their first-born infants (18 females) participated in this short-term (three month) longitudinal study. Recruited from prenatal classes, the mothers were white, middle-class women in their late twenties ($M$ = 27.09 years, $SD$ = 4.65) with some college education ($M$ = 15.34 years, $SD$ =2.01). The majority of mothers (87.5%) were married. More than half (65.6%) of the mothers were employed full-time when they were first recruited. The infants in this study were all delivered at full-term (mean gestational age = 39.94 weeks and mean birth weight = 3419.68 grams) with no major complications.

### Research Design and Procedure

The data collection took place when the infants were three and six months of age ($\pm 1$ week). At three months, infants and their mothers took part in the maternal still face procedure. At six months, mother-infant dyads engaged in floor play with age appropriate toys. The behavioral observations and coding are described as follows.

*Maternal Still Face Procedure.* Maternal still face procedure, a widely used experimental procedure designed to assess young infants' emotional competence (e.g., Tronick et al., 1978; Mayes & Carter, 1990; Weinberg, Tronick, Cohn, & Olson, 1999) was conducted in a laboratory room. The infant was placed in an infant seat sitting across from his/her mother at an eye level with no toys. In the first three-minutes of social interaction, the mother played with her infant as they normally would. Upon receiving a signal from the experimenter, the mother stopped playing and looked at her infant with a neutral expression. The mother remained in this still-face posture for three minutes. After the still-face episode, the mother resumed playing with her infant for another three minutes. The still face and resumption of play episodes were curtailed when the infant exhibited continuous crying for thirty seconds. Two infants were too fussy to finish the first episode of routine play. Two mothers failed to follow the instructions for the maternal still face episode. Two babies were extremely distressed and were unable to resume the social interaction with their mothers; thus, the sample size varied in subsequent analysis.

*Behavioral Coding.* Infant affect exhibited during mother-infant play before and after the maternal still face was coded second by second. Based on the Facial Action Coding System (Ekman & Friesen, 1978), the expression of positive affect was defined as the contraction of zygomatic major muscle, which retracts the lip corners back and upward (e.g., Fogel, Hsu, Shapiro, Nelson-Goens, & Secrist, 2006). Infant negative affect was identified as a cry face with knitted eyebrows and squinted eyes. The measures of infant positive and negative affect were derived as the percentage of the total duration for each episode. Twenty percent of infants were randomly selected for checking coding reliability. The average percentage of agreement was 98% and the average kappa was .72.

*Mother-Infant Play.* At six months of age, infants and their mothers engaged in free play on the floor in a laboratory room with age appropriate toys for about ten minutes. One infant was too fussy to begin the floor play. Maternal actions were coded from videos.[1]

*Maternal Actions.* The first step in coding was to identify the occurrence of four maternal actions (Bornstein & Tamis-LeMonda, 1990; Bornstein et al., 1992) second by second: (1) *Social*: Mothers spontaneously guide their infant's attention to their face for social games or face-to-face interaction; (2) *Didactic*: Mothers direct their infant to focus attention to an object or event in the environment; (3) *Monitoring*: Mothers quietly observe their infant without initiating any verbal or physical activities; and (4) *Caregiving*: Mothers perform caregiving activities such as cleaning the infant's face. Because of the rare occurrences of maternal caregiving behavior, it was dropped from further analysis. The frequency of maternal actions was computed and derived as rate per minute. The average percentage of agreement was 79% and the average kappa was .72 on the basis of 26% of randomly selected and coded play sessions.

*Temporal measures of maternal actions.* Second, to capture the dynamics in maternal actions, three temporal characteristics were identified: (1) *Activation:*

Mothers shift out of inactive monitoring and initiate didactic or social actions. (2) *Termination:* Mothers stop didactic or social actions and begin monitoring the infant. (3) *Switch:* Mothers make a transition between didactic and social actions. Yule's Q statistic was calculated to index the odds for the change in maternal actions (see Bakeman, McArthur, & Quera, 1996; Bakeman & Robinson, 1997). These three temporal measures were computed separately for maternal social and didactic actions.

## RESULTS

### Characteristics of Maternal Action

*Frequency Characteristics.* Consistent with previous research (e.g., Bornstein & Tamis-LeMonda, 1990), mothers as a group engaged in more frequent didactic than social actions during play. There was no concordance in maternal social and didactic actions, and the frequency of maternal social and didactic actions was not significantly correlated (see Table 3.1).

*Temporal Characteristics.* Mothers were more likely to activate didactic than social actions and to terminate didactic rather than social actions. Nevertheless, they were equally likely to switch from social to didactic actions or vice versa (see Table 3.1). In addition, maternal switches between social and didactic actions showed a pattern of concordance: those who were more likely to switch from social to didactic actions were more likely to switch from didactic to social actions. By contrast, the likelihood for mothers to activate or terminate social and didactic actions was not significantly correlated (see Table 3.1).

Because no significant main or interaction effects involving infant gender for infant affect and maternal actions were found, data from male and female infants were combined for all subsequent analysis.

### Infant Affect and Maternal Actions

*Associations with frequency measures.* Results from the correlational analysis showed that infants' positive affect displayed before and after the still face was associated with increased maternal social actions; whereas, their negative affect exhibited before and after the still face was associated with increased maternal didactic actions (see Table 3.2). A valence-specific pattern characterized the respective correlations between infant positive and negative affect with the frequency of maternal social and didactic actions.

**Table 3.1.  Characteristics of Maternal Social and Didactic Actions at Six Months**

| Characteristics | Social Actions Mean (SD) | Didactic Actions Mean (SD) | Difference | | Concordance (r) |
| --- | --- | --- | --- | --- | --- |
| | | | F Value | Effect Size ($\eta^2$) | |
| Frequency | .57 (0.40) | 2.29 (0.58) | 164.98** | .86 | -.03 |
| Temporal | | | | | |
| Activation | .26 (0.53) | .92 (0.10) | 6.64** | .57 | -.12 |
| Termination | .20 (0.64) | .88 (0.24) | 5.55** | .54 | .00 |
| Switch | -.28 (0.58) | -.17 (0.58) | 1.04 | .04 | .43* |

*$p<.05$    **$p<.01$

**Table 3.2.   Correlations between Maternal Actions and Infant Affect in Different Interactive Contexts**

| Action Mode | Action Characteristics | Infant Affect | | | |
|---|---|---|---|---|---|
| | | Before Maternal Still Face | | After Maternal Still Face | |
| | | Positive | Negative | Positive | Negative |
| Social | Frequency | .37* | −.24 | .34+ | .18 |
| | Temporal | | | | |
| | Activation | −.21 | .09 | .31 | −.66** |
| | Termination | −.07 | −.43* | .30 | −.65** |
| | Switch | .21 | −.11 | −.23 | .69** |
| Didactic | Frequency | .08 | .40* | −.27 | .41* |
| | Temporal | | | | |
| | Activation | −.23 | .19 | −.31 | .08 |
| | Termination | −.08 | .20 | −.04 | .25 |
| | Switch | -.01 | −.16 | −.17 | .30 |

$+p<.10$    $*p<.05$    $**p<.01$

*Associations with temporal measures.* Infant negative affect, but not positive affect, exhibited before and after the "still face" was significantly correlated with the temporal measures of maternal social actions. Specifically, infant negative affect observed before the "still face" was linked to the reduced likelihood for mothers to terminate social actions. Infant negative affect observed after the "still face" was linked to a reduced likelihood for mothers to activate and terminate social actions and an increased likelihood to switch from social to didactic actions (see Table 3.2). A valence-specific pattern also characterized the respective correlations.

## Infant Affect and Maternal Action Style

Our results show that individual mothers exhibit a configuration of social and didactic actions, which work jointly to form distinctively different action styles. Literature on socialization makes the conceptual distinction between parenting actions and parenting style (see Darling & Steinberg, 1993, for a review). The dimensions model of parental style focuses on the underlying organizational structure of actions. Within this model, parenting style has been defined and operationalized as a linear combination of multiple dimensions of parental actions highlighting the similarity in their underlying dimensions (e.g., Maccoby & Martin, 1983; McGroder, 2000).

Cluster analysis was selected as the strategy to ascertain each mother's action style by analyzing the measures of each mother's social and didactic actions in a configuration. This statistical method previously has been applied to identify mothers with different parenting patterns in infancy and early childhood (e.g., Fish & Stifter, 1995; Fish & Stifter, & Belsky, 1993; McGroder, 2000; Smith, Landry, & Swank, 2000; Symons, 2001). A two-step process was carried out: a hierarchical cluster analysis was performed first, which was followed by a K-means cluster analysis. To determine the appropriate number of clusters, the dendrogram resulting from hierarchical cluster analysis using Ward's method was inspected. This suggested a two-cluster solution. K-means cluster analysis was then performed to assign mothers into groups.

Eleven mothers classified in the first cluster (Didactic-Oriented mothers) represented a style primarily focused on didactic actions. Twenty mothers classified in the second cluster (Social-Oriented mothers) showed a preference for social actions. Compared to Didactic-Oriented mothers, Social-Oriented mothers engaged in less frequent didactic actions, were more likely to terminate and activate social actions, and made less switches between social and didactic actions, Wilks' $\Lambda = 0.229$, $F(8,22) = 8.22$, $p =< .001$, partial $\eta^2 = .77$ (see Table 3.3).

To examine whether infant affect contributed to mothers' action styles three months later, a 2 (Mother Cluster) $\times$ 2 (Episode) mixed-design MANOVA was performed, with infant positive and negative affect as the dependent variables. Results indicated that as described previously, infants' affect became more negative from before to after the still face, Wilks' $\Lambda = 0.561$, $F(2,22) = 8.62$, $p < .01$, partial $\eta^2 = .40$. Infants of didactic-oriented mothers showed significantly more negative affect than those of social-oriented mothers, Wilks' $\Lambda = 0.582$, $F(2,22) = 7.89$, $p < .01$, partial $\eta^2 = .34$. The interaction effect between Mother Cluster and Still-Face Episode was also marginally significant, Wilks' $\Lambda = 0.901$, $F(2,22) = 2.73$, $p < .10$, partial $\eta^2 = .20$. Follow-up analyses revealed that although infants of didactic-oriented mothers did not differ from those of social-oriented mothers in their positive and negative affect before the still-face, they displayed significantly more negative affect, $F(1,24) = 32.90$, $p < .001$, partial $\eta^2 = .59$, and less positive affect, $F(1,24) = 7.55$, $p < .01$, partial $\eta^2 = .25$, than those of social-oriented mothers after the still-face (see Table 3.4).

These findings indicated that infant affect at age three months was associated with maternal action styles three months later and that the interactive context moderated the developmental association between infant affect and maternal action style.[2]

**Table 3.3.  Differences between Didactic-Oriented and Social-Oriented Mothers**

| Action Mode | Action Characteristics | Cluster of Mothers | | Difference (F) | Effect Size ($\eta^2$) |
| --- | --- | --- | --- | --- | --- |
| | | Didactic-Oriented Mean (SD) | Social-Oriented Mean (SD) | | |
| Social | Frequency | .54 (0.32) | .59 (0.44) | 0.09 | .00 |
| | Temporal | | | | |
| | Activation | −.15 (0.51) | .49 (0.40) | 14.65** | .34 |
| | Termination | −.39 (0.55) | .52 (0.41) | 27.71** | .49 |
| | Switch | .25 (0.52) | −.39 (0.48) | 11.91** | .29 |
| Didactic | Frequency | 2.73 (0.42) | 2.05 (0.51) | 14.31** | .33 |
| | Temporal | | | | |
| | Activation | 0.95 (0.04) | 0.91 (0.11) | 1.42 | .05 |
| | Termination | 0.87 (0.29) | 0.88 (0.22) | 0.02 | .00 |
| | Switch | 0.07 (0.58) | −.48 (0.49) | 7.84** | .21 |

*$p < .05$     **$p < .01$

**Table 3.4.   Differences in Infant Affect between Didactic-Oriented and Social-Oriented Mothers Before and After the Challenge of Maternal Still Face**

| | Infant Affect (%) | | | |
| | Before Maternal Still Face | | After Maternal Still Face | |
| Cluster of Mothers | Positive | Negative | Positive | Negative |
| --- | --- | --- | --- | --- |
| Didactic-Oriented | 13.47 (13.03) | 15.16 (31.20) | 1.45 (2.96) | 59.59 (45.32) |
| Social-Oriented | 10.08 (12.25) | 5.39 (10.95) | 7.53 (9.18) | 15.57 (25.85) |

## DISCUSSION

The two primary modes of actions observed in mothers during play at six months were social and didactic. While social actions were characterized by mothers' engagement of their infants' attention to themselves for prolonged social interactions, didactic actions were characterized by mothers' engagement of their infants' attention to objects or events in the environment. Close examination in this study revealed that maternal actions during play are a multidimensional phenomenon with unique frequency and temporal characteristics. Guided by the theorization of infant affect as social and communicative signals in regulating parental actions, the present study extended previous work to understand the contribution of infant affect at three months to maternal-infant action characteristics and style at six months . Overall, our findings support the social-regulatory function of infant affect and further suggest that the developmental association of early infant affect with later maternal-infant actions may be valence specific and context sensitive.

### Characteristics and Style in Maternal Actions During Play

Consistent with previous findings, we found that mothers engaged in significantly more frequent didactic actions than social actions during play in early infancy (e.g., Bornstein et al., 1990). In addition, mothers' actions during play were characterized by a greater likelihood to activate and terminate didactic actions than social actions. Together, these findings may reflect a developmental phenomenon that triadic interaction involving mother, infant, and object replaces dyadic social interaction starting at 3 to 4 months of age (e.g., Cohn & Tronick, 1988; Kaye & Fogel, 1980). Despite a moderate concordance in switching behaviors, the activation and termination between maternal social and didactic actions are independent. The disparity and disassociation between social and didactic actions suggest that they are distinctively different constructs. For mothers to be sensitive and responsive to their infants during play they may need to modulate both types of action appropriately, depending on the needs, interests and developmental age of the child. Detailed analyses have revealed qualitative differences in maternal social actions (e.g., Keller et al., 2004): whereas some are distal in nature (e.g., eye contact), some are proximal (e.g., physical contact). Distal and proximal social actions in mothers have implications for later development. Infants in cultures where their caregivers prefer distal social actions, when compared to children in cultures where their caregivers prefer proximal social actions (e.g., physical contact), tend to develop self-regulation earlier and self-recognition later in toddlerhood (Keller, Yovsi, Borke, Kartner, Jensen et al., 2004). Future research needs to further explore the frequency and temporal characteristics of maternal distal and proximal social actions during play.

Mothers in this study also showed two distinctive action styles: didactic-oriented and social-oriented. A didactic-oriented style is characterized by frequent didactic actions and quick transitions between social and didactic actions. A social-oriented style is featured by less frequent didactic actions and frequent engagement and disengagement of social actions. Cross-culture comparative studies demonstrate that mothers with different socio-cultural orientations differ in their action styles (Keller, Lohaus, Kuensemueller, Abels, Yovsi et al., 2004). Our findings indicated that mothers with relatively homogeneous socio-cultural background may also differ in their preferred action styles during play with their infants. Factors other than the larger cultural value system such as characteristics of the infant, the mother, and the family and non-familial (e.g., child care experience) context may shape maternal action style. The role of infant affect and social interactive context is discussed below.

## Infant Affect and Characteristics of Maternal Actions

Social functional accounts of affective expressions have hypothesized that infant positive affect serves interpersonal functions through eliciting emotional matching in partners and providing incentives for partners to continue social actions (Shiota et al., 2004). Focusing on the concurrent relations between maternal and infant actions, previous still-face research demonstrated that mothers respectively respond to their infants' positive and negative affect with increased and decreased sensitivity and positivity (e.g., Miller et al., 2002; Rosenblum et al., 2002). In this study, we found that a valence-specific pattern characterized the respective associations of infant positive and negative affect with the frequency of maternal social and didactic actions. Infant positive affect observed both before and after the still face was associated with increased social actions in mothers three months later, which provides support for the evocative and incentive functions of infant positive affect in promoting parental social engagements. By contrast, we found that infant negative affect observed both before and after the still face was related to mothers' frequent didactic actions three months later. These findings are consistent with the results reported by Jahromi et al. (2004) that increased intensity and duration of infant cry was concurrently related to increased maternal distracting behavior and decreased maternal touching.

A valence-specific pattern also features the associations between infant positive and negative affect with the temporal characteristics of maternal social parenting. Whereas infant positive affect was not significantly associated with the temporal features of maternal social actions, infant negative affect demonstrated strong associations. Infant negative affect observed both before and after the still-face challenge predicted a decrease in mothers' termination of social actions. Infant negative affect observed after the still face was further associated with mothers' tendency not to initiate social actions and to increase the switch from social to didactic actions. These findings suggest that when interacting with emotionally difficult infants, mothers may need to exert additional effort by adopting a strategy of blending social actions with didactic actions. When social actions fail, mothers tend to quickly shift to didactic actions.

## Infant Affect and Maternal Action Style

Infants of mothers with a didactic-oriented action style showed less positive affect and more negative affect after, not before, the still-face, as compared to infants of mothers with a social-oriented action style. One explanation for these findings is a "mothers-as-external-regulators" hypothesis (cf. Calkins & Fox, 1992; Spangler, Schieche, Ilg, & Maier, 1994). By six months, although infants are capable of engaging in self regulation, mothers still play a significant role in regulating infant emotions. In response to infants' heightened interests in objects, two didactic strategies are found to be effective in reducing infant distress at six months of age (Crockenberg & Leerkes, 2004). One strategy is to maintain infant attention on the source of stress in the environment with maternal verbal support, and the other is to distract infant attention to a new object. It has been documented that infants displaying low positive affect and high negative affect after the still-face challenge are those who demonstrate ineffective physiological regulation during the still-face. The arousal levels of these infants can not be reduced by maternal social engagement after the still-face (Moore & Calkins, 2004). Mothers of infants who displayed low positive affect and heightened negative affect after the still-face may perceive their infants as less efficacious in self-regulation of emotions and requiring effortful maternal regulation. These mothers prefer to engage in didactic activities with frequent shifts between social and didactic actions. Over time, this didactic strategy may gradually become an adaptive action style for these mothers.

## Moderating Role of Interactive Context

Infant negative affect observed after the "still face" as compared to that observed before the "still face" was a stronger predictor of the temporal features of maternal social actions. Mothers are more emotionally involved during dyadic social engagements than during mother-infant-object interactions (Miller et al., 2002). Consequently, infant affect may play a more influential role in the temporal dynamics of maternal social actions than those of didactic actions. Together with our finding that infant affect displayed after the still-face challenge differentiated maternal-infant action style at age six months, it appears that the interactive context plays a moderating role in the linkage between early infant affect and later maternal-infant action.

One explanation for the differential contribution of infant affect in different interactive contexts to the characteristics and style in maternal actions highlights the role of parenting cognition. Maternal actions during play are likely to be guided by their attribution and interpretation of infant signals (cf. Wood & Gustafson, 2001; Donovan, Leavitt, & Walsh 1997; Rosenblum et al., 2002). Recent evidence shows that maternal impressions of infant emotionality are contextually based (Hane, Fox, Polak-Toste, Ghera, & Gunner, 2006). The salience of infant affect to mothers differs across interactive contexts. The finding of a strong link between infant affect observed after the still-face challenge to maternal actions and style implicates that infant affect observed in the situation where the infant is emotionally challenged is more salient to mothers. This may be due to the differences in the intensity of infant negative affect perceived by mothers. After experiencing the stress of "still face," infants demonstrate a configuration of concomitant behaviors indicating intensified distress (Weinberg & Tronick, 1994, 1996). The formulation and consolidation of maternal impressions of infant emotionally is likely to be based on intense infant signals. Cognitive representation of infant emotionality may further serve as a guide for mothers to select action strategies and form a stylistic preference.

In summary, results from the present study offer new information regarding the frequency and temporal characteristics of maternal actions during play, as well as infant affect as a contributor to mothers' actions. The conclusions drawn from this study, however, may be limited. First, parenting is a joint process between parent and child, and the contribution of maternal characteristics (e.g., Clark, Kochanska, & Ready, 2000) and beliefs (e.g., Donovan et al., 1997) that were not considered in this study. Infant affective expressions were observed in an experimental condition rather than in a naturalistic situation. Thus, the current findings need to be replicated with observations of infant affect during the course of home-based interactions with mothers. The generalizability of the two maternal action styles examined in this study may be limited by the small sample size and by the specific characteristics of the relatively homogeneous cultural background and low-risk socioeconomic status of the mothers in the current sample. Additionally, some of the non-significant findings need to be viewed with caution due to concerns related to the adequacy of statistical power (e.g., small sample size). Only large effect sizes can be detected with the current sample. Overall, the present study provides supportive evidence for the social regulatory effect of infant affect on maternal actions, related to both emotional valence and interactive context.

## NOTES

1. Infant affect was also coded. Because the focus of the floor play was on maternal social and didactic actions, the play was terminated when the infant became visibly distressed. The infants were predominantly neutral ($M=85.6\%$, $SD=12.98$) in their affect during floor play. Only one concurrent correlation (out of 16) between infant positive and negative affect and measure of maternal actions was found to be significant. Thus, infant affect observed at 6 months was not considered in the analysis.

2. The infants displayed more positive ($M = 12.36\%$) than negative affect ($M = 7.70\%$) during play with their mothers before the "still face," but exhibited more negative ($M = 31.30\%$) than positive ($M = 5.22\%$) affect after the "still face," Wilks' $\Lambda = 0.706$, $F(2,24) = 4.99$, $p<.05$, partial $\eta^2 = .29$. The change pattern of decreased positive affect and increased negative affect in infants' response to the "still-face" challenge was consistent with the literature (e.g., Weinberg et al., 1999), indicating that the experiment was successful in manipulating infant affect.

## REFERENCES

Bakeman, R., McArthur, D., & Quera, V. (1996). Detecting group differences in sequential association using sampled permutations: Log odds, kappa, and phi compared. *Behavior Research Methods, Instruments, & Computers, 28*, 446–457.

Bakeman, R., & Robinson, B. F. (1997). When Ns do not justify means. In L. B. Adamson & M. A. Romski (Eds.), *Communication and language acquisition: Discoveries from atypical development* (pp. 49–72). Baltimore, MD: Paul H. Brookes.

Barr, R. G. (1990). The normal crying curve: What do we really know? *Developmental Medicine and Child Neurology, 32*, 356–362.

Bornstein, M. H. (2002). Parenting infants. In M. H. Bornstein (2nd ed.), *Handbook of parenting, vol. 1: Children and parenting* (pp. 1–43). Mahwah, NJ: Lawrence Erlbaum.

Bornstein, M. H., Cote, L. R., & Venuti, P. (2001). Parenting beliefs and behaviors in Northern and Southern groups of Italian mothers of young infants. *Journal of Family Psychology, 15*, 663–675.

Bornstein, M. H., Hendricks, C., Haynes, M., & Painter, K. M. (2007). Maternal sensitivity and child responsiveness: Associations with social context, maternal characteristics, and child characteristics in a multivariate analysis. *Infancy, 12*, 189–223.

Bornstein, M. H., & Tamis-LeMonda, C. S. (1990). Activities and interactions of mothers and their firstborn infants in the first six months of life: Covariation, stability, continuity, correspondence, and prediction. *Child Development, 61*, 1206–1217.

Bornstein, M. H., Tamis-LeMonda, C. S., Pascual, L., Haynes, M., Painter, K. M., Galperin, C. Z., & Pecheux, M.-G. (1996). Ideas about parenting in Argentina, France, and the United States. *International Journal of Behavioral Development, 19*, 347–367.

Bornstein, M. H., Tamis-LeMonda, C. S., Pecheux, M.-G., & Rahn, C. W. (1991). Mother and infant activity and interaction in France and in the United States: A comparative study. *International Journal of Behavioral Development, 14*, 21–43.

Bornstein, M. H., Tamis-LeMonda, C. S., Tal, J., Ludemann, P., Toda, S., Rahn, C. W., Pecheux, M.-G., Azuman, H., & Vardi, D. (1992). Maternal responsiveness to infants in three societies: The United States, France, and Japan. *Child Development, 63*, 808–821.

Bornstein, M. H., Toda, S., Azuma, H., Tamis-LeMonda, C. S., & Ogino, M. (1990). Mother and infant activity and interaction in Japan and in the United States: II. A comparative microanalysis of naturalistic exchanges focused on the organization of infant attention. *International Journal of Behavioral Development, 13*, 289–308.

Calkins, S. D., & Fox, N. A. (1992). The relations among infant temperament, security of attachment, and behavioral inhibition at twenty-four months. *Child Development, 63*, 1456–1472.

Clark, L. A., Kochanska, G., & Ready, R. (2000). Mothers' personality and its interaction with child temperament as predictors of parenting behavior. *Journal of Personality and Social Psychology, 79*, 274–285.

Crockenberg, S. C., & Leerkes, E. M. (2004). Infant and maternal behaviors regulate infant reactivity to novelty at 6 months. *Developmental Psychology, 40*, 1123–1132.

Darling, N., & Steinberg, L. (1993). Parenting style as context: An integrative model. *Psychological Bulletin, 113*, 487–496.

Donovan, W. L., Leavitt, L. A., & Walsh, R. O. (1997). Cognitive set and coping strategy affect mothers' sensitivity to infant cries: A signal detection approach. *Child Development, 68,* 760–772.

Ekman, P. & Friesen, W. V. (1978). *Facial action coding system.* Palo Alto, CA: Consulting Psychologists Press.

Fish, M., & Stifter, C. A. (1995). Patterns of mother-infant interaction and attachment: A cluster-analytic approach. *Infant Behavior and Development, 18,* 435–446.

Fish, M., Stifter, C. A., & Belsky, J. (1993). Early patterns of mother-infant dyadic interaction: Infant, mother, and family demographic antecedents. *Infant Behavior and Development, 16,* 1–18.

Fogel, A., Hsu, H., Shapiro, A. F., Nelson-Goens, C., & Secrist, C. (2006). Effects of normal and perturbed social play on the duration and amplitude of different types of infant smiles. *Developmental Psychology, 42,* 459–473.

Hane, A. A., Fox, N. A., Polak-Toste, C., Ghera, M. M., & Gunner, B. M. (2006). Contextual basis of maternal perceptions of infant temperament. *Developmental Psychology, 42,* 1077–1088.

Horstmann, G. (2003). What do facial expressions convey: Feeling states, behavioral intention, or action requests? *Emotion, 3,* 130–166.

Hsu, H., & Fogel, A. (2003). Stability and transitions of mother-infant face-to-face communication during the first six months: A micro-historical approach. *Developmental Psychology, 39,* 1061–1082.

Hubbard, F. O., & van Ijzendoorn, M. H. (1991). Maternal unresponsiveness and infant crying across the first 9 months: A naturalistic longitudinal study. *Infant Behavior & Development, 14,* 299–312.

Jahromi, L. B., Putnam, S. P., & Stifter, C. A. (2004). Maternal regulation of infant reactivity from 2 to 6 months. *Developmental Psychology, 40,* 477–487.

Kaye, K., & Fogel, A. (1980). The temporal structure of face-to-face communication between mothers and infants. *Developmental Psychology, 16,* 454–464.

Keller, H., Lohaus, A., Kuensemueller, P., Abels, M., Yovsi, R., Voelker, S., Jensen, H., Papaligoura, Z., Rosabal-Coto, M., Kulks, D., & Mohita, P. (2004). The Bio-culture of parenting: Evidence from five cultural communities. *Parenting: Science and Practice, 4,* 25–50.

Keller, H., Yovsi, R., Borke, J., Kartner, J., Jensen, H., & Papaligoura, Z. (2004). Developmental consequences of early parenting experiences: Self-recognition and self-regulation in three cultural communities. *Child Development, 75,* 1745–1760.

Keller, H., & Scholmerich, A. (1987). Infant vocalizations and parental reactions during the first four months of life. *Developmental Psychology, 23,* 62–67.

Lavelli, M., & Fogel, A. (2005). Developmental changes in the relationship between the infant's attention and emotion during early face-to-face communication: The 2-month transition. *Developmental Psychology, 41,* 265–280.

Mayes, L. C., & Carter, A. S. (1990). Emerging social regulatory capacities as seen in the still-face situation. *Child Development, 61,* 754–763.

Maccoby, E. E., & Martin, J. A. (1983). Socialization in the context of the family: Parent-child interaction. In P. H. Mussen (Series. Ed.) & E. M. Hetherington (Vol.

Ed.), *Handbook of child psychology: Vol. 4. Socialization, personality, and social development* (4th ed., pp. 1–101). New York: Wiley.

Messinger, D. S., Fogel, A., & Dickson, K. L. (2001). All smiles are positive, but some smiles are more positive than others. *Developmental Psychology, 37,* 642–653.

McGroder, S. M. (2000). Parenting among low-income, African American single mothers with preschool-age children: Patterns, predictors, and developmental correlates. *Child Development, 71,* 752–771.

Miller, A. L., McDonough, S. C., Rosenblum, K. L., & Sameroff, A. J. (2002). Emotion regulation in context: Situational effects on infant and caregiver behavior. *Infancy, 3,* 403–433.

Moore, G. A., & Calkins, S. D. (2004). Infants' vagal regulation in the still-face paradigm is related to dyadic coordination of mother–infant interaction. *Developmental Psychology, 40,* 1068–1080.

Moore, G. A., Cohn, J. F., & Campbell, S. B. (2001). Infant affective responses to mother's still face at 6 months differentially predicted internalizing and externalizing behavior at 18 months. *Developmental Psychology, 37,* 706–714.

Rosenblum, K. L., McDonough, S., Muzik, M., Miller, A., & Sameroff, A. (2002). Maternal representations of the infant: Associations with infant response to the Still Face. *Child Development, 73,* 999–1015.

Sameroff, A. J., & Chandler, M. J. (1975). Reproductive risk and the continuum of caretaking casualty. In F. D. Horowitz, E. M. Hetherington, S. Scarr–Salapatek, & G. Siegal (Eds.), *Review of child development research,* Vol 4, (pp. 187–244). Chicago: University of Chicago Press.

Sameroff, A. J., & Mackenzie, M. J. (2003). Research strategies for capturing transactional models of development: The limits of the possible. *Development & Psychopathology, 15,* 613–640.

Shiota, M. N., Campos, B., Keltner, D., & Hertenstein, M. J. (2004). Positive emotion and the regulation of interpersonal relationships. In P. Philippot & S. Feldman (Eds.), *The regulation of emotion* (p.127–155). Mahwah, NJ: Lawrence Erlbaum.

Smith, K., Landry, S. H., & Swank, P. R. (2000). The influence of early patterns of positive parenting on children's preschool outcomes. *Early Education & Development, 11,* 147–169.

Spangler, G., Schieche, M., Ilg, U., & Maier, U. (1994). Maternal sensitivity as an external organizer for biobehavioral regulation in infancy. *Developmental Psychobiology, 27,* 425–437.

Symons, D. K. (2001). A dyad-oriented approach to distress and mother-child relationship outcomes in the first 24 months. *Parenting: Science & Practice, 1,* 101–122.

Symons, D., & Moran, G. (1994). Responsiveness and dependency are different aspects of social contingencies: An example from mother and infant smiles. *Infant Behavior & Development, 17,* 209–214.

Tronick, E. Z., Als, H., Adamson, L., Wise, S., & Brazelton, B. (1978). The infants' response to entrapment between conflictory messages in mother-infant interaction. *American Academy of Child Psychiatry, 1,* 1–13.

Van Ijzendoorn, M. H., & Hubbard, F. O. (2000). Are infant crying and maternal responsiveness during the first year related to infant-mother attachment at 15 months? *Attachment & Human Development, 2*, 371–391.

Weinberg, M. K., & Tronick, E. Z. (1994). Beyond the face: An empirical study of infant affective configurations of facial, vocal, gestural, and regulatory behaviors. *Child Development, 65*, 1503–1515.

Weinberg, M. K., & Tronick, E. Z. (1996). Infant affective reactions to the resumption of maternal interaction after the still face. *Child Development, 67*, 905–914.

Weinberg, M. K., Tronick, E. Z., Cohn, J. F., & Olson, K. L. (1999). Gender differences in emotional expressivity and self-regulation during early infancy. *Developmental Psychology, 35*, 175–188.

Wood, R. M., & Gustafson, G. E. (2001). Infant crying and adults' anticipated caregiving responses: Acoustic and contextual influences. *Child Development, 72*, 1287–1300.

*Part II*

# THE COMPLEXITIES OF CHILD-CHILD PLAY IN DIFFERENT CONTEXTS

## Chapter Four

# The Reality of Pretend Play: Ethnic, Socioeconomic, and Gender Variations in Young Children's Involvement

### Rachana Karnik and Jonathan Tudge

Young children's play activities have received substantial attention in early childhood research because of their positive contributions to children's development. Many scholars have suggested that play has more value than simply being an activity for amusement. Piaget's theory of cognitive development in children underpins much of the research on children's play (Pellegrini, 1982; Rubin, Watson, & Jambor, 1978). Children's play has been linked to their representation of reality through pretend (Piaget, 1962). This development is seen in the emergence of pretend play as children progress from simple and concrete to complex and abstract types of play—for example, pretend play precedes games with rules—(Clift, Stagnitti, & DeMello, 1998). According to Piaget, pretend play emerges around two years of age. It increases in the fifth and sixth year of life and then declines. Researchers and practitioners have applied Piaget's developmental theory to observe and explain children's growth and development on the basis of children's play patterns (Pellegrini & Smith, 2003). Pretend play is "the projecting of a supposed situation onto an actual one, in the spirit of fun rather than for survival" (Lillard, 1993, p. 349). Lillard outlined five features necessary for pretend play to occur—there should be a pretender, a reality that is pretended (e.g., pretending a war), an idea or a mental representation different from reality (e.g., considering sticks as guns), projecting the idea or mental representation as reality (e.g., using the sticks as guns), and being aware of the difference between reality and non-reality.

Pretend play has received a good deal of attention from researchers in the fields of both developmental and cross-cultural psychology. Many developmental psychologists have explored the correlates of pretend play. In the area of cognitive skills, for example, pretend play has been linked to creativity, academic competence/achievement, linguistic competence, mathematical skills, problem-solving skills, and organizational skills (e.g., Bergen, 2002; Brown, Rickards, & Bortoli, 2001; Lloyd & Howe, 2003). In the area of social skills, it has been linked with turn-taking, perspective-taking, and peer relations (e.g., Colwell & Lindsey, 2005; Farver, Kim, & Lee-Shin, 2000). Some of this research has been conducted in naturalistic settings. For example, Haight and Miller (1993) observed pretend play at home with the mother present during the observational periods.

There is also some research on children's play in parts of the "majority" world (Kağitçibaşi, 2005) from a socio-cultural or cultural–anthropological perspective (Bloch, 1989; Farver, 1993; Gaskins, 1999; Göncü, Mistry, & Mosier, 2000; Göncü, Tuermer, Jain, & Johnson, 1999; Lancy, 1996; Rogoff, Mistry, Göncü, & Mosier, 1993; Roopnarine, Hooper, Ahmeduzzaman, & Pollack, 1993; Schwartzman, 1978). Some of this research is based simply on naturalistic observations of children's naturally occurring activities (Bloch, 1989; Gaskins, 1999), although other work, albeit set within the home, features quasi-experimental procedures. The method developed by Rogoff and her colleagues, for example, involves the introduction of some novel play objects to mothers and their toddlers as well as observation of what naturally occurs during interviews with the mothers (Rogoff et al., 1993).

It is not only essential to compare pretend play across different societies, but it is equally important to study children's pretend play within a given society (Tudge, Lee, & Putnam, 1998). Some scholars have therefore compared the relations between children's pretend play and parental beliefs of immigrant and non-immigrant populations (e.g., Cote & Bornstein, 2005; Farver et al, 2000; Parmar, Harkness, & Super, 2004). However, given the ethnic and social class diversity in the United States, one does not have to study immigrant groups to discover links among pretend play and within-society cultural differences. Defining culture as shared values, beliefs, and practices (Tudge, 2008) both ethnicity and social class may be viewed as different cultural contexts for the developing child. This definition of culture is supported empirically, as extant literature in the area of ethnic research suggests differential home environment and socialization provided by European American and African American parents to their children (e.g., Quintana et al., 2006). Juxtaposing the understanding from previous research findings that differences in home environment and parental socialization of their children are linked with different pretend play experiences of children (Parmar et al., 2004), we hypothesize that frequency and content of children's pretend play will be different for European American and African American children (treated subsequently as ethnic differences).

In addition, the family investment model supports the idea that children of different socioeconomic status (SES) backgrounds are exposed to different home environments including the availability of toys and games that stimulate learning (Conger & Donnellan, 2007). Given this perspective, we assume that children from middle-class and working-class families may have different opportunities for pretend play and we hypothesize social class differences in frequency and content of children's pretend play. Scholars of pretend play have rarely considered the impact of social context on pretend play, especially the intersection of class and ethnicity. Hence, the present study is a step in this direction.

Lastly, the children's play literature suggests that there are differences in the pretend play of girls and boys. These differences are not only in the frequency of play but also in the content of such play among girls and boys (see Colwell & Lindsey, 2005; Fabes, Martin, Hanish, Anders, & Madden-Derdich, 2003; Gosso, Morais, & Otta, 2007). Therefore, in this chapter, we hypothesize gender differences both in the frequency and content of children's pretend play.

Most of the research literature outlined here has several limitations in regards to theoretical, methodological, and conceptual issues in studying children's pretend-play activities. A major theoretical drawback of these studies has been that the bulk of research conducted by developmental psychologists has been carried out in laboratory settings where "induced" pretend play is studied rather than naturally occurring pretend play (e.g., Bornstein, Haynes, Legler, O'Reilly & Painter, 1997; Smith & Whitney, 1987; Lillard, 1993) or in semi-structured settings in children's homes (e.g., Bornstein, Haynes, Pascual, Painter, & Galperín, 1999; Cote & Bornstein, 2005) and preschools (e.g., Wyer & Spence, 1999).

Overall, then, there is a lacuna in the pretend-play literature in terms of the actual frequency and description of naturally occurring pretend play in children's homes as well as in other social settings. There is also limited cross-cultural or intra-societal research on children's pretend play that has looked at different patterns of pretend play as a function of their ethnicity and social class.

A major conceptual contribution of this study is that our position on pretend play fits explicitly within a broader theoretical framework which has everyday activities and interactions (including pretend play) as critical for development, and that the nature of these everyday activities and interactions (including pretend play) varies by virtue of both the context (i.e., culture) and individual characteristics (e.g., gender). A second major contribution of the study is the ethnographic observational method of data collection. This method of data collection is in keeping with our paradigmatic (i.e., contextualist) and theoretical position.

# THEORETICAL FRAMEWORK

The data for this paper are drawn from part of the Cultural Ecology of Young Children (CEYC) Project. The CEYC project is based on cultural–ecological theory (Tudge, 2008), a theory derived from Bronfenbrenner's bioecological theory (Bronfenbrenner, 1995, 1999, 2005; Bronfenbrenner & Morris, 2006) and Vygotsky's cultural–historical theory (Tudge & Scrimsher, 2003; Vygotsky, 1987, 1997a, 1997b). At the core of cultural–ecological theory are the everyday activities and interactions in which children take part in the various contexts in which they are typically situated. Cultural–ecological theory conceptualizes that peoples' everyday activities and interactions are influenced by the mutual influence of their own individual characteristics and the context, both culture and the immediate setting, in which the individuals are situated. The theory postulates that individuals' characteristics as well as the characteristics of significant others in the lives of the children (e.g., parents, siblings, friends, and teachers) influence the choice of activities in which they engage and the ways in which the individuals transform these activities. On the other hand, these activities can only occur in a context, and these contexts in turn are influenced by the occurrence of the activities. This shows the complex interaction between the individual and the context. The ongoing analyses of the data aim to explore these complex influences of children's characteristics and their context for children's development. Cultural–ecological theory will be used to study the occurrence and content of pretend play in children's everyday activities.

In summary, on the basis of cultural–ecological theory, culture is defined as a shared set of values, beliefs, practices, identity, and access to similar resources that parents attempt to transmit to their children (Tudge, 2008). According to this definition of culture, ethnicity and social class may be considered as providing different cultural contexts to the extent to which they fulfill the above criteria. We examine the interaction between ethnicity and social class (cultural variables) and children's gender (a socially influenced individual characteristic) as influencing children's pretend-play activities. We hypothesize that pretend play in children will vary according to their ethnicity, social class, and gender.

# METHOD

The CEYC Project is an ongoing longitudinal study using ethnographic observations to study preschool-aged children's typically occurring everyday activities and interactions in their natural settings. One of the many aims of the project is to explore similarities and differences both within and between cultures in parents' child-rearing values and their children's everyday activities and interactions. Children were observed in a single city in each of seven different countries: the United States, Russia, Estonia, Korea, Finland, Kenya, and Brazil. Half of the children were from middle-class families (as determined by education and occupation criteria) and half from working-class backgrounds. In addition, in the U.S. city half the children were African-American and half were European-American. This selection was equally divided by social class (for more details, see Tudge, 2008).

## Participants

Participants in this study were selected from four cultural groups residing in the city of Greensboro, North Carolina, in the United States. A total of 39 children from European American ($n = 20$) and African American ($n = 19$) communities (2 middle class and 2 working class) were observed. There were 9 girls and 11 boys from middle-class families and 10 girls and 9 boys from working-class families (see Table 4.1). Families were selected for the study if they clearly fit either working-class or middle-class criteria, by Hollingshead (1975) standards (see Table 4.1), and if their children had been born within one of four neighborhoods of the city that were relatively homogeneous (by ethnicity and social class). Social class status was determined by parents having a college degree and employment, if working outside the home, in a professional job (middle class), or no college degree and a job in

Table 4.1.   Participant Characteristics (N = 39)

| Characteristics | European American Families | African American Families |
|---|---|---|
| Families contacted | 46 | 50 |
| Did not meet requirements | 12 | 15 |
| Declined to participate (% rejected) | 14 (30.4%) | 16 (32%) |
| Recruited | 20 | 19 |
| Middle-class participants | 11 | 9 |
| Age of children, M (SD) | 36.6 (7.0) | 38.3 (5.7) |
| Girls | 6 | 3 |
| Boys | 5 | 6 |
| Hollingshead M (SD) | 52.1 (8.0) | 50.2 (4.3) |
| Working-class participants | 9 | 10 |
| Age of children, M (SD) | 36.9 (4.5) | 39.8 (6.4) |
| Girls | 5 | 5 |
| Boys | 4 | 5 |
| Hollingshead, M (SD) | 28.9 (4.8) | 28.6 (4.0) |

the semi-skilled or skilled labor sector (working class). All parents meeting our criteria were invited to participate in the study, with an acceptance range of 64–78% from the four neighborhoods. For this paper, we are therefore able to examine similarities and differences in children's engagement in pretend play in these four different cultural groups.

## Data Collection Procedures

Children's everyday activities and interactions were observed and video-taped. Children were observed for 20 hours, of which 18 hours involved live coding that took place over one week per child, with the final two hours videotaped. These observations were carried out by a single observer per child over the course of a week. They took place in two 2-hour blocks, four 4-hour blocks (one block per day), to cover the equivalent of one complete day in the child's life. To achieve this goal each target child was observed once early in the morning, typically starting before he or she woke up, once during the end of the day when the child was getting ready to go to bed, and the rest of the observations spread over the remainder of the day, with children observed anywhere that they were situated during the observational block. Approximately 180 observations of every child were carried out.

The observers were trained using live and videotaped observations of children from families with a preschool-aged child. Any discrepancies in coding were resolved through discussion of disagreements until consensus was reached. Reliability was assessed using videotaped observations both before and during data collection. Coders had to attain and retain a minimum *kappa* of .75 on all codes. Observers coded activities, partners, roles in activity, initiation of activity, etc. for a 30-second period ("window") every 6 minutes. The activities and interactions in which the children engaged were coded under broad categories of lessons, work, play, conversation, and other, each of which had various subcategories (see Table 4.2).

Coding took place immediately after each window and was followed by written field notes that described the activities and interactions in more detail. In a single "window" period it was possible to code more than one activity. For example, an observer could observe and code play as well as conversation and/or academic lessons as well as work within a single "window."

We defined pretend play as play in which a child was emulating either a role from the adult world or any other type of pretend play such as re-enacting everyday routines. Specifically, play involving the pretending of adult roles from various aspects of adult life (such as occupation, celebrity, war-related, adult social, and domestic roles) was coded as *adult pretend* whereas play that involved the enactment and reproduction of various daily activities that

Table 4.2. Definitions of Major Activities

| Activities | Definition |
|---|---|
| Lessons | Deliberate attempts to impart or elicit information relating to: |
|   Academic | School (spelling, counting, learning shapes, comparing quantities, colors, etc.); |
|   World | How things work, why things happen, safety; |
|   Interpersonal | Appropriate behavior with others, etiquette etc.; |
|   Religious | Religious or spiritual matters. |
| Work | Household activities (cooking, cleaning, repairing, etc.), shopping, etc. |
| Play | Activities engaged in for their own enjoyment: |
|   Toys | Objects designed specifically for play or manipulation by children; |
|   Pretend | Play involving evidence that a role is being assumed, whether prosaic (mother shopping), mythical (super-hero), or object (animal); |
|   Natural objects | Playing with objects that are easily available in the natural surroundings such as sand, pebbles, etc.; |
|   Adult-oriented objects | Playing with objects not designed for the play or use of children. Specifically objects used by adults such as kitchen utensils. |
|   Academic | Play with academic object (looking at a book, playing with shapes, numbers, etc.), with no lesson involved; |
|   TV, entertainment | Watching TV, listening to radio, going to a ball-game, circus, etc. |
|   Other play | Objects not designed specifically for children, such as household objects, natural objects, or no object at all (rough and tumble, chase); |
| Conversation | Talk with a sustained or focused topic about things not the current focus of engagement. |
| Other | Activities such as sleeping, eating, bathing, etc. and those that were uncodable. |

did not feature adults (fictional characters or settings, animals, and taking on other children's roles) was coded as *generic play*. Our coding of pretend play was conservative. That is, for a child to be coded as engaging in pretend play he or she had to display verbal or nonverbal evidence of pretence. A child, simply moving a block along the ground, would have been coded as playing with a child-oriented object; adding the sounds of a car being driven or a dog barking would have allowed us to code the activity as pretend. We are therefore likely to have underestimated the extent to which the children were actually involved in pretend play.

Although the initial coding of pretend play as "adult" or "generic" was made immediately after each observational window closed, we coded the field notes in order to provide data on the specific subcategories that are the focus of this paper. To establish inter-rater reliability, 20 excerpts from the field notes and videotape transcripts were coded separately by three coders (two of whom transcribed the videotape data) of the research team. Any discrepancy in coding was resolved through a consensus of the research group.

## RESULTS

### Analysis

The pretend-play activities were coded into the various subcategories using a qualitative data analysis software, NVivo Version 2.0 (QSR International, 2002). Thereafter, the computed frequency of the occurrence of different types of pretend play (based on the content of their play) for each child was entered into SPSS (Statistical Package for the Social Sciences). Using this data, we conducted multivariate analysis (MANOVAs) and followed significant MANOVAs with univariate ANOVAs.

Because these children were drawn purposefully from four specific communities in Greensboro they cannot be considered to be randomly drawn from some known populations. In this case statistics, whose purpose is to infer from samples to populations, are neither relevant nor appropriate. Our sole reason for using inferential statistics is to allow us to discuss group differences that are large enough to be considered meaningful. As the second author has argued elsewhere (Tudge, 2008), given the ways in which these data were collected, using time-sampling methods, differences that can be seen as meaningful are likely to have a clear impact on children's development.

The observations of African American and European American children's everyday activities were examined to understand the frequency and content of pretend play. The results are presented in three sections (a) types of everyday activities, (b) types of play, and (c) types of pretend play content. The quantitative multivariate results as well as vignettes from the field notes and video transcripts have been interspersed to give a more nuanced understanding of the reported data.

### Types of Everyday Activities

Everyday activities and interactions of the children were categorized into lessons (7% of the observations), work (11%), play (71%), and conversation (11%). The three-way 2 X 2 X 2 (Ethnicity X Gender X Class) MANOVA revealed statistically significant main effects of Ethnicity, $F(4, 28) = 3.94$, $p < .05$ and

**Table 4.3.  Means for Types of Activities**

| Communities | Lessons | Work | Play | Conversation |
|---|---|---|---|---|
| | European American (*n* = 20) | | | |
| Middle-Class Girls | 6.42 | 5.03 | 46.74 | 14.39 |
| Middle-Class Boys | 8.84 | 10.43 | 44.04 | 12.43 |
| Working-Class Girls | 5.24 | 8.72 | 59.39 | 8.85 |
| Working-Class Boys | 5.56 | 7.63 | 66.7 | 6.07 |
| | African American (*n* = 19) | | | |
| Middle-Class Girls | 6.42 | 11.61 | 64.52 | 9.59 |
| Middle-Class Boys | 5.83 | 10.32 | 61.06 | 3.86 |
| Working-Class Boys | 4.32 | 8.72 | 59.7 | 9.14 |
| Working-Class Boys | 3.08 | 7.63 | 63.97 | 4.46 |

of Class, $F(4, 28) = 2.8, p < .05$. The univariate ANOVAs for play revealed a significant main effect of Class, $F(1, 31) = 4.31, p <.05$, and an interaction effect of Ethnicity X Class, $F(1, 31) = 5.35, p < .05$. Overall, children from working-class families engaged significantly more in play activities than did those from middle-class families. European American middle-class children engaged in significantly less play than did children from any other group.

## Types of Play Activities

Play (including entertainment) activities were initially classified into seven categories: playing with toys (e.g., objects designed for children such as dolls), engaging in pretend play (generic play and emulation of adult roles), playing with natural objects (e.g., sand), playing without any objects, playing with adult oriented objects (e.g., playing with kitchen utensils), playing with academic objects (e.g., alphabet blocks), and watching TV (see Table 4.2).

Children played most with toys, followed by watching TV, and playing with adults. They engaged least in pretend play. The three-way MANOVA indicated a significant main effect of Ethnicity, $F(8, 24) = 6.44, p < .001$, and of Class, $F(7, 25) = 2.55, p < .05$. The univariate ANOVAs for pretend play did not reveal any significant main or interaction effects based on children's ethnicity and class.

## Types of Pretend Play

As noted earlier, pretend play was initially coded into two types, namely generic and adult. One example of generic pretend play was provided by Patty. Patty, a European American working-class girl, and her friend pretended to be frogs.

**Table 4.4.  Means for Types of Play Activities**

| Communities | Toys | Pretend | Natural | No object | Adult | Acad. | TV |
|---|---|---|---|---|---|---|---|
| | | | European American (*n* = 20) | | | | |
| Middle-Class Girls | 19.26 | 3.47 | 3.05 | 3.81 | 2.44 | 6.58 | 7.37 |
| Middle-Class Boys | 16.63 | 4.0 | 1.52 | 3.33 | 3.75 | 3.67 | 9.46 |
| Working-Class Girls | 25.11 | 3.97 | 2.82 | 4.23 | 6.25 | 2.67 | 13.88 |
| Working-Class Boys | 31.21 | 2.24 | 3.84 | 3.37 | 7.08 | 6.41 | 12.14 |
| | | | African American (*n* = 19) | | | | |
| Middle-Class Girls | 24.47 | 4.05 | 3.45 | 6.03 | 6.52 | 7.54 | 10.8 |
| Middle-Class Boys | 25.7 | .77 | 3.19 | 7.97 | 8.46 | 2.54 | 11.1 |
| Working-Class Girls | 20.06 | 1.88 | 3.53 | 9.31 | 10.13 | 2.21 | 12.15 |
| Working-Class Boys | 19.82 | .78 | 2.72 | 9.45 | 7.62 | 5.17 | 17.53 |

Patty's friend is jumping like a frog and making noises from his mouth. Patty watches him and sits on the ground with her feet behind her and jumps like a frog behind him. Both children are hopping like a frog. Patty's friend invites Patty to race like a frog, and he does the countdown and both race like frogs. Both children reach the adults standing nearby and stop their game by standing up on their feet.

By contrast, Una, a girl from the European American, working-class community, emulated adult roles around the farmhouse.

Una is singing to the toy cow, "Here we go inside the house." She finds another toy animal from inside the farmhouse. She asks her mother if this is the mother cow, but the mother replies "Looks like a horse to me." Una is playing farmhouse. She puts the toy horse in it and shuts the house door saying "I am going to lock you up in the cage." She opens the door again and says "Yes, I am going to lock you monkey and then get mama monkey." Una fixes the fence of the farmhouse. Una opens the door of the farmhouse and walks the brown toy (toy horse) in the farmhouse. Una jumps to the farmhouse play, and her mother joins her. Una says "I am the farmer lady you are the farmer man." Una then asks, "Who is going to be the animal?" The mother replies "I don't know, I will drive the tractor." The mother says, "peep peep," and drives the tractor. Una also makes tractor noises. Now the mother leaves the tractor trailer/wagon behind the farmhouse, and comes with the driver ahead and asks Una if she will do it. Una affirms and takes the tractor and latches the trailer/wagon on to it. Una drives the tractor making noises (brrr prrr). The mother meanwhile has fenced the cow. Una now asks her mother, "Why he can't get out" and the mother replies, "Because I fenced him up." Una picks another animal from the trailer and walks into the farmhouse.

In terms of generic pretend, the children pretended to carry out daily activities (making a phone call to granny), to be fictional characters (e.g., Wendy)

*Table 4.5.    Means for Types of Pretend Play*

| Communities | Adult | Generic |
|---|---|---|
| European American (*n* = 20) | | |
| Middle-Class Girls | 2.17 | 2.49 |
| Middle-Class Boys | 3.2 | 1 |
| Working-Class Girls | 2.6 | 2.1 |
| Working-Class Boys | 1.5 | 1.5 |
| African American (*n* = 19) | | |
| Middle-Class Girls | 2.67 | 1.67 |
| Middle-Class Boys | .67 | .83 |
| Working-Class Girls | .8 | .62 |
| Working-Class Boys | .4 | .2 |

or pretended to be in fictional settings (e.g., going to "Neverland"), to be animals (e.g., making noises like a dog), and to pretend that they were at some type of special occasion (e.g., celebrating Easter). MANOVAs showed a significant main effect of Class, $F(4, 28) = 3.1, p < .05$. Follow-up univariate ANOVAs indicated that the effect of Class, $F(1, 31) = 6.67, p < .05$ was significant only for children pretending to be animals, with working-class children being involved in significantly more animal play than were children from middle-class families.

In terms of adult pretend, children emulated occupational (e.g., firemen, teacher), celebrity (e.g., football player), war-related (e.g., killing pirates), adult social (e.g., pretending to be a bride), and domestic (e.g., cooking), roles. John, a boy from a European American, middle-class background, provides an interesting example.

John is playing post-office with his mother. He is the postal worker, and his mother is a customer. John reads a letter to his mother. There is a lot of talk

**Table 4.6.    Means for Types of Generic Play**

| Communities | Daily | Fiction | Animal | Special |
|---|---|---|---|---|
| European American (*n* = 20) | | | | |
| Middle-Class Girls | 0.83 | 1 | 0.33 | 0.33 |
| Middle-Class Boys | 0.4 | 0.4 | 0 | 0.2 |
| Working-Class Girls | 0.6 | 0 | 1 | 0.4 |
| Working-Class Boys | 0 | 0.5 | 1 | 0 |
| African American (*n* = 19) | | | | |
| Middle-Class Girls | 0.67 | 0.67 | 0 | 0.33 |
| Middle-Class Boys | 0 | 0.67 | 0.17 | 0 |
| Working-Class Girls | 0 | 0.2 | 0.2 | 0.22 |
| Working-Class Boys | 0 | 0 | 0.2 | 0 |

about stamps. Mother tells him that he will be "fired" if he doesn't do his post-man job. John is about to call a fireman. Mother says if he does not give her the three stamps which she has asked for that he will get "fired." He understands the threat. After some time John is playing alone, and mother is doing her laundry. John is playing with his post office set and mother after sometime comes and sits on the floor with him and he is getting her mail ready.

Raymond, from an African American working-class family, illustrates an instance of emulating a celebrity.

> Raymond is running into the yard and announcing if anyone wants to play foot-ball. He and another child are seen running up and down. Raymond is saying "I have got the football" and holds out an empty hand. In reality there is no football between the boys.

Another example is provided by Georgina, a girl from a European American, middle-class background engaged in domestic pretend play.

> Georgina is "baking a cake" in a child kitchen in the playroom. She is inter-rupted by a girl who comes over to her and asks what she is making and whether she can help her. Georgina says "yes," and the little girl sits down and Georgina tells her she is on her way in her car to get some hot dogs. Georgina then gets out a set of toy dishes and pots and pans. She is holding the lids of each pot while the girl stirs it with a spoon. She pretends to stir food and puts spoonsfuls on a plate. She is asking the other child "Do you want some more?" and the other girl asks her back "Are you going to cook some more?"

The three-way MANOVA revealed a significant main effect of Gender, $F(5, 27) = 3.04$, $p < .05$. As expected, the subsequent univariate ANOVAs appeared to be significant for the effect of Gender on children's social [$F(1, 31) = 8.28$, $p < .01$] and domestic [$F(1, 31) = 7.62$ $p < .01$] adult pretend play with more girls than boys involved in social and domestic play. A typical example is provided by Felicia, a girl from a European American middle-class background, who was dressed up as a bride.

> Felicia has on a child-sized white lace dress (costume) and she has put on a pair of wings to go with it saying that "the brides wear wings." She asks if Grandma will go with her to the wedding.

Another example is that of Brianna, a girl from an African American middle-class family, who was observed giving a party.

> Brianna has pulled out some toys and is sitting at her little table. So then mother asks her "Are you going to feed the babies?" To this Brianna replies, "No," and

**Table 4.7. Means for Types of Adult Role Pretend**

| Communities | Occupation | Celebrity | War | Social | Domestic |
|---|---|---|---|---|---|
| European American (n = 20) | | | | | |
| Middle-Class Girls | 0.17 | 0 | 0 | 0.5 | 1.5 |
| Middle-Class Boys | 1.8 | 0 | 0.6 | 0 | 0.8 |
| Working-Class Girls | 0.6 | 0.4 | 0 | 0.2 | 1.4 |
| Working-Class Boys | 0.5 | 0 | 1 | 0 | 0 |
| African American (n = 19) | | | | | |
| Middle-Class Girls | 0 | 0 | 0 | 1 | 1.67 |
| Middle-Class Boys | 0 | 0.17 | 0 | 0 | 0.5 |
| Working-Class Girls | 0.4 | 0.2 | 0 | 0 | 0.2 |
| Working-Class Boys | 0.2 | 0.2 | 0 | 0 | 0 |

tells the mother that she is having a tea party but has no tea to give to her babies (dolls). She tells the mother that she is having a birthday party and is going to invite the rabbit and the elephant.

## DISCUSSION

As we had anticipated, children were observed playing in the majority of observations, but they did not often engage in pretend play. Although children were observed playing in 44% to 63% of the observations, they were only engaged in pretend play about 4% of the time, a surprisingly low amount when compared to the results of many previous studies on pretend play. The most likely reason for the difference is that most research related to children's play in the past has explored the content of pretend play in laboratory settings where pretend play is induced (e.g., Smith & Whitney, 1987; Wyer & Spence, 1999), rather than the frequency and occurrence of pretend play in real-life settings.

As described earlier, there were no significant mean differences by ethnicity, class, or gender in the extent to which the children engaged in the two broadest categories of pretend play, namely the generic pretend play and the emulation of adult roles. However, social class and gender (but not ethnicity) significantly influenced the extent to which these children were involved in the various subcategories of pretend play.

An interesting finding that emerged was related to the gender and social class of children. We found that girls seemed to differ from boys in their pretend play activities. When observed in their natural settings, girls tended to engage in more gender stereotypical play activities. In the category of generic pretend play, middle-class girls pretended to involve themselves in daily activities (e.g., bathing a doll), social pretend play (e.g., pretending to be a bride), and domestic pretend play (e.g., cooking) more than did their male counterparts. No such difference was found for working-class girls. Furthermore, we examined the patterns of the content of boys' emulation of adult roles and we found that middle-class boys tended (though not significantly so) to be involved in more occupation-related emulation.

An important strength of the study is the method used for data collection — ethnographic observations. The validity of observations as a method of data collection has been questioned in research as leading to socially desirable responses and behaviors from participants. We propose to counter-argue that young pre-school children as well as their parents became accustomed to the observer's presence for two reasons. First, the observer spent a good deal of time with each child, not interacting in any way, but simply observing what the children were doing and the people with whom they were interacting. Because the children were so young, they appeared to become accustomed to the observer's presence very quickly. Second, because each child was equipped with a small wireless microphone, the observer was able to observe and listen to the child without being very close in proximity. This may have allowed normal activities and interactions to occur.

We noted that the children and those with whom they interacted seemed to be at ease with the observer's presence. They gave no indication of behaving differently because of the observer. Although human error in perceiving the interactions may have occurred, we felt that we were observing the types of activities and interactions in which the children were typically involved. Because researchers observed children and their naturally occurring activities and interactions in their natural environments and contexts, we believe that our data are ecologically valid (Bronfenbrenner, 1977).

There are several other possible limitations of this study. First, the children in our study were only three years old and thus should not be expected to have engaged in as much pretend play as would children a year or more older. On the other hand, researchers such as Haight and Miller (1993), who studied children solely in their home environments at times when their mothers were with them, may have overestimated the extent to which pretend play occurs in the everyday lives of very young children. Children, after all, do not typically spend all of their time at home with their mothers, but are to be found in many other contexts and often not with their mothers.

A second limitation of the study is the likelihood that we have underreported the frequency of pretend play occurring in children's lives. We only coded pretend play when the children made it apparent, either verbally or behaviorally, that they were taking on some type of pretend role. There may have been other situations in which they simply did not signal that they were pretending. For example, a child walking on hands and feet may have been pretending to be a dog, but without barking, we would not have known nor would we have coded the behavior as pretend.

A third limitation of the study is the small number of participants. However, these participants were chosen purposefully from specific neighborhoods of the city and from families that met specific racial/ethnic and socioeconomic conditions (see Tudge, 2008). Given that we were able to recruit approximately 70% of the families that satisfied our criteria in each of the neighborhoods, we are really describing small populations rather than samples that have been randomly selected from some broader population. Clearly, this restricts the extent to which we are able to generalize our findings. However, as discussed in the earlier section about data analysis, generalizability was not our goal.

There is one sense, however, in which we are willing to generalize our findings—not across other groups but across time. It should be remembered that although we observed for 18 hours, we only coded what occurred during a 30-second window every six minutes, or a total of 90 minutes in total. Given our time-sampling approach there is no reason to think that what we observed during these 30-second windows would not have taken place during any other time period that we were observing (but not coding). For example, we found that (on average) European American children engaged in pretend play in about 4.1 of their observations and African American children in about 1.9 of their observations during the 90 minutes of total observations. Assuming that children are awake for about 14 hours per day at this age, we might assume that these children engaged in pretend play almost 40 times vs. about 18 times during an entire day. As Hart and Risley (1995, 1999) argued regarding early language experience, these types of regular differences in the experiences of young children may come to have a profound impact on their development, particularly if pretend play does have the type of positive impact that many scholars have described.

## CONCLUSION

We examined the occurrence, frequency, and type of pretend-play activities of three and four-year-old children in their natural settings using cultural–ecological theory. We found that although children engaged in play in over half of our observations, the types of play varied by ethnicity, social class, and gender. Children engaged relatively infrequently in pretend play, but middle-class children (both European American and African American), and particularly girls, engaged in more pretend play than did working-class children. Various scholars have found a link between children engaging in pretend play and subsequent social and cognitive development, but the assessment of pretend play has largely taken place under controlled or semi-controlled contexts. As Bronfenbrenner (1977) argued, we need to be concerned about the ecological validity of findings that are derived solely from studies using methods of tight control. More research is therefore needed to examine the extent to which young children engage in pretend play in their normal, everyday contexts and the types of pretend in which they engage. It is also necessary to conduct more longitudinal research that examines the impact on children's social and cognitive development of the types of pretend play in which children engage in their everyday lives.

# REFERENCES

Bergen, D. (2002). The role of pretend play in children's cognitive development. *Early Childhood Research & Practice, 4*(1). Retrieved http://ecrp.uiuc.edu/v4n1/bergen.html.

Bloch, M. N. (1989). Young boys' and girls' play at home and in the community: A cultural-ecological framework. In M. N. Bloch & A. D. Pellegrini (Eds.), *The ecological context of children's play* (pp. 120–154). Norwood, NJ: Ablex.

Bornstein, M. H., Haynes, O. M., Pascual, L., Painter, K. M., & Galperín, C. (1999). Play in two societies: Pervasiveness of process, specificity of structure. *Child Development, 70,* 317–331.

Bornstein, M. H., Haynes, O. M., Legler, J. M., O'Reilly, A. W., & Painter, K. M. (1997). Symbolic play in childhood: Interpersonal and environmental context and stability. *Infant Behavior and Development, 20*(2), 197–207.

Bronfenbrenner, U. (1977). Toward an experimental ecology of human development. *American Psychologist, 32,* 513–531.

Bronfenbrenner, U. (1995). Developmental ecology through space and time: A future perspective In P. Moen, G. H. Elder, Jr., & K. Lüscher (Eds.), *Examining lives in context: Perspectives on the ecology of human development* (pp. 619–647). Washington, DC: American Psychological Association.

Bronfenbrenner, U. (1999). Environments in developmental perspective: Theoretical and operational models. In S. L. Friedman & T. D. Wachs (Eds.), *Measuring environment across the life span: Emerging methods and concepts* (pp. 3–28). Washington, DC: American Psychological Association Press.

Bronfenbrenner, U. (2005). The bioecological theory of human development. In U. Bronfenbrenner (Ed.), *Making human beings human: Bioecological perspectives on human development* (pp. 3–15). Thousand Oaks, CA: Sage.

Bronfenbrenner, U., & Morris, P. A. (2006). The bioecological model of human development. In W. Damon (Series Ed.) & R. M. Lerner (Vol. Ed.), *Handbook of child psychology: Vol. 1. Theoretical models of human development* (6th ed., pp. 793–828). New York: John Wiley.

Brown, P. M., Rickards, F. W., & Bortoli, A. (2001). Structures underpinning pretend play and word production in young hearing children and children with hearing loss. *Journal of Deaf Studies and Deaf Education, 6,* 15–31.

Clift, S., Stagnitti, K., & DeMello, L. (1998). A validational study of the test of pretend play using correlational and classificational analyses. *Child Language Teaching and Therapy, 14,* 199–209.

Colwell, M. J., & Lindsey, E. W. (2005). Preschool children's pretend and physical play and sex of play partner: Connections of peer competence. *Sex Roles, 52,* 497–509.

Conger, R. D. & Donnellan, M. B. (2007). An interactionist perspective on the socioeconomic context of human development. *The Annual Review of Psychology, 58,* 175–199.

Cote, L. R., & Bornstein, M. H. (2005). Child and mother play in cultures of origin, acculturating cultures, and cultures of destination. *International Journal of Behavioral Development. 29,* 479–488.

Fabes, R. A., Martin, C. L., Hanish, L. D., Anders, M. C., & Madden-Derdich, D. A. (2003). Early school competence: The roles of sex-segregated play and effortful control. *Developmental Psychology, 39,* 848–858.

Farver, J. M., Kim, Y. K., & Lee-Shin, Y. (2000). Within cultural differences. Examining individual differences in Korean American and European American preschoolers' social pretend play. *Journal of Cross-Cultural Psychology, 31,* 583–602.

Farver, J. M. (1993). Cultural differences in scaffolding pretend play: A comparison of American and Mexican mother–child and sibling–child pairs. In K. MacDonald (Ed.), *Parent–child play: Descriptions and implications* (pp. 349–366) Albany, NY: SUNY Press.

Gaskins, S. (1999). Children's daily lives in a Mayan village: A case study of culturally constructed roles and activities. In A. Göncü (Ed.), *Children's engagement in the world: Sociocultural perspectives* (pp. 25–61). New York: Cambridge University Press.

Göncü, A., Mistry, J., & Mosier, C. (2000). Cultural variations in play of toddlers. *International Journal of Behavioral Development, 24,* 321–329.

Göncü, A., Tuermer, U., Jain, J., & Johnson, D. (1999). Children's play as cultural activity. In A. Göncü (Ed.), *Children's engagement in the world: Sociocultural perspectives* (pp. 148–170). New York: Cambridge University Press.

Gosso, Y., Morais, M. L. S., & Otta, E. (2007). Pretend play of Brazilian children: A window into different cultural worlds. *Journal of Cross-Cultural Psychology, 38,* 539–558.

Haight, W., & Miller, P. J. (1993). *Pretending at home: Early development in a sociocultural context.* Albany, NY: State University of New York Press.

Hart, B., & Risley, T. R. (1995). *Meaningful differences in the everyday experiences of young American children.* Baltimore, MD: Brookes Publishing.

Hart, B., & Risley, T. R. (1999). *The social world of children learning to talk.* Baltimore, MD: Brookes Publishing.

Hollingshead, A. B. (1975). Four factor index of social status. Unpublished manuscript, Department of Sociology, Yale University, New Haven, CT.

Kağitçibaşi, Ç. (2005). Autonomy and relatedness in cultural context: Implications for self and family. *Journal of Cross-cultural Psychology, 36,* 403–422.

Lancy, D. F. (1996). *Playing on the mother ground: Cultural routines for children's development.* New York: Guilford Press.

Lillard, A. S. (1993). Young children's conceptualization of pretense: Action or mental representational state? *Child Development, 64,* 372–386.

Lloyd, B. & Howe, N. (2003). Solitary play and convergent and divergent thinking skills in preschool children. *Early Childhood Research Quarterly, 18,* 22–41.

Parmar, P., Harkness, S., & Super, C. M. (2004). Asian and Euro-American parents' ethnotheories of play and learning: Effects on preschool children's home routines and school behavior. *International Journal of Behavioral Development, 28,* 97–104.

Pellegrini, A. D. (1982). Development of preschoolers' social-cognitive play behaviours. *Perceptual and Motor Skills, 55,* 1109–10.

Pellegrini, A. D., & Smith, P. (2003). Development of play. In J. Valsiner & K. J. Connolly (Eds.), *Handbook of psychology* (pp. 276–291). London: Sage Publications.

Piaget, J. (1962). *Play, dreams and imitation in childhood.* New York: Norton.

QSR International Pty Ltd. (2002). NVivo (Version 2.0). [Computer software]. Victoria, Australia: Author.

Quintana, S. M., Aboud, F. E., Chao, R. K., Contreras-Grau, J., Cross Jr., W. E., Hudley, C. et al. (2006). Race, ethnicity, and culture in child development: Contemporary research and future directions. *Child Development, 77,* 1129–1141.

Rogoff, B., Mistry, J., Göncü, A., & Mosier, C. (1993). Guided participation in cultural activity by toddlers and caregivers. *Monographs of the Society for Research in Child Development, 58* (Serial No. 236).

Roopnarine, J. L., Hooper, F. H., Ahmeduzzaman, M., & Pollack, B. (1993). Gentle play partners: Mother–child and father–child play in New Delhi, India. In K. MacDonald (Ed.) *Parent–child play: Descriptions and implications* (pp. 287–304). Albany, NY: SUNY Press.

Rubin, K. H., Watson, K. S., & Jambor, T. W. (1978). Free play behaviors in preschool and kindergarten children. *Child Development, 49,* 534–536.

Schwartzman, H. G. (1978). *Transformations: The anthropology of children's play.* New York: Plenum.

Smith, P. K., & Whitney, S. (1987). Play and associative fluency: Experimenter effects may be responsible for previous positive findings. *Developmental Psychology, 23,* 49–53.

Tudge, J. R. H. (2008). *The everyday lives of young children: Culture, class, and child rearing in diverse societies.* New York: Cambridge University Press.

Tudge, J. R. H., & Scrimsher, S. (2003). Lev S. Vygotsky on education: A cultural-historical, interpersonal, and individual approach to development. In B. J. Zimmerman & D. H. Schunk (Eds.), *Educational psychology: A century of contributions* (pp. 207–228). Mahwah, NJ: Lawrence Erlbaum Associates.

Tudge, J. R. H., Lee, S., & Putnam, S. (1998).Young children's play in socio-cultural context: South Korea and the United States. In S. Reifel (Series Ed.) & Duncan M. C., G. Chick & A. Aycock (Vol. Ed.), *Play and Culture Studies, Vol. 1. Diversions and divergences in fields of play* (pp.77–90). Greenwich: Albex Publishing Corporation.

Vygotsky, L. S. (1987). *The collected works of L. S. Vygotsky: Vol. 1, Problems of general psychology* in R. W. Rieber & A. S. Carton, Eds., N. Minick, trans. New York: Plenum. (Original publication, 1934, written between 1929 and 1934).

Vygotsky, L. S. (1997a). *The collected works of L. S. Vygotsky: Vol. 3, Problems of the theory and history of psychology* (R. W. Rieber & J. Wollock, Eds., & R van der Veer, trans.). New York: Plenum. (Chapters originally written or published between 1924 and 1934).

Vygotsky, L. S. (1997b). *The collected works of L. S. Vygotsky: Vol. 4, The history of the development of higher mental functions* (R. W. Rieber, Ed., & M. J. Hall, trans.). New York: Plenum. (Originally written in 1931; chapters 1–5 first published in 1960, chapters 6–15 first published in 1997).

Wyer, S. R., & Spence, S. H. (1999). Play and divergent problem solving: Evidence supporting a reciprocal relationship. *Early Education & Development, 10,* 419–444.

*Chapter Five*

# Children's Pretend Play with Media-Based Toys

## Sandra Chang-Kredl and Nina Howe

When children engage in pretend play, they communicate, through enactment and storytelling, the narratives and motifs that they have absorbed from a plethora of cultural sources. This study focuses on one narrative template: toys derived from children's television and films. The authors investigate the influence of media-based and generic toys on the pretend play of 5-year-old children, specifically the roles, themes, and types of communication in their pretend play. Over the past 50 years, marketing industries and mass media have inundated the child's world with toys representing images of television and film cartoon characters. More than 70% of American gross profits from toy sales are based on tie-in merchandise derived from television and films (Steinberg & Kincheloe, 2004). The 1980's deregulation of commercial television in the United States resulted in a mass marketing strategy whereby characters and character-based products are developed before, after, or simultaneously with the creation of animated television programs (and films) that function to promote these products (Cross, 1997; Cross & Smits, 2005; Kline, 1993). A cartoon media phenomenon, such as the *Powerpuff Girls* or *SpongeBob SquarePants*, combines the cartoon program with its product line (e.g., toys, clothes, lunchboxes) in what Van Fuqua (2003) calls "a seamless loop of reception and consumption" (p. 210).

The relationship between pretend play and mass media has been described from two largely opposing perspectives. On the one hand, education scholars argue that media representations direct and limit children's pretend play by providing them with ready-made storylines and characters around which they can organize their imaginative experiences, rather than allowing them the opportunity to develop fantasies based on their own real-life experiences or to create their own ideas (Sutton-Smith, 1988; Greenfield et al., 1993; Kline,

1993). On the other hand, communication and media scholars, advancing a model of audience agency, argue that children are not passive consumers of media who simply mimic media representations, but that they actively negotiate media in individually meaningful ways (Walkerdine, 1997; Buckingham, 2003). Further, communication scholars contend that *play* is the child's means of actively transforming media images, roles, and themes (Kline, 1993; Buckingham, 2003).

The authors of the present study integrated education and communication perspectives and methodology from a tradition of play theories and research (see Rubin et al., 1983; Howe, Petrakos, & Rinaldi, 1998) to examine the specific mechanisms of children's pretend play with media-based toys. This approach contributes to a complex, dynamic view of how children engage with media representations; specifically, how children use play to emulate or alter the roles and themes they are offered through toys derived from television and films.

## PRETEND PLAY, SEMIOTICS, AND COMMUNICATION

The ability to pretend, according to Piaget (1962), is based on semiotic functioning, or the reading of signs, which Danesi (1994) describes as the basic tool of communication: a means for constructing knowledge and transmitting that understanding to others. Play researchers, such as Rubin et al. (1983) and Garvey & Berndt (1976), have described pretend play as involving the transformation of objects, situations, or identities using "as if" behavior. Children's pretend play was described by Howe et al. (1998) (adapting Doyle and Connelly's 1989 scale) as taking place in three forms: (1) *enactment*, in which the child acts out story events and simulates the characteristics or identity of another person through voice, speech or action (e.g., the child picks up a character toy and makes it fly in the air, while pretending to speak for the character: "I'll save you, Princess!"); (2) *low-level negotiation*, in which the child arranges toys and props with a connection to narrative or pretense (e.g., the child lines up 20 character toys in a row for a parade); and (3) *high-level negotiation*, considered the most sophisticated level of pretend play, in which a child narrates or acts as the stage manager directing and explaining events (e.g., the child tells the story of how the parade celebrates the arrival of Santa Claus).

## OBJECT USE IN PRETEND PLAY

There is a strong motoric quality to young children's symbolic and communicative activities, such that interacting with objects is an integral part of how children engage with concepts and symbols (Bergen, 2002). Piaget (1962) and Vygotsky (1966) reasoned that objects or props are required to support young children's pretend play. Rather than assuming a role him/herself, the child depends on an object to make the transition from reality to pretense, and ascribes the qualities and identities of a role to that object. For example, in pretending that a stick or a wooden horse is an actual horse, the child uses an object (the stick or wooden horse) as a pivot to separate the meaning of the symbolic horse from the actual horse.

Past research on objects used in pretend play indicate that low-realism objects (e.g., home-sewn figures with very few facial details) elicit more varied pretend play themes than high-realism objects (e.g., Barbie-type dolls with features explicitly represented) (Phillips, 1945; Pulaski, 1973). Moreover, younger preschoolers were found to depend on the support offered by realistic objects to engage in make-believe (McLoyd, 1983; Woodard, 1984). The significant difference between the present study's media-based toys and the toys used in the high versus low realism studies, conducted by researchers such as Pulaski (1973) and Woodard (1984), is the source of the toy's meaning. The meaning of media-based toys is conveyed to the child via the television programs, films, books, and advertising. The meaning of toys *not* based on specific cartoons or films is demonstrated to the child through other channels, such as real-life or generalized exposure to these objects.

## MEDIA INFLUENCES ON PRETEND PLAY

Greenfield et al. (1993) distinguished between *imitative* and *creative* pretense in their study of the audio-visual impact of television on children, by comparing the imaginative elements of children's play after either viewing a television program or playing a game. According to Greenfield et al., imitative pretense elicits straightforward recall of narratives and roles. For example, a child may be "transported" into a cartoon (in their case, *The Smurfs*), and re-enact or imitate the televised characters and script viewed earlier. Creative pretense, on the other hand, involves a transformative process beyond recall or reenactment of pre-scripted ideas and identities. In other words, rather than imitating a television representation, the child will develop a character or event unrelated to a specific media text.

## THE PRESENT STUDY

Children draw from a plethora of scripts to help shape their play. The goal of the present study is to examine closely *one* form of influence—namely, toys derived from children's television and films. A unique quality about the toys used in this study is that they are part of a political economy that thrives on marketing, in part, through purposely connecting toys with specific children's media narratives and motifs. In taking into account debates over limitations in children's play with toys (Greenfield et al., 1993; Kline, 1993; Buckingham, 2003), the central question of the present study was: how do media-based toys affect the communicative behaviors (physical and verbal) of children engaging in pretend play? Specifically, we examined the influence of toy type (character toys derived from commercial television or films versus generic toys unrelated to mass media) on the types of roles, variety of themes, and categories of pretend play engaged in by 5-year-olds.

Children's play has been studied through diverse research approaches, including ethnography (Dyson, 2003), empirical studies (Howe et al., 1993), and observations (Singer & Singer, 1981). The present study followed a long-standing research tradition examining children's use of objects in pretend play through an empirical paradigm that allows for the control of various factors that may influence the association between toy type and children's pretend play (Pulaski, 1973; Petrakos & Howe, 1996). We selected an empirical method in order to replicate a tradition of play studies largely ignored by cultural and communication studies (see Buckingham, 2003; Dyson, 2003).

In order to identify the level of media influence that the toys may have on the children's play, and partially based on previous studies, we delineated three types of pretend play: (1) enactment, (2) low-level negotiation, and (3) high-level negotiation, and three types of pretend roles and themes: (1) manufactured, (2) archetypal, and (3) reality-based. Manufactured roles are roles that are directly related to a story character *as intended* by the toys' manufacturers (e.g. Cinderella, Shrek), carrying a unique history (e.g., Cinderella is the stepdaughter whose father dies); similarly, manufactured themes are directly related to a named story theme (e.g., the glass slipper must fit Cinderella's foot). Archetypal roles have a fictional nature, but are not related to a specific fictional character (e.g., a witch, a prince). Archetypal themes are fictional, but are not derived from a known fictional narrative (e.g. a knight rescues a princess). Reality-based roles are derived from the child's concrete, real-life experiences rather than being related to fictional stories (e.g., mommy, teacher, family dog). Reality-based themes are related to real-life experiences (e.g. going to the grocery store).

The study focused on 5-year-olds since this is the period of development when there is a peak interest in symbolic play (Piaget, 1962) and it also falls into the 5–8 year age range targeted by toy marketers (see Kline, 1993). Given the compelling research that media-based toys and children's television encourage gender-specific roles and play (Carlson-Paige & Levin, 1987; Paley, 1984, 2004), gender effects were also taken into consideration. The experimental design of the study was based on Pulaski's (1973) work on children's play with toys varying in levels of realism.

Rather than focusing on short-term audio-visual effects (e.g., Greenfield et al., 1993), we took the perspective that the average child is familiar with targeted television and film toys through a 'total marketing' system, which includes not only the television programs and movies, but also advertisements, store displays, licensed goods, and peer influence (Kline, 1993). The measures of categories of pretend play and types of roles and themes were based on observations of the stories that individual children enacted and communicated while playing with the objects in the two toy type conditions.

Two critical issues were addressed. First, because previous play research has generally examined roles and themes rather than the quantity or type of pretense, and has not addressed differences between enactment and negotiation, we had no basis to predict such differences. Second, taking into account findings that role play tends to correspond to the specific setting (Howe et al., 1998; Dodge & Frost, 1986; Petrakos & Howe, 1996), it was anticipated that there would be a higher number of manufactured roles (i.e., roles depicting an intended fictional character, such as Woody from Pixar's *Toy Story*) and manufactured themes (i.e., storylines depicting an intended fictional theme, such as Spiderman throwing a web from his wrists) in the media-based toy condition.

## METHOD

### Participants

Twenty-eight children (14 boys, 14 girls) five years of age ($M = 60.29$ mos., $SD = 4.16$ mos., range 54–66 mos.) participated. The children were recruited from three daycare centers in a metropolitan, bilingual (English/French) city (pop = 3,000,000). The children were from ethnically diverse families (22 Caucasian, 1 African-American, 4 Asian, 2 Hispanic), which is reflective of the municipal population (Statistics Canada, 2001). The children were from middle class families based on parental job descriptions. Two of the daycares were affiliated with English language universities, and the third daycare was located in a largely Anglophone neighborhood. Twenty-six of the children communicated in English during their play sessions and two communicated in French.

### Procedure

Children were individually introduced to the experimental procedures. As the literature indicates that children usually play with media-based and superhero toys outside of the classroom (in non-classroom settings) (see Levin & Rosenquest, 2001), each child was brought from his/her daycare classroom to another familiar playroom where toys were set up on a table. The child sat down with the first author, who played a number of warm-up puzzle activities with the child. After the child was comfortable, the toys were brought out with an introduction similar to the Pulaski (1973) procedure: "You may play with anything you choose. Would you like to make up a story or put on a play for me?" Play sessions lasted eight minutes per toy condition. After the first session, the child was offered a second puzzle task in order to change his or her focus. The author then presented the child with toys from the second toy condition. Conditions were presented in counterbalanced order: (a) media-based toys and (b) generic toys. Play sessions were videotaped and the children's pretend play, roles, and themes were coded.

To ensure that the toys used in this study reflected the children's previous exposure to the television and films from which the toys in the study were derived, parents completed a questionnaire regarding their children's familiarity with a list of popular films and television programs. The parental questionnaire was sent home before the play data were collected and was returned to the daycare director.

Gender was not a primary concern in this study, but because gender has been shown to impact pretend play behaviors (Paley, 2004), the differences between the boys and girls' play were taken into account. The factor of ethnicity was beyond the scope of this study.

## Materials

The objects in both toy conditions (media-based versus generic) were balanced for number and type of figures, and accessory materials. Level of realism in both conditions was also matched so that measures were based on the toys' relation to media source rather than differences in levels of object realism. For example, the media-based Spiderman toy was balanced in the generic condition with a muscular, red-colored, male figure; the media-based Woody from Toy Story was matched in the generic condition with a cowboy figure unrelated to popular media narratives; and Blue, the dog from the animated program Blue's Clues, in the media-based toy condition was matched with a cartoonish dog in the generic toy condition (see Table 5.1 for a list of toys).

## Measures

*Play.* Play measures were assessed using a time sampling method in which the children's videotaped sessions (i.e., verbalizations, play, non-play behaviors)

**Table 5.1.   Description of Media-Based Versus Generic Toys in Play Sessions**

| Media-based | Generic |
|---|---|
| Spiderman | Muscular, red male figure |
| Batman | Muscular, grey knight |
| Cinderella | Young woman in gown |
| Prince Charming from *Cinderella* | Young man in tuxedo |
| Woody from *Toy Story* | Cowboy |
| Princess Fiona from *Shrek* | Young woman in gown |
| Donkey from *Shrek* | Donkey |
| Powerpuff girls (3) | Girl figures (3) |
| Maleficent from *Sleeping Beauty* | Witch |
| Blues' Clues dog | Dog |
| Dalmatian from *101 Dalmatians* | Dalmatian |
| Madeline | Girl |
| Arthur and D.W. | Boy and girl |
| Harry Potter | Boy |
| Curious George | Monkey |
| Franklin | Turtle |
| Thomas the Tank Engine | Train |

were scored every 10 seconds. The play coding scheme was based on an adaptation and combination of (1) Rubin & Wolf's (1979) play observation scale (i.e., pretend play, constructive play, manipulative play, other play, and non-play) and (2) Howe et al.'s (1998) adaptation of Doyle and Connolly's (1989) scale for pretend play (i.e., enactment, low-level negotiation, and high-level negotiation) (see Table 5.2).

For each 10-second interval, the child was rated for the type of play (pretend, other play) or nonplay he/she was observed in for the majority of the interval. If a child was observed in pretend play, then the interval was further coded as enactment, low-level negotiation, or high-level negotiation. Pretend enactment included pretense involving verbal enactment (i.e., through content of speech or exaggerated tone of voice, such as "Waah! I hurt myself!") or physical enactment (i.e., making a toy gesture or move). Pretend negotiation (low and high level) was defined by the procedural or preparatory behaviors related to pretense, rather than enactment. Low-level pretend negotiation was coded for intervals when the child physically arranged toys, but was not enacting pretense (e.g., a child quietly lining up characters for a parade). High-level pretend negotiation was coded when the child demonstrated verbal procedural behaviors, initiated pretend scenarios, assigned roles, or narrated a story (e.g., "Let's say this is the princess and she is in the high tower and then she gets sad"). If two or more types of play were observed in one

10-second interval, the type of play that predominated was coded. Once the intervals of pretense were identified, they were coded for roles and themes as described below.

*Roles and themes.* Role measures were assessed using the time sampling method described above. In this case, for each 10-second interval in which pretend play was observed, the pretend role that the child engaged in predominantly, through performance or story-telling, was coded as (a) manufactured (i.e., based on a specific media character, such as Harry Potter or Princess Fiona), (b) archetypal (i.e., based neither in reality nor on a specific media character, such as the mean witch or the knight), or (c) reality-based (i.e., derived from a child's real-life experience, such as Mommy or Teacher) (see Table 5.2).

To consider role transformations in both toy conditions, manufactured roles that were scripted by the media-based toys (e.g., using the Cinderella toy to play Cinderella) were distinguished from roles that were created by the child with no pre-scripted cue from the toys (e.g., using a generic toy *or* the Princess Fiona toy to play Cinderella) (see Table 5.2 for definitions). While the authors acknowledge that reality itself is a cultural construction, the term is used in this study as a way of distinguishing the three forms of play: manufactured, archetypal, and reality-based.

Similarly, each pretend play interval was coded for the predominant theme the child generated, as (a) manufactured (e.g., Harry Potter arrives at the Hogwarts School for Witchcraft and Wizardry), (b) archetypal (e.g., the witch threatens the boy), or (c) reality-based (e.g., the boy goes to school) (see Table 5.2).

*Parent Questionnaire.* Parents were given a list of 30 popular children's television programs and films and asked to rate the number of times their child was exposed to each program (none, one viewing, two viewings, three or more viewings). The questionnaire provided information about the children's current television and film-viewing habits, and also was used to ensure that the toys selected matched the children's experiences with mass media.

## Inter-coder Reliability

Using the videotaped play sessions, two observers were trained on the coding schemes described above; one rater was naïve to the study's purpose. Interrater reliability was assessed for 25% (7/28) of observational sessions. Reliability was first calculated as the number of agreements/number of agreements + disagreements (play = 83%, roles = 84.5%, themes = 86%). An overall *kappa* coefficient of .80 was achieved.

**Table 5.2.   Definitions and Examples of Measures**

Play Variables

1. *Pretend enactment:* Exaggerated voice (e.g., "Waah!"); content of speech (e.g., "the princess says hello"; actions and gestures (e.g., making a figure walk).
2. *Low-level pretend negotiation:* Arrangement of props with a connection to narrative or pretense (e.g., lining up characters for a parade).
3. *High-level pretend negotiation:* Preparatory or procedural behaviors; initiation of pretense; storytelling; assignment of roles, termination of pretense (e.g., "Let's play Spiderman", "and the girl gets angry and he starts to cry").
4. *Other play:* Constructive, exploratory, functional, games-with-rules (e.g., balancing figures on top of each other with no reference to narrative or pretense).
5. *Non-play:* child does not engage in play behavior.

Role Variables

1. *Manufactured roles:* In media-based and generic conditions. Use of proper name (e.g., Cinderella, Shrek) or directly related to a named story character (e.g., Cinderella's stepmother) with a unique history.
   1a. *Scripted as manufactured:* In media-based condition ONLY. Child assigns or enacts a role to a figure scripted by the fictional story from which the figure is derived (e.g., the figure of Fiona is used to represent the Princess Fiona).
   1b. *Media-derived and transformed:* In media-based condition ONLY. Child transforms a media-based figure to enact a character from a *different* fictional story (e.g., Fiona is made to enact the role of Cinderella's stepsister, Drizella).
2. *Archetypal roles:* Child assigns or enacts a role unrelated to a definite fictional story but not in a child's concrete reality (e.g., Cinderella figure or generic lady figure made to say, "This is a queen").
3. *Reality-based roles:* Child assigns or enacts a role unrelated to a fictional story (e.g., Cinderella figure or generic lady figure made to say, "This is Mommy").

Theme Variables

1. *Manufactured themes:* In media-based and generic conditions. Must be directly related to a named story theme (e.g., Arthur).
   1a. *Scripted as manufactured:* In media-based condition ONLY. Child uses media-based figures to describe or enact a fictional story theme sequence from which the figure is derived (e.g., Fiona is being rescued by an Ogre named Shrek).
   1b. *Media-based and transformed:* In media-based condition ONLY. Child uses media-based figures to describe or enact a fictional story theme sequence from a *different* fictional story (e.g., Cinderella is being rescued by an Ogre named Shrek).
2. *Archetypal themes:* Child uses figures to describe or enact a theme that is not derived from a known fictional narrative but clearly not based on a child's lived reality (e.g., knight rescues princess).
3. *Reality-based themes:* Child uses figures to describe or enact a reality based story theme (e.g., Cinderella figure or generic lady figure to go to grocery store).

## RESULTS

Comparisons were made between the media-based and generic toy conditions on: (a) categories of pretend play (i.e., enactment and negotiation), and (b) roles and themes. The factors used in this design were: (a) toy type (media-based versus generic), and (b) gender (boys versus girls). The dependent variables were (a) pretend play, (b) roles, and (c) themes (see Table 2). Statistical analyses were based on 2 x 2 (gender by toy type) factorial designs with repeated measures on each child across levels of toy type. Analyses of variance and $t$-tests were performed with a level of significance set at $p = .05$, 1-tailed. Samples of the children's verbal play narratives are in the Appendix.

### Descriptive Statistics

The means and standard deviations for play, role, and theme variables in the media-based versus generic toy conditions are found in Table 5.3.

### Pretend Play Measures

To test Question 1, whether there are differences in enactment and negotiation behaviors, $2 \times 2$ repeated-measures ANOVAs were performed with the following dependent measures: (1) pretend enactment, (2) low-level pretend

Table 5.3.  Means and Standard Deviations of Variables by Toy Type

|  | Media-Based | | Generic | |
|---|---|---|---|---|
|  | Mean | SD | Mean | SD |
| Manufactured Roles | 41.40 | 26.27 | 8.03 | 12.69 |
| Manufactured (as scripted) | 34.29 | 23.41 | N/A | N/A |
| Manufactured (transformed) | 7.11 | 12.38 | N/A | N/A |
| Archetypal Roles | 9.36 | 13.95 | 18.98 | 19.80 |
| Reality Roles | 12.05 | 17.77 | 32.45 | 30.43 |
| Manufactured Themes | 16.86 | 13.01 | 4.31 | 8.54 |
| Archetypal Themes | 4.63 | 6.41 | 8.89 | 7.58 |
| Reality Themes | 9.66 | 9.13 | 13.20 | 12.10 |
| Pretend Play | 30.53 | 11.71 | 27.69 | 15.11 |
| Enactment | 16.10 | 9.87 | 10.20 | 8.93 |
| Low-level negotiation | 5.94 | 6.46 | 5.64 | 6.35 |
| High-level negotiation | 8.49 | 6.91 | 11.85 | 9.50 |

negotiation, and (3) high-level pretend negotiation. The within-subjects factor was toy type (media-based versus generic) and the between-subjects factor was gender.

The analyses did not support the null Question 1, and revealed that toy type and/or gender *did* influence the three subcategories of pretend play (see Table 5.3 for toy type means). Specifically: (1) more pretend enactment was found with media-based toys than with the generic toys, $F(1, 26) = 18.25, p < .01$, and (2) a trend revealed that more frequent high-level negotiation was found with generic toys than with media-based toys, $F(1, 26) = 3.73, p = .07$.

### Role and Theme Measures

To test Question 2, that more manufactured roles and themes would be observed in the media-based toy condition, as well as to investigate for gender associations, $2 \times 2$ repeated-measures ANOVAs were performed. In the case of roles, the dependent variables were the mean scores of: (1) manufactured roles, (2) reality-based roles, and (3) archetypal roles; the between-subjects factor was toy type and the within-subjects factor was gender (see Table 3 for toy type means). Significantly more manufactured roles were observed in the media-based compared to the generic toy condition, $F(1, 26) = 44.35, p < .01$, supporting Question 2. Separate *t*-tests indicated that the overall significant difference in media-derived roles observed was due to the manufactured roles scripted by the toys in the media-based toy condition (e.g., Child #15 used the Woody toy to enact a scene as Woody from *Toy Story*) and not by transformed roles (e.g., using a Princess Fiona or generic doll to play Cinderella) (see the Appendix for examples of children's verbal play).

The results also revealed more archetypal roles, $F(1, 26) = 11.70, p < .01$, and reality roles, $F(1, 26) = 14.72, p < .01$, in the generic toy condition compared to the media-based toys. A significant gender effect was found with reality-based roles whereby girls were observed in more reality-based roles than boys, $F(1, 26) = 6.50, p = .02$ (*M* girls $= 62.10$, *M* boys $= 26.90$), particularly in the generic toy condition. There was also a significant gender by toy type interaction effect for archetypal roles, $F(1, 26) = 13.17. p < .01$. Follow-up *t*-tests revealed that boys in the generic toy condition (*M* boys generic $= 28.04$) engaged in the significantly greatest number of archetypal roles (*M* boys media-based $= 8.21$, *M* girls media-based $= 10.50$, *M* girls generic $= 9.92$).

In the case of themes, three separate $2 \times 2$ repeated-measures ANOVAs were performed on the theme variables as dependent measures. The within-subjects factor was toy type and the between-subjects factor was gender.

First, significant toy type main effects indicated more manufactured themes were observed in the media-based condition, $F(1, 26) = 30.17$, $p < .01$ (see Table 5.3 for toy type means). Second, a significant toy type main effect revealed more archetypal themes were observed in the generic condition, $F(1, 26) = 9.18$, $p < .01$. A gender by toy type interaction effect for archetypal themes was also found, $F(1, 26) = 4.06$, $p = .05$. Follow-up *t*-tests showed that boys in the generic condition ($M$ boys generic $= 12.04$) were observed in the highest number of archetypal themes ($M$ boys media-based $= 4.93$, $M$ girls media-based $= 4.32$, $M$ girls generic $= 5.75$).

## Parent Ratings on Children's Exposure to Fictional Narratives

A total score for parents' ratings of their child's exposure to fictional narratives was calculated by adding up the scores per child. In order to measure the relationship between parent ratings of their children's exposure to the narratives from which the media-based toys were derived and children's manufactured role and theme enactments with the toys, bivariate correlations were conducted between the parent score and the child's observed roles and themes (i.e., manufactured and non-manufactured). No significant correlations between parent ratings on children's narrative exposure and roles or themes were found ($rs = -.15$ to $.20$, *ns*, 2-tailed).

## DISCUSSION

The goal of this study was to apply empirical methods of analysis, based on a long-standing tradition of play studies, to examine the communicative behaviors and mechanisms of pretend play in children's engagement with media-based toys. More specifically, the study examined how children emulated or transformed the roles and themes offered to them through film and television-based character toys.

The research on object use in pretend play did not provide a basis for predicting differences in enactment and negotiation, as researchers focused on roles and themes, rather than categories of pretend play (e.g., Pulaski, 1973; Petrakos & Howe, 1996). An important finding of this study is that significantly more pretend enactment was observed with media-based toys and more high-level negotiation was observed with generic toys. Pretend enactment took place when the child assumed the identity of another person by speaking, moving, or acting as that character. High-level pretend negotiation involved procedural behaviors; the child initiated and set up pretense scenarios, assigned roles, and told the story (Howe et al., 1998) (e.g., Child # 27 assigned roles to character toys as follows: "He's the groom. She's the bride. He's the priest", and then narrated the marriage: "The guests show up and the priest talks").

In support of the second hypothesis, more manufactured roles and themes were observed in the media-based toy condition than in the generic toy condition. In other words, in the media-based toy condition, the role children assigned to the Princess Fiona toy was generally Princess Fiona (e.g., Child #23: "Fiona, she does karate too") and the Spiderman toy *was* played as Spiderman (e.g., Child # 6 made a Spiderman toy gesture a webbing motion and spoke in a pretense voice: "I'm going to web you now!"). In contrast, in the generic toy condition, the young woman in the long green gown was usually not given a role from a popular film or television program, and the red, muscular figure was often a "bad guy", but rarely one already named and scripted by a media program (e.g., Child 2: "Horsey, go get the bad guy") (see the Appendix for further examples). While it is not surprising that the media-based toys, being defined in this study as carrying a script intended by the toys' manufacturers, encouraged more 'manufactured pretense,' this finding combined with the higher level of pretend enactment (with media-based toys) is particularly relevant to our aim of examining how children engage with media toys.

## Imitative versus Transformational Pretend Play

One of the main arguments against television viewing is that television narratives limit children's creativity by providing them with ready-made storylines and characters around which to organize their imaginative experience (Kline, 1993). Implicit in this argument is the distinction between *imitative* and *creative* imagination as described by Greenfield et al. (1993). If children playing with media-based toys engage in significantly more frequent pretend enactment, manufactured roles, and manufactured themes, one might argue that their play is, in large part, emulating the scripts and identities depicted by the television programs or films. If the children playing with generic toys are engaged in significantly more high-level pretend negotiation with characters not derived from television or film, it is likely that the children were transforming and creating characters and ideas. In the media-based toy condition, rather than *transforming* the identities and narratives depicted by the toys, the children seemed to be *transported* into the prefabricated television or film world. This distinction may reflect the differences, using Greenfield et al.'s (1993) terms, between imitative and transformative imagination.

While one perspective is that children are active agents, rather than passive consumers, of media (Buckingham, 2003), the current study's findings tentatively support arguments by Kline (1993) and Steinberg and Kincheloe (2004) that television toys, in fact, do direct children's role enactments. Kline (1993) argued that character marketing results in a type of scripted play, in which children are provided with the tools to recreate animated narratives seen in films and television, and the toy is emphasized as the necessary tool for pretense. According to Kline, if children play with the toys in ways that market industries intend, rather than being objects of transformation, the toys become the child's means for being 'transported' into the film or television program's fictional world.

An important caveat should be noted here. While toys based on media narratives may act as artifacts with scaffold-like qualities, it would be an over-simplification to assume that long-term play with the same artifacts would not later develop into more transformative forms of symbolic and communicative behaviors—an interesting possibility for future studies.

## Archetypal Roles and Themes

While the children (especially the girls) engaged in more reality-based play in the generic toy condition, they also engaged in significantly more archetypal roles and themes in the generic toy condition. This finding is interesting because it suggests that the children's pretend play tended to break the boundaries of their own realities. In other words, the children were compelled to pretend in a fantasy mode beyond their daily reality. When the toys did not offer a clear manufactured script for fictional pretense, the children combined elements of a non-specific fictional nature. For example, Child #18 enacted and narrated a story of a knight, named Keith, who rescues a princess from a witch. Archetypal roles were not prevalent in the media-based toy condition. This leads one to compare the creative aspects of manufactured play (e.g., Spiderman webbing) versus archetypal play (e.g., the knight rescuing).

Piaget (1962) described pretend or symbolic play as taking place when a child evoked his or her experiences of the outside world and reinvented them in an imaginary world. Does archetypal play reflect more closely the notion of reinventing (Piaget, 1962) and transforming ideas (Greenfield et al., 1993)? Can archetypal play be described as transformative or creative if the link to a specific script is not apparent? Finally, combined with the finding that more high-level negotiation (considered by play theorists to be a more sophisticated level of pretend play than enactment) was found in the generic toy condition, do children pretend more creatively (seeing things "in a new light"; generating "new" ideas) with generic toys compared to media toys? If future research is to consider the connections between pretend play and creativity, these questions must be examined.

An association with gender was found for the children's observed play, roles, and themes and for the most part, our findings were consistent with previous research (see Carlson-Paige & Levin, 1987; Kline, 1993): the boys' action play was more pronounced in the media-based condition, an indication of gender-specific action narratives directed at boys. The influence of media-based versus generic toys on the frequency of high-level pretend negotiation was stronger for girls. High-level negotiation involves extensive use of verbal skills, thus our finding corresponds to evidence that girls engage in more verbal communication than boys. In contrast, mass media's sex-typed toys encourage boys to fight, kill, and dominate (Carlson-Paige & Levin, 1987), which are activities requiring stronger physical enactment skills than verbal negotiation or storytelling ability.

## FUTURE RESEARCH DIRECTIONS AND CONCLUSIONS

Some further limitations should be noted, including the sample size and the children's middle-class backgrounds. Also, although all efforts were made to select a range of toys reflecting current children's media and toy culture, perhaps a study employing a different set of media-based toys would have produced different results. The use of dyads or small groups would have provided the opportunity to observe more complex social pretend play than individual sessions, although play with media-based toys is more often a solitary form of play (Kline, 1993). Conducting the study in an early childhood classroom setting may also have resulted in different findings; however, teachers typically do not allow children to play with media-based toys in classrooms (Carlson-Paige & Levin, 1987). Finally, future studies could examine social class or cultural differences and preferences in the play of children related to a variety of media-based toys.

This study raises important questions about children's play and media, specifically in terms of the connections between: (1) pretend enactment and imitative imagination and (2) high-level pretend negotiation and creative imagination. Play is a complex phenomenon as reflected in the need for children to pretend in a fantasy mode beyond their daily reality. In addition, in Western cultures, their lives have been inundated with pre-scripted identities and ideas. Future research, including longer-term studies, could examine whether media-based toys are narrowing or broadening children's opportunities to develop fictional identities and ideas.

In conclusion, a main finding of this study was that during individual short-term play sessions, media-based toys elicited pretend enactment with manufactured roles and themes, whereas generic toys encouraged high-level negotiation and archetypal or reality-based roles and themes. Play with the generic toys did not follow a script (or a script directly derived from the toy), involved higher level pretense behaviours, and therefore was a less imitative and more transformative form of pretense. We argue that these findings may suggest that television and film-scripted toys promote imitative imagination, whereas generic toys encourage more transformative imagination. A deeper understanding of the mechanisms and dynamics of both pretend play and children's consumer culture would contribute to a better understanding of children's experiences within their media-filled worlds.

# REFERENCES

Bergen, D. (2002). The role of pretend play in children's cognitive development. *Early Childhood Research and Practice, 4,* 193–204.

Buckingham, D. (2003). *Media education : literacy, learning, and contemporary culture.* Cambridge, UK: Polity Press.

Carlson-Paige, N., & Levin, D. (1987). *The war play dilemma: Children's needs and society's future.* NY: Teachers College Press.

Cross, G. (1997). *Kids' stuff. Toys and the changing world of American childhood.* Cambridge, MA: Harvard University Press.

Cross, G. & Smits, G. (2005). Japan, the US and the globalization of children's consumer culture. *Journal of Social History, 38*(4), 873–890.

Danesi, M. (1994). *Messages and Meanings: An Introduction to Semiotics.* Toronto, Canada: Canadian Scholars' Press.

Dodge, M.K., & Frost, J.L. (1986). Children's dramatic play: Influence of thematic and non-thematic settings. *Childhood Education, 62,* 166–170.

Dyson, A.H. (2003). "Welcome to the jam": Popular culture, school literacy, and the making of childhoods. *Harvard Educational Review, 73,* 328–361.

Doyle, A. B., & Connolly, J. (1989). Negotiation and enactment in social pretend play. *Early Childhood Research Quarterly, 4,* 289–302.

Garvey, C., & Berndt, R. (1976). *The organization of pretend play.* (ERIC Document Reproduction Service No. ED 114 891).

Greenfield, P., Yut, E., Chung, M., Land, D., Kreider, H., Pantoja, M., & Horsley, K. (1993). The program-length commercial: A study of the effects of television/toy tie-ins on imaginative play. Psychology *& Marketing, 7*(4), 237–255.

Howe, N., Moller, L., Chambers, B., & Petrakos, H. (1993). The ecology of dramatic play centers and children's social and cognitive play. *Early Childhood Research Quarterly, 8,* 235–251.

Howe, N., Petrakos, H., & Rinaldi, C. (1998). "All the sheeps are dead. He murdered them": Sibling pretense, negotiation, internal state language, and relationship quality. *Child Development, 69*(1), 182–91.

Kline, S. (1993). *Out of the garden: Toys, TV and the children's culture in the age of marketing.* NY: Verso.

Levin, D. E., & Rosenquest, B. (2001). The increasing role of electronic toys in the lives of infants and toddlers: Should we be concerned? *Contemporary Issues in Early Childhood, 2*(2), 242–247.

McLoyd, V. C. (1983). The effects of the structure of play objects on the pretend play of low-income preschool children. *Child Development, 54,* 626–635.

Paley, V. (1984). *Boys and girls: Superheroes in the doll corner.* Chicago, IL: University of Chicago Press.

Paley, V. (2004). *A child's work: The importance of fantasy play.* Chicago, IL: University of Chicago Press.

Petrakos, H., & Howe, N. (1996). The influence of the physical design of the dramatic play center on children's play. *Early Childhood Research Quarterly, 11,* 63–77.

Phillips, T. (1945). Doll play as a function of the realism of the materials and the length of the experimental session. *Child Development, 16,* 123–143.

Piaget, J. (1962). *Play, dreams, and imitation in childhood.* NY: Norton.

Pulaski, M.A. (1973). Toys and imaginative play. In J. L. Singer (Ed.), *The child's world of make-believe: Experimental studies of imaginative play* (pp. 74–103). NY: Academic.

Rubin, K. H., Fein, G. G., & Vanderberg, B. (1983). Play. In P. H. Mussen (Ed.), *Handbook of child psychology Vol. 4* (pp. 694–775). NY: Wiley.

Rubin, K. H., & Wolf, D. (1979). The development of maybe: The evolution of social roles into narrative roles. In E. Winner & H. Gardner (Eds.), *New directions for child development, 6* (pp. 15–28). San Francisco, CA: Jossey-Bass.

Singer, J. L. & Singer, D. G. (1981). *Television, imagination, and aggression: A study of preschoolers.* Hillsdale, NJ: Lawrence Erlbaum Associates.

Statistics Canada (2001). Population by selected ethnic origins, by census metropolitan areas (Montreal). Retrieved http://www40.statcan.ca/101/cst01/demo27h.htm.

Steinberg, S. R., & Kincheloe, J. L. (Eds.) (2004). *Kinderculture: The corporate construction of childhood.* Boulder, CO: Westview Press.

Sutton-Smith, B. (1988). War toys and childhood aggression. *Play and Culture, 1,* 57–69.

Van Fuqua, J. (2003). "What are those little girls make of?": *The Powerpuff Girls* and consumer culture. In C.A. Stabile & M. Harrison (Eds.) *Prime time animation: Television animation and American culture* (pp. 205–219). NY: Routledge.

Vygotsky, L. S. (1966). Play and its role in the mental development of the child. In M. Cole (Ed.), *Soviet developmental psychology.* NY: Sharpe.

Walkerdine, V. (1997). *Daddy's little girl.* Cambridge, MA: Harvard University Press.

Woodard, C. Y. (1984). Guidelines for facilitating sociodramatic play. *Childhood Education, 60,* 172–177.

## APPENDIX

## Forms of Verbal Play Transcribed from Play Sessions

1. Scripted as manufactured:
   a. "Cinderella got so scaredy of the stepmother and hid." (Child 3)
   b. "The queen watches as Sleeping Beauty is getting dead." (Child 15)
   c. "Lord Farquaard, you've chosen Princess Fiona!" (Child 7)
   d. "Fiona, she does karate too." (Child 23)
   e. "The PowerPuff girls fly there. They rescue the mean monkey." (Child 22)
   f. "I'm going to web you now!" (Child 6)
2. Archetypal:
   a. "Horsey, go get the bad guy." (Child 2)
   b. "The witch needs to be in the evil, evil place." (Child 9)
   c. "He's the knight and he fights." (Child 19)
   d. "The other prince is gonna come for me." (Child 1)
   e. "Let's say this is the princess and she is in the high tower and then she gets sad." (Child 9)
   f. "He's the groom. She's the bride. He's the priest." (Child 27)
3. Reality-based:
   a. "The mom says, 'Tidy up these but not these.'" (Child 14)
   b. "Um, um, first the little boy and the little girl have to live in a house." (Child 9)
   c. "Come here sweetie. It's Mommy." (Child 1)
   d. "The house is broken. She made the house broken." (Child 21)
   e. "The girl is stronger because she eats her vegetables." (Child 6)
   f. "Him, he's the salesman." (Child 13).

## Chapter Six

# Young Children's Emotional Responses to Cheating in Game Play[1,2]

## Robyn Holmes

The play theorist, Brian Sutton-Smith (1995) suggested that instead of searching for explanations and interpretations of play through broad and generalizing theories, the future of play theory might be better served via "persuasive discourses" (p. 277). Sutton-Smith (1997) further elaborated on these discourses or rhetorics of play. These included play as progress, power, self, identity, festival, imaginary, frivolity, and fate. In contemporary times, the rhetoric of play as progress tends to dominate much of Western thinking and the play literature (Sutton-Smith, 1997). In this rhetoric, play is linked to learning and has educational value. Many educators and psychologists employ this framework and recent works in play have addressed this perspective (e.g., Lytle, 2003; Johnson, Christie & Wardle, 2005; Singer, Golinkoff & Hirsch-Pasek, 2006).

Each of the other rhetorics address particular types of play or other related ludic behavior. For example, play as power is typically applied to sports events and contests (Sutton-Smith, 1997) and can be broadly extended to power issues in all play (Sluss, 2007). Play as identity is associated with festivals and celebrations and those linked to the identification process (e.g., Dell Clark, 2005). Play as imaginary is associated with the performance arts such as music and dance and explores the relationship between play and creativity. Play as self is associated with clinical disciplines and explores the relationship between play and the personality. Play as frivolity is pursued by folklorists and historians and includes humorous or ludic behaviors such as the antics of tricksters and clowns (Sutton-Smith, 1997).

One of the lesser explored rhetorics whose historical origins can be traced back to ancient Greek times is play as fate (Frost, Wortham & Reifel, 2005). This includes play activities whose outcomes are determined by destiny such as gambling (e.g., slots, horse racing, poker), table games, bingo, and sanctioned gambling such as state-run lotteries and the stock market. Play as fate reflects the darker side of play and includes conflict and unhealthy competition (Sutton-Smith, 1997). By logical extension this includes cheating in play and sports (e.g., blood doping, steroid use). Examples of children and adolescents' cheating include those that violate game rules or the rules of fairness. Some forms of cheating are actually legitimized such as the cable show "Cheat!" which provides shortcuts and special codes for gamers and publications that distribute game cheats to its' readers.

## CHEATING AND PLAY

There are multiple theoretical stances that provide explanations for and interpretations of cheating behaviors. Consequently, there are several definitions of cheating that appear in the literature. If one takes a moral stance to cheating, it is frequently defined as behaving inappropriately and violating social norms. In this view, actions and behaviors are evaluated as being right or wrong, appropriate or inappropriate (e.g., Waugh, Godfrey, Evans, & Craig, 1995). From a psychoanalytical perspective, cheating is associated with internalizing parental values and norms and the violation of these standards. Freud (1938), Erikson (1966), and Woolgar, Steele, Steele, Yabsley, and Fonagy's (2001) works reflect this tradition. Other psychotherapists have defined cheating as "creative play" where the player bends or stretches the rules (Bellinson, 2002, p. 68).

Individual reasons for cheating by children vary and motivations to cheat are dependent upon context. Even moral children may cheat to win or be the best under certain circumstances such as not being caught doing so (e.g., Lobel & Levanon, 1988). Age may also play a role in children's cheating behavior. Younger children often prefer games with rule structure but aren't cognitively able to follow the rules for long periods of time (Bellinson, 2002). Consequently, children will cheat when games are too difficult for them (American Academy of Pediatrics, 2008). Younger children are also learning to internalize their culture's values and seek adult approval and may cheat if their culture values competition and winning (American Academy of Pediatrics, 2008; Meeks, 1970). However, younger children often do not fully comprehend the emotional consequences that follow a moral transgression. Thus they are likely to report that a person who cheats and wins will feel happy even though they committed a transgression. They focus upon the outcome rather than the moral implications of their actions (Lourenco, 1997; Woolgar, et al., 2001)

Socialization may also play a role in the pervasiveness of cheating. For example, in individualistic cultures such as the United States, competitiveness and winning is rewarded. In their early experiences, children in individualistic cultures are socialized to learn that losing has negative consequences (American Academy of Pediatrics, 2008; Sommers & Satel, 2005). Finally, gender is an important factor in the socialization process. In the US, boys are socialized to be more competitive than most girls are and may be more susceptible to succeeding through any means (e.g., Bellinson, 2002). Some empirical studies have found boys more likely than girls to cheat at game playing (e.g., Rubin & Hubbard, 2001).

Much of the literature on cheating has concentrated on two specific settings: academe (e.g., Evans & Craig, 1990; Lin & Wen, 2007; Lupton & Chapman, 2002; Strom & Strom, 2007; Taylor, Pogrebin, & Dodge, 2002) and organized or professional sports (e.g., Carstairs, 2003; Hembree, 2007; LePage, 2006; Mewett, 2002; Roberts, 1996). Although cheating is relatively common in children's game play in contrast to other scholarly topics of play, the relationship between cheating and play is relatively unexplored.

For example, Rubin and Hubbard (2003) investigated the relationship between gender, socioeconomic status, and aggression on children's language use and cheating during game playing. They found that peer-rejected children cheated and were more likely to use negative language more than children of average status. Other studies on cheating have qualitatively observed children in natural settings. These include Mechling's (1988) work with games, "cutting corners" and manipulating game rules and Holmes, Valentino-McCarthy and Schmidt's (2007) work with young children's perceptions of cheating during play. Through participant observation they found that children cheat in certain situations and contexts and the children's decisions to cheat during play were primarily based upon their desire to win, fairness, and whether cheating was deemed appropriate by the playgroup. In their group of kindergartners, morality, social expectations, and fairness played a major role in the children's decision to cheat during play and perceptions of cheating.


## FAIRNESS

Play, like all social behavior, is rule governed. This is reflected in the importance of fairness in play. Fairness is simply playing by the rules. Piaget's (1932) description of marble play is a testimony to how players strategically use rules by manipulating or modifying them during play. Hughes' (1989) work on "gaming" or how players manipulate the rules of play of the ball game, Four Square highlights how players modify game rules in real-life settings and focuses upon social status and friend relationships. In children's game play, rule violations are a common transgression that frequently leads to conflict.

There are consequences to not playing fairly and cheaters may be prohibited from playing in the game (e.g., Feezell, 1988). As Meeks (1970; 2000) noted, some children have difficulty in abiding by the rules of the game if it means they will not win. In these cases, playing for fun is supplanted by the desire to win. Most children who do not play fairly are aware of a game's rules and cognizant of the fact they are breaking or manipulating them (Bellinson, 2002). However, children who do not play fairly also know that play is an altered state of reality. Although their cheating may be tolerated in play (e.g., Zan & Hildebrandt, 2005) or the consequences for being caught will not be severe, they are aware in other contexts this would not be the case (Bellinson, 2002).

## EMOTIONS AND PLAY

Play has been linked to children's emotional expressions and affective processing in several ways. First, unhealthy play in the form of "spoilsports, cheats, bullies" has been associated with negative emotional responses, specifically anger (Sutton-Smith, 2003, p. 6). Second, empirical studies have established a connection between pretend play and children's social and emotional development such as emotional regulation (e.g., Berk, Mann, & Ogan, 2006; Galyer & Evans, 2001; Russ & Kaugars, 2001). Second, pretend play provides an altered state of reality in which children can express negative emotions without consequences (Haight & Miller, 1993) or cope with painful real life experiences such as chronic illness (Dell Clark, 2003).

Pretend play is not the only play form linked to emotional expression. Bellinson (2002) addressed the use of board games in children's psychotherapy and noted that some children are more comfortable using structured games such as board games rather than verbal means to express themselves. She argued that board games can be utilized to analyze children's emotional expressions and unconscious wishes and conflicts. She suggested that cheating at board games such as children's motivations to cheat, how they violate game rules, the duration of the cheating, and when children cheat can reveal information about the child's emotional state.

Few, if any studies have pursued the topic of children's cheating during game play (e.g., Holmes, Valentino-McCarthy, & Schmidt, 2007; Mechling, 1988; Rubin & Hubbard, 2003) and more rare are those that explore the relationship between cheating associated with game play and emotion. Hubbard's work (2001) that explored the relationship between children's emotional expressions during game play in contrived cheating and fair playing conditions is an exceptional case.

This pilot study pursues two research questions: First, it explores young children's feelings about cheating during game play from both the player and victim's perspective. Past research has demonstrated that children, even young children, can identify with and attribute negative feelings to a victim in both artificial (Keller, Gummerum, Lindsey, 2004; Núñez, 1999) and real-life settings (Dunn, 1988) though younger children may still associate positive feelings with the violator (Keller, et al., 2004). In addition, girls are slightly more prone to report secondary emotions for transgressors than boys are (Kochanska, Gross, Lin, & Nichols, 2002).

Based upon past research literature, it was expected that all the children in this study would be more inclined to associate negative, primary emotions with another person's cheating but younger children would be more inclined to associate their own cheating with positive, primary emotions. Kindergarten children were expected to associate their own cheating with secondary emotions such as embarrassed or ashamed (Lewis & Haviland-Jones, 2006; Keller, et al., 2004). In addition, girls were expected to report more secondary emotions than boys (Kochanska, et al., 2002).

Second, this pilot study explores children's perceptions of and ability to define fairness during play. It was expected that the kindergarten children would be more capable of verbally expressing their understanding of fairness and rule violations than the preschoolers (e.g., Bellinson, 2002; Covrig, 1996; Piaget, 1962).

## METHOD

### Participants

Twenty-one preschoolers and 11 kindergarten children enrolled in two different northeastern institutions were participants. In the nursery school, one 4-year-old and pre-K class were included. In the 4-year-old class there were ten children (5 boys, 5 girls). All of the children were European American and ages ranged from 4.1–4.7 years with a mean of 4.37 years (SD = .41). In the pre-K class there were 11 children (5 boys, 6 girls). All were European American and ages ranged from 4.1–5.2 years with a mean age of 4.62 years (SD = .42). The total preschool sample was 10 boys and 11 girls with an age range of 4.1–5.2 years with a mean age of 4.7 years (SD = .47). Parental consent return rate was 75.86% (22/29 for the total sample; 11/16 for the 4-year-olds and 11/13 for the 5-year-olds).

In the kindergarten sample, there were seven boys and four girls. All of the children were European American with the exception of one African American child. Ages ranged from 5.3–5.8 years with a mean age of 5.5 years (SD = .22). A Vietnamese child arrived very late in the school year and was not included in the study. Parental consent return rate was 100%. An Institutional Review Board granted approval for this project and director and parental/guardian consent were also obtained. Participants were treated according to American Psychological Association (1992) ethical codes of conduct. All names used in this chapter are pseudonyms.

## Stimulus Materials

The following board games and cards were introduced to the children during free play periods. These stimuli were selected for their developmental appropriateness, their presence in many preschool and kindergarten toy inventories, and their ability to facilitate cheating. They were: CandyLand, Go Fish, Chutes and Ladders, Checkers, Chess, Trouble, and a regular deck of playing cards. Early childhood educators, the play literature, and the children's teachers confirmed the appropriateness of the game selections using criteria such as developmental norms and complexity of the game. All of the classrooms had most of these games in their play inventories and these games were employed in a previous project on cheating (Holmes, Valentino-McCarthy & Schmidt, 2007).

## Design and Procedure

This study employed a qualitative design and methodological approaches including participant observation, unstructured interviewing, and a Smiley Face Picture Task.

*Participant Observation.* Participant observation typically involves some type of fieldwork and is both a method and process. In this approach the researcher enters a group with the intention of learning to experience the world the way they do. The researcher seeks to establish relationships, record and observe behavior, and become directly involved in the children's lives (Bernard, 2006).

*Unstructured Interviewing.* Unstructured interviewing is also sometimes called ethnographic interviewing. The interviewer has clear goals and questions in mind but the interviewee is given the flexibility to converse about related topics and at a comfortable pace (Bernard, 2006).

*The Smiley Face Task.* Picture tasks have been employed with children to help them communicate their understanding of an event, concept, or phenomenon. Sometimes these tasks are used to complement verbal methods; at other times they are employed in place of verbal methods when children are unable to express their understanding and perceptions of their world. Recent works that have utilized picture or visual tasks with children include Dell Clark's (2004) use of the Metaphor Sort Technique (a picture task) to reveal the children's understanding of their chronic illness and Toren's (2007) work in which she asked children to draw pictures of Sunday brunch to help reveal their cognitive notions about household relationships and the cultural meanings of this event. In the present study, given the difficulty young children may have in verbally expressing their knowledge and understanding of emotions, a picture task was designed to complement observations and interviews.

In the Smiley Face Task children were shown smiley faces depicting primary and secondary emotions. These consisted of the primary emotions of HAPPY, ANGRY/MAD, SAD, and the secondary emotions of EMBARASSED, ASHAMED, and CONFUSED (a neutral response). Smiley faces were employed for the following reasons. First, they are an image with which many young children are familiar and they are gender neutral. Some studies have reported that a person's gender influences preschoolers' perception of emotion (e.g., Widen & Russell, 2002). Second, facial expressions are important in communicating emotional states (e.g., Pollak & Sinha, 2002) and the ability to associate facial expression with emotion emerges in infancy, develops rapidly, and improves markedly through the preschool years (e.g., Thomas, De Bellis, Graham, & LaBar, 2007). In addition, consultation with several early childhood educators and a pilot study with similar-aged children were conducted to determine whether the task was developmentally appropriate. Positive responses from both sources resulted in the design of the following procedure.

During free play individual children were led to a quiet table in the classroom. The six smiley faces were individually displayed on the table and placed in front of the child. Prior to the task, the researcher named each face's emotional expression for the child. Then each child went through a few trials to make sure he/she could accurately identify the smiley face's emotion. If he/she could correctly identify them all, the task proceeded. Individual children were asked two questions whose order was counterbalanced. They were: "Please point to the face that shows: How do you feel when you cheat while you are playing?" And "Please point to the face that shows: How do you feel when someone else cheats while you are playing?" Both questions were followed with "Why?"

These were considered developmentally appropriate questions since the awareness of the self and the emergence of self-conscious emotions are linked to the cognitive ability to compare one's behavior to societal norms. For many children, this emerges developmentally by age three (Lewis & Haviland-Jones, 2006). Finally, asking children to verbally express how they and another person would potentially feel about a given situation via the use of interviews has been employed in previous studies with young children (Karniol & Koren, 1987). This task was performed at a quiet classroom table away from ongoing activity in all classrooms. Responses were tallied for each child and grouped by gender.

*The Preschool Fieldwork Period.* The preschool fieldwork period began in September 2006 and ended in June 2007. Each class was visited on two separate days for three hours per week. Observations lasted 15 weeks for approximately 45 hours of total observation time. All observations were recorded as written field notes during indoor free play periods. Two research assistants worked independently with the 4-year-old and pre-K classes. The author visited both classes.

The author and two assistants initially met with the children in each class at the start of the school year and the children were told these individuals would be visiting their class to play with them. Upon meeting the children, the researchers learned the children's names, played with them, and participated in classroom activities to allow the children to adjust to their presence and become comfortable with them. This introductory period lasted several weeks. After that, stimulus games such as CandyLand, Go Fish, Chutes and Ladders, and Trouble were introduced for the children to select during free play. These games were played on classroom tables and the fieldworkers sat with the children and observed them as they were playing. All activities were continuously monitored and the fieldworkers recorded all instances of cheating at play and verbal material related to cheating and fairness in the form of written field notes.

During play, children were informally asked questions such as:

1. What do you do when someone cheats while you're playing?
2. How do you feel about people who cheat while they're playing with you? Why?
3. Do you like it when people cheat while you're playing? Why or Why not?
4. When you're playing fair what does that mean?
5. What do you mean when you say "that's not fair?

In November 2006, the children were administered the Smiley Face Task.

*The Kindergarten Fieldwork Period.* The kindergarten fieldwork period began in September 2006 and ended in June 2007. The author visited the

children one day a week for 2 hours over 19 sessions for a total of approximately 40 hours of observation. Visits took place on different days of the
week. At the beginning of the project, the author was introduced to the children and they were also told that she would be playing with them and asking
them questions while they were playing.

For the first few visits the author learned the children's names, played with
them, and participated in classroom activities to allow the children to adjust to
her presence and become comfortable with her. Following this acquaintance
period, stimulus games such as *CandyLand*, *Go Fish*, *Chutes and Ladders*,
and *Trouble* were introduced to the children. The children could now voluntary select these games for use during free play. These games were played on
classroom tables and the author sat with the children and observed them as
they were playing. All activities were continuously monitored and the author
recorded all instances of cheating at play and verbal material related to cheating and fairness in the form of written field notes.

While they were playing, these children were informally asked the same
questions described above. The Smiley Face task was individually administered to the children in December 2006.

## Coding

The coding process employed was adopted from Holmes, Valentino-McCarthy and Schmidt's work (2007). The author taught two assistants the coding
procedure for the field notes that included observational and interview material. All three served as coders to ensure reliability. First, the author randomly
selected one question and its' accompanying responses to demonstrate the
coding process. She explained that the informal interview questions were the
anchor in the coding process. Next, categorical domains were formed from
the children's verbatim responses to these questions and similar responses
were subsumed into their respective domains.

For example, when asked the question "How do you feel about people who
cheat while they're playing with you?" some children responded with "sad"
or "I get angry when people cheat on me." These were coded and tallied as
separate responses. Sometimes a child's response might contain two separate
domains such as in the response, "Sometimes I get mad and then sometimes I
just say that's not fair." Such a response was coded for each separate domain
and then tallied separately as well. The two assistants were given interview
material with which to practice the procedure. This lasted one week. The author and her assistants then independently coded another question together in
one room and then compared their domains and tallies. Only one discrepancy

arose and this was immediately discussed and resolved. Coding field notes began immediately following this session and coders worked independently.

## RESULTS

Data from the two preschool classes were combined to represent the preschool sample. Two facts supported this decision to blend the classes. First, these children all shared a preschool educational experience. Second, only a few children in the pre-K class were over 5 years of age and were closer in age to the children in the 4-year-old class.

In Table 6.1, frequencies for preschoolers' responses to the Smiley Face Task regarding their feelings about another person's cheating are presented. For both boys and girls, ANGRY/MAD was the emotion most frequently reported. ANGRY/MAD accounted for 54.5% of all responses with girls reporting this emotion slightly more than boys (58.3%/50.0%). For example, Vincent responded, "I get mad when someone else does (cheat)." Similarly, Melissa responded, "I get mad. Cheating is mean." SAD was the second most frequently reported emotion and accounted for 27.3% of all responses. For example, MaryAnne responded, "Sad—I don't play with people who cheat 'cause it's not fair." Boys were twice as likely as girls to proffer this response (40.0%/16.7%). ASHAMED and HAPPY were least reported for both boys and girls.

In Table 6.1, frequencies for kindergarteners' responses to the Smiley Face Task regarding their feelings about another person's cheating also are presented. For these kindergarteners SAD was the emotion reported with the greatest frequency. It accounted for 66.7% of all responses with girls more than twice as likely as boys to do so (83.3%/42.9%). For example, Jill responded, "Sad because I wanted to win." Similarly, Tim responded

**Table 6.1. Frequencies for Preschoolers' and Kindergartner's Responses to the Smiley Face Task: "How do you feel when someone else cheats while you're playing?"**

| | Emotions | | | | |
|---|---|---|---|---|---|
| Classroom | Angry (Mad) | Sad | Ashamed | Happy | Confused |
| PRESCHOOLERS | | | | | |
| Boys (n = 10) | 5 | 4 | 2 | 0 | 0 |
| Girls (n = 11) | 7 | 2 | 1 | 1 | 0 |
| KINDERGARTENERS | | | | | |
| Boys (n = 7) | 2 | 3 | 1 | 0 | 1 |
| Girls (n = 4) | 1 | 5 | 0 | 0 | 0 |

sad but for different reasons, "Sad, because it wasn't fair." ANGRY/MAD, ASHAMED, and CONFUSED were the least reported. A common response for MAD was, "I get mad 'cause someone is doing something they were not opposed to." Some children made a connection between their own feelings and the cheater's behavior. For example, Brian responded, "I get mad at them and tell the teacher 'cause they hurt my feelings."

In Table 6.2, frequencies for preschoolers' responses to the Smiley Face Task regarding their feelings about their own cheating are presented.

The most frequently reported emotion was HAPPY. It accounted for 40.9% of all responses. Gender differences emerged. Fifty percent of all girls and 30% of all boys reported feeling happy when they cheated. For example, Wendy replied, "I'm happy when I cheat because that means I'm going to win and when you win you are the best." Other children reported feeling happy but with reservations. For example, Christie responded, "Happy but I didn't win fairly so it's not really winning." MAD and ASHAMED were the second most frequently reported emotions. Boys were three times as likely to report being mad than girls were. For example, Brent was "mad, because I was losing and I had to cheat." Girls were three times more likely than boys to report feeling ashamed when they cheated. Christie responded, "Ashamed, 'cause my daddy says cheating is bad." EMBARASSED was not reported by boys.

In Table 6.2, frequencies for kindergartners' responses to the Smiley Face Task regarding their feelings about their own cheating also are presented. Kindergarteners' responses were more dispersed than preschooler responses to this query. MAD was the most frequently reported emotion and accounted for 54.5% of all responses. Gender differences emerged. Seventy-five percent of all girls reported feeling mad when they cheated whereas only 42.8% of all boys did. For example, Rose responded, "Mad—I was doing something

**Table 6.2.  Frequencies for Preschoolers' and Kindergarteners' Responses to the Smiley Face Task: "How do you feel when you cheat while you're playing?"**

| Classroom | Emotions | | | | |
|---|---|---|---|---|---|
|  | Happy | Sad | Angry (Mad) | Ashamed | Embarrassed |
| PRESCHOOLERS |  |  |  |  |  |
| Boys   (n = 10) | 3 | 1 | 3 | 1 | 0 |
| Girls   (n = 11) | 6 | 2 | 1 | 3 | 1 |
| KINDERGARTENERS |  |  |  |  |  |
| Boys   (n = 7) | 0 | 1 | 3 | 1 | 2 |
| Girls   (n = 4) | 0 | 1 | 3 | 2 | 1 |

I wasn't supposed to." Other girls were angry at themselves because they thought "nobody would play with me." EMBARASSED and ASHAMED were the second most frequently reported emotions. These accounted for 27.2% of all responses.

In addition, there were gender differences. Girls were twice as likely as boys to report feeling ashamed when they cheated than boys were. For example, Michele responded, "Ashamed—the other person was close to winning and it wasn't fair." Justin also responded with "Ashamed because I wasn't playing nicely. Cheating is bad." Boys were twice as likely as girls to be embarrassed when they cheated. For example, Brian replied he was "Embarrassed—you're not supposed to even if it makes you happy."

## Definitions of Fairness

Playing fair and cheating are concepts that spontaneously emerged in the children's conversations while they were playing. For example, preschoolers Richard, Sarah, and Kevin were playing Trouble. Richard moved Sarah's man the incorrect number of spaces so she would avoid sending his man back to home base. Sarah spoke to Richard, "You're cheating. That's not how you play." Kevin then interjected, "Yeah, that's not fair. You're not opposed to do that." Fairness emerged in the children's explanations of cheating and both preschool and kindergarten children could identify rule and turn taking violations.

For example, when kindergarteners Rose and James were playing Checkers, James moved his man two spaces. Immediately after the move, Rose said, "You only move one space." Looking for verification, she turned to Michael who was seated to her immediate right. He replied, "I play Checkers and you only move one space." However, even though most of the preschool children acknowledged rule violations in game play they had difficulty in verbally expressing their knowledge of and defining the concept of fairness. Most simply echoed the question in their responses or replied, "Because". Only the kindergarten children were capable of providing responses to questions about fairness.

For this group of children, fairness and playing fair involved maintaining and following the rules of play. Violation of the norm or rules of play emerged in the children's responses. For example, to the question "What does it mean when you're not playing fair?" Ricky responded, "You're not playing by the rules." Justin supported his understanding. He replied, "It's not right, that's not how you play." Some children equated fairness with behaving inappropriately. For example, Ashley replied, "Doing something you think is okay but it really isn't."

Fairness and playing fair were also associated with cheating for these children. For example, to the question what does playing fair mean, Loretta replied, "It's not fair when you cheat." Joseph was much more explicit. He responded, "When you're not playing fair it means you're cheating." Finally, James explained why it was important to win fairly. He replied, "It's no fair when someone gets to cheat so that makes you want to cheat too. You gotta win fair."

## DISCUSSION

This pilot study explored the relationship between cheating during game play and children's ability to identify their feelings about cheating. In addition, the children's perceptions and understanding of fairness were also explored. The findings support the first research question that addresses whether preschool and kindergarten children can identify and explain their feelings about their own cheating and how they feel when they are playing with a cheater. For them, cheating at game play was associated with particular emotions and the reporting of either primary or secondary emotions was dependent upon several factors which included cognitive maturity, whether the self or another person was doing the cheating, and the motivations for cheating. In addition, as expected, preschool children were unable to verbally convey their understanding of the abstract concept of fairness in contrast to the kindergarten children who were able to do so.

The preschoolers reported getting angry or mad when they were the victim of cheating and girls reported this emotion more than boys did. This supports Sutton-Smith's (2003) view that cheating is associated with the primary emotion, anger. For these children, the response "mad" was accompanied by explanations that focused upon meanness or the fact that they weren't able to win when someone cheated. Frustration is clearly a trigger for anger (e.g., Segall, Dasen, Berry & Poortinga, 1999) and the children may have linked frustration to the cheater who blocked their opportunity to win. In addition, these children considered cheating a form of trickery and were adamantly opposed to being tricked by playmates. Victims often responded with anger rather than humor.

In addition, albeit with lesser frequency, preschoolers reported feeling sad when they were victimized by a cheater. Explanations that accompanied the response SAD focused upon the fact that the cheaters violated the game rules and weren't playing fair. Thus the emotion ANGER was directly linked to the act of cheating whereas the emotion SAD was indirectly linked to cheating via the concept of fairness.

By contrast, kindergarteners overwhelming reported feeling sad when they were the victim of cheating and girls were more likely to report this emotion than boys. For the kindergartners the rationale behind SAD included being deprived of winning. Kindergarten children also reported feeling MAD with much less frequency but employed the same rationale preschoolers did for feeling sad—feelings of anger were linked to fairness, "not playing the way you're supposed to" and winning unfairly. The age differences in reported emotional responses may be due to developmental patterns of dealing with frustration where younger children get mad and somewhat older children evaluate the situation using different criteria. Thus the kindergartners reported feeling sad when someone else cheats against them.

When asked how they felt about their own cheating, preschoolers overwhelming reported feeling happy, with girls twice as likely to report this emotion than boys. The preschoolers were happy when they cheated because it helped them to win and winning was linked to personal achievement. For example, Loretta responded, "I'm happy when I win 'cause when you win, you are the best." For the preschoolers, individual accomplishments outweighed internalized norms. This supports Lobel and Levanon's (1998) view that children will cheat to win or be the best. In line with developmental norms, the younger children focused upon outcome rather than moral consequences of their behavior (Lourenco, 1997; Keller et al., 2004). The primary emotion, ANGER and the secondary emotion SHAME were also reported with lesser frequency. In these instances, girls were more likely than boys to report feeling ashamed. This pattern is in line with other reported findings (e.g., Kochanska et al., 2002).

For the kindergarteners, ANGRY or MAD were reported with equal frequencies for girls and boys. Again this supports Sutton-Smith's (2003) relationship between specific emotions and forms of play—anger and cheating. However the kindergarteners reported feeling ashamed and embarrassed when they cheated more so than the preschoolers did. The secondary, cognitive emotions such as EMBARASSED and ASHAMED reported by kindergarteners may presumably be due to the fact that they have acquired broader social experiences, internalized parental and societal norms, and understand the consequences of cheating in an academic setting more than preschoolers (Freud, 1938; Lewis & Haviland-Jones, 2006). No kindergarten child reported feeling happy when he or she was the cheater. Clearly this is an emotion that would not be condoned by authority figures and societal standards. In fact, ASHAMED and EMBARASSED were accompanied by explanations that focused upon violating game rules and not winning fairly. So the children were cognizant of not only societal norms but also fairness within the context of the game (e.g., Feezell, 1988).

One commonality that surfaced between the two groups of children was their preoccupation with winning. Exclamations of "I'm winning" and "I'm the winner" were constantly heard during free play. Children just entering a game would frequently ask, "Whose winning?" The children's emphasis on winning may be due in part to American socialization pressures that emphasize being the best and personal achievements. In an individualistic culture such as the US, children learn early on that winning is important, losing has negative consequences, and they will be judged on their own accomplishments (Sommers & Satel, 2005). Thus the desire to win could be a powerful motivation to cheat as children come to learn and internalize their cultural values.

One could also argue that the decision to cheat may produce a conflict situation for these children. Play is a social activity and children need playmates to engage in a multiplayer game. When asked if you should cheat to win, Lauren responded, "No...you play to have fun and play with your friends." But the desire to win can be the motivation for some children's cheating, a behavior which can also result in peer conflict and the loss of playmates. For example, Anthony and Ben were playing the card game War, and Ben had been cheating throughout the game. Ben stated, "He's (Anthony) upset 'cause I got all the cards. It's just the way you play the game. I didn't cheat. He doesn't want to lose." Anthony countered, "You are too cheating. I'm tellin' on you." They ended the game and then within seconds started to play again. Ben began, "I won that round, wanna play again?" He and Anthony played diplomatically until the next instance of cheating had to be negotiated. It is possible that cheating in game play crosses into two discourses — play as fate and play as progress. In game play with peers, children learn about rule structure and the consequences and cultural meaning of playing fairly and cheating.

With respect to notions of fairness, for this group of children, the verbal ability to express concept of fairness was also linked to cognitive maturity, linguistic competency, and wider social experiences. For these kindergarteners, fairness is understood and expressed as following the rules. This parallels children's notions of fairness reported by Holmes, Valentino-McCarthy and Schmidt (2007). Playing by the rules with players who play fairly was highly valued by the children (e.g., Feezell, 1988). Failure to do so resulted in the protest, "Hey no fair", "That's not fair. You're not supposed to do that" and "You're not playing by the rules." Sometimes not playing fairly resulted in termination of the game.

For example, Joey and Brian were playing a game of Checkers. When they began they were laughing, smiling, and talking through their checker moves. Joey began to cheat repeatedly. After Brian called his attention to his cheating and challenged Joey on his moves, Joey adamantly denied cheating claiming that the number of spaces he moved his checker was fair. Brian's body language changed drastically. He frowned, pouted, and folded his arms across his chest. At one point he said to Joey, "If you do that one more time I'm not playing" after which he turned his chair around with his back facing Joey. Joey walked around to him and swore he wouldn't cheat anymore. Play continued until the next cheating instance and then Brian ended the game with "I'm not playing with you anymore. You're cheating."

There were several limitations to this study. First, both sub-samples were small and homogeneous with respect to ethnicity and socio-economic status (SES). Second, the same fieldworker did not administer all three tasks though all fieldworkers were female and trained by the author. In addition, the children were asked to report their feelings about hypothetical cheating situations and not when they were actually cheating or the victim of cheating during game play. This hypothetical perspective may have been too cognitively demanding for the young children although some studies with slightly older children have reported their ability to respond to hypothetical scenarios (Lewis & Haviland-Jones, 2006). Finally, the facial images employed clearly illustrated only one single emotion for each image. In real-life settings, facial expressions may be processed as a mixed response and sometimes facial expressions are accompanied by other non-verbal cues which may convey a different emotion (e.g., Pollak & Sinha, 2002).

The relationship between play and emotion is a relatively unexplored topic (Haight, Black, Ostler & Sheridan, 2006) and cheating during game play and its link to emotion is a particular case. Future research might consider developmental and cross-cultural explorations in cheating during game play and its relationship to emotion. Additional attention might be given to conducting studies in natural settings such as home and school and employing different visual stimuli and tasks. Learning to play fairly is an important lesson for children and one which would further our understanding of the meaning and function of play in children's lives.

## NOTES

1. The author warmly thanks the children, teachers, directors, and field sites for their participation in this project. She also expresses her thanks to her student assistants, Allison McGorry and Christina Shaheen. Finally, the author also kindly thanks the editor and reviewers for their thoughtful comments and suggestions.
2. An abbreviated version of this work was presented at the IPA/TASP International Meeting for the Study of Play in April, 2007 at Rochester, New York.

# REFERENCES

American Academy of Pediatrics. (2008). *Parenting corner Question and Answer: Cheating.* Retrieved http://aap.org/publicized/BK_5Cheating.html.

American Psychological Association. (1992). Ethical principles of psychologists and code of conduct. *American Psychologist, 47,* 1597–1611.

Bellinson, J. (2002). *Children's use of board games in psychotherapy.* Northvale, NJ: Jason Aronson Inc.

Berk, L., Mann, T., & Ogan, A. (2006). Make-believe play: Wellspring for development of self-regulation. In D. Singer, R. Golnikoff, & K. Hirsch-Pasek (Eds.), *Play = Learning: How play motivates and enhances children's cognitive and social-emotional growth* (pp. 74–100). New York: Oxford University Press.

Bernard, R. (2006). *Research methods in anthropology: Qualitative and Quantitative Approaches* (4th ed.). Walnut Creek, CA: AltaMira Press.

Carstairs, C. (2003). The wide world of doping: Drug scandals, natural bodies, and the business of sports entertainment. *Addiction Research & Theory, 11,* 263–281.

Covrig, D. (1996). Sport, fair play, and children's conceptions of fairness. *Journal for a Just & Caring Education, 2,* 263–279.

Dell Clark, C. (2003). *In sickness and in play: Children coping with chronic illness.* New Brunswick, NJ: Rutgers University Press.

Dell Clark, C. (2004). Visual metaphor as method in interviews with children. *Journal of Linguistic Anthropology, 14,* 171–185.

Dell Clark, C. (2005). Tricks of Festival: Children, Enculturation, and American Halloween. *Ethos 33,*180–205.

Dunn, J. (1988). *The beginnings of social understanding.* Cambridge, MA: Harvard University Press.

Erikson, K., (1966). *Wayward Puritans; a study in the sociology of deviance.* New York: Wiley.

Evans, E., & Craig, D. (1990). Teacher and student perceptions of academic cheating in middle and senior schools. *Journal of Educational Research, 84,* 44–50.

Feezell, R. (1988). On the wrongness of cheating and why cheaters can't play the game. *Journal of the Philosophy of Sport, XV,* 57–68.

Freud, S. (1938). *A general introduction to psychoanalysis.* (English translation revised ed. By J. Riviere). New York: Garden City Publications.

Frost, J., Wortham, S., & Reifel, S. (2005). *Play and Child Development* (2nd ed.). Upper Saddle River, NJ: Pearson Publishing.

Galyer, K., & Evans, I. (2001). Pretend play and the development of emotion regulation in preschool children. *Early Child Development and Care, 166,* 93–108.

Hembree, M. (2007). If they cheat, sit them down. *Sporting News, 231,* 47–48.

Haight, W., Black, J., Ostler, T., & Sheridan, K. (2006). Pretend play and emotion: Learning in transition in traumatized mothers and children. In D. Singer, R. Golnikoff & K. Hirsch-Pasek (Eds.), *Play = Learning: How play motivates and enhances children's cognitive and social-emotional growth* (pp. 209–230). New York: Oxford University Press.

Haight, W., & Miller, P. (1993). *Pretending at home: early development in a socio-cultural context.* Albany: State University of New York Press.

Holmes, R., Valentino-McCarthy, J., & Schmidt, S. (2007). "Hey, no fair": Young children's perceptions of cheating. In D. Sluss & O. Jarrett (Eds.), *Investigating play in the 21ˢᵗ century: Play and Culture Studies, Vol. 7* (pp. 259–276). Lanham, MD: University Press of America, Inc.

Hubbard, J. (2001). Emotion expression processes in children's peer interaction: The role of peer rejection, aggression, and gender. *Child Development, 72,* 1426–1438.

Hughes, L. (1989). Foursquare: A Glossary and "Native" taxonomy of game rules. *Play & Culture, 2,* 103–136.

Johnson, J., Christie, J., & Wardle, F. (Eds.). (2005). *Play, development, and early education.* Boston: Pearson Education Inc.

Karniol, R., & Koren, L. (1987). How would you feel?: Children's inferences regarding their own and others' affective reactions. *Cognitive Development, 2,* 271–278.

Keller, M., Gummerum, X., & Lindsey, S. (2004). Understanding perspectives and emotions in contract violation: Development of deontic and moral reasoning. *Child Development, 75,* 614–635.

Kochanska, G., Gross, J., Lin, M., & Nichols, K. (2002). Guilt in young children: Development, determinants, and relations with a broader system of standards. *Child Development, 73,* 461–482.

Le Page, M. (2006). Only drugs can stop the sports cheats. *New Scientist, 191,* 18–1.

Lewis, M., & Haviland-Jones, J. (2006). *Handbook of emotions* (2ⁿᵈ ed.). New York: The Guilford Press.

Lin, C., & Wen, L. (2007). Academic dishonesty in higher education: A nationwide study in Taiwan. *The International Journal of Higher Education and Educational Planning, 54,* 85–97.

Lobel, T. E., & Levanon, I. (1988). Self-esteem, need for approval, and cheating behavior in children. *Journal of Education Research, 80,* 122–123.

Lourenço, O. (1997). Children's attributions of moral emotions to victimizers: Some data, doubts and suggestions. *British Journal of Developmental Psychology, 15,* 425–438.

Lupton, R., & Chapman, K. (2002). Russian and American college students' attitudes, perceptions and tendencies toward cheating. *Educational Research, 44,* 17–27.

Lytle, D. (Ed.). (2003). *Play and educational theory and practice. Play & Culture Studies, Vol. 5.* Westport, CT: Praeger.

Mechling, J. (1988). On the relation between creativity and cutting corners. *Adolescent Psychiatry, 15,* 346–366.

Meeks, J. (1970). Children who cheat at games. *Journal of the American Academy of Child Psychiatry, 9,* 157–170.

Meeks, J (2000). Reflections on children who cheat at games: A commentary. *Journal of Infant, Child, and Adolescent Psychotherapy, 1,* 71–75.

Mewett, P. (2002). Discourses of deception: Cheating in professional running. *Australian Journal of Anthropology, 13,* 292–309.

Nunez, M. (1999, April). *Young psychologists & dealers: Early conditional reasoning on reciprocal exchanges and the emotions involved.* Poster session presented at the biennial meeting of the Society for Research in Child Development, Albuquerque, NM.

Piaget, J. (1932). *The moral judgment of the child.* Oxford, England: Harcourt Brace.

Piaget, J. (1962). *The language and thought of the child* (M. Gabain, Trans.). Cleveland, OH: Meridian (Original work published in 1923).

Pollak, S., & Sinha, P. (2002). Effects of early experience on children's recognition of facial displays of emotion. *Developmental Psychology, 38,* 784–791.

Roberts, T. (1996). Cheating in sport: Recent considerations. *Sport Science Review, 5,* 72–87.

Rubin, R., & Hubbard, J. (2003). Children's verbalizations and cheating behavior during game playing: The role of socioeconomic status, aggression, and gender. *Journal of Abnormal Child Psychology, 31,* 65–78.

Russ, S., & Kaugars, A. (2001). Emotion in children's play and creative problem solving. *Creativity Research Journal, 13,* 211–219.

Segall, M., Dasen, P., Berry, J., & Poortinga, Y. (1999). *Human behavior in global perspective.* (2nd ed.). Boston: Allyn and Bacon.

Sluss, D. (2007). Conceptualizing play investigations in the 21st century. In D. Sluss & O. Jarrett (Eds.), *Investigating play in the 21st century: Play and Culture Studies, Vol. 7* (pp. 307–314). Lanham, MD: University Press of America, Inc.

Singer, D., Golnikoff, R., & Hirsch-Pasek, K. (2006). *Play=Learning: How play motivates and enhances children's cognitive and social-emotional growth.* New York: Oxford University Press.

Sommers, C., & Satel, S. (2005). *One nation under therapy: How the helping cultures is eroding self-reliance.* New York: St. Martin's Press.

Strom, P., & Strom, R. (2007). Cheating in middle school and high school. *The Educational Forum, 71,* 104–116.

Sutton-Smith, B. (1995). Conclusion: The persuasive rhetorics of play. In A. Pellegrini (Ed.), *The future of play theory* (pp. 275–295). Albany, New York: SUNY Press.

Sutton-Smith, B. (1997). *The ambiguity of play.* Cambridge, MA: Harvard University Press.

Sutton-Smith, B. (2003). Play as a parody of emotional vulnerability of play. In D. Lytle (Ed.), *Play and Educational Theory and Practice. Play & Culture Studies, Vol. 5* (pp. 3–18). Westport, CT: Praeger.

Taylor, L., Pogrebin, M., & Dodge, M. (2002). Advanced placement-advance pressures: Academic dishonesty among elite high school students. *Educational Studies: Journal of the American Educational Studies Association, 33,* 403–421.

Thomas, L., De Bellis, M., Graham, R., & LaBar, K. (2007). Development of emotional facial recognition in late childhood and adolescence. *Developmental Science, 10,* 547–558.

Toren, C. (2007). Sunday lunch in Fiji: Continuity and transformation in ideas of the household. *American Anthropologist, 109,* 285–295.

Waugh, R.F., Godfrey, J. R., Evans, E. D., & Craig, D. (1995). Measuring students' perceptions about cheating in six countries. *Australian Journal of Psychology, 47,* 73–80.

Widen, S., & Russell, J. (2002). Gender and preschoolers' perceptions of emotion. *Merrill-Palmer Quarterly, 48,* 248–262.

Woolgar, M., Steele, H., Steele, M., Yabsley, S., & Fonagy, P. (2001). Children's play narrative responses to hypothetical dilemmas and their awareness of moral emotions. *British Journal of Developmental Psychology, 19,* 115–128.

Zan, B., & Hildebrandt, C. (2005). Cooperative and competitive games in constructivist classrooms. *The Constructivist, 16,* 1–13.

*Chapter Seven*

# Contribution of Theory of Mind to Pretend Play: Concordance between Preschool Play Partners

Hui-Chin Hsu and Patricia K. Janes

*Theory of mind* (TOM) refers to children's ability to understand that people may have mental states such as desires, feelings, and beliefs and that people's mental states may be different from their own. Several theories have been developed to explain the mechanisms of theory of mind development in early childhood. For example, theory-theory (e.g., Perner, 1991), modularity theory (Scholl & Leslie, 1999), and simulation theory (e.g., Harris, 1991) take a within-individual approach highlighting cognitive processes within the individual child, whereas other theories taking a social constructive perspective emphasize the importance of interpersonal processes between the child and other people (e.g., Carpendale & Lewis, 2004).

During pretend play, children create a shared imaginary world with their play partners (e.g., Astington & Baird, 2005; Jarrold, Carruthers, Smith, & Boucher, 1994; Taylor, 1996). Beginning at age 3, children increasingly choose same-sex playmates (Maccoby, 1998). Children who engaged in more same-sex pretend play tend to be socially more competent (Colwell & Lindsey, 2005). Children's ability to collaborate and integrate their ideas with partners during pretend play demonstrates a fundamental understanding of the minds of others (Forbes, Katz, & Paul, 1986; Giffin, 1984; Jarrold et al., 1994; Lillard, 1998; Sawyer, 1997). Dunn and her colleagues (e.g., Dunn & Cutting, 1999; Dunn & Dale, 1984; Slomkowski & Dunn, 1996; Youngblade & Dunn, 1995) have demonstrated that the establishment and maintenance of shared pretend play depend on the quality of the relationship between two same-gender players, either siblings or friends.

Connected communication, prosocial actions, low levels of conflict, and discourse about inner states between children and their play partners were found to be associated with children's better performance at TOM assessment (Cutting & Dunn, 2006). However, little is known about whether the match or mismatch between two play partners' TOM abilities may also alter children's pretend play patterns. Focusing on the concordance between two play partners' theory of mind abilities, the present preliminary study was an experiment designed to explore whether the contribution of 4-year-olds' understanding of mind to their pretend play is beyond the effect of relationship quality.

## PEER PRETEND PLAY

Pretend play is a social activity that requires participants' joint attention, reciprocity, and use of communication pragmatics. Pretense play created by preschool-aged partners whether explicitly or implicitly depicted contains three basic components: the *elements* of pretend play, the *enactment* of the pretend play, and the *metaplay* strategies used to create and maintain the pretense scenario (Fein & Rivkin, 1986; Garvey, 1982; Forbes et al., 1986). The elements of the pretend play are the *roles, props, action sequences, and themes*, reflecting symbolic representations of a non-real world (Fenson, 1984; Goncü & Kessel, 1988). The *enactment* component refers to the assuming of role characters and acting out of the pretense scenarios, which is similar to a theatrical performance as the children transform into character roles in response to their play partners (Auwarter, 1986; Sawyer, 1997). During enactment, some or all elements of pretend play are incorporated into children's acting and mutually accepted by play partners. The *metaplay* is strategies implemented by the children as they set up the play scenario, attempt to negotiate the thematic production, and maintain its continuity during enactment (Trawick-Smith, 1998).

Play partners' communication during enactment is distinctively different from their mutual exchanges during metaplay. During enactment, the play partners not only interact as actors assuming attitudes and behaviors with the aid of voice, face, gesture, and/or props to represent the role characters, but also accept the imaginary transformations of identity, object, action plan, or situation by each other. In essence, play partners are not only required to apply their presentational abilities in more than one aspect of the play, but also to collaborate with each other in more than one aspect of the play. Children's pretense enactment seems to reflect their effortless interaction with a peer in an imaginary world demonstrating a greater understanding of each other's perspectives and a better anticipation of each other's response. During metaplay, the play partners step out of the pretend play frame to plan and negotiate various elements of the play (Trawick-Smith, 1998). It has been reported that greater enactment is associated with greater metaplay (Doyle & Connelly, 1989) and that metaplay tends to precede enactment (Doyle, Doehring, Tessier, de Lorimier, & Shapiro, 1992). Although enactment and metaplay are both positively correlated with peer social acceptance, the effect of enactment is relatively greater than metaplay (Doyle & Connelly. 1989). It appears that metaplay functions as a support to the play partners' enactment within the pretend frame.

## PRETEND PLAY AND THE THEORY OF MIND

Pretend play appears to be associated with theory of mind development. One hypothesis, termed the metarepresentation model (for a review, see Lillard, 2001), argues that children gain more practice at manipulating mental representations of the world during pretend play and later apply their conceptual understanding of mental representations outside of pretense domains. Lillard (2001) further proposes a social-cognitive hypothesis, which argues that symbolic functioning and specific social-cognitive skills such as intention reading, social referencing, and joint attention are involved in this developmental process. She suggests that together with the ability of decoupling between pretense and reality, children gain the understanding that pretense is mental in the context of social pretend play with peers.

Pretend play is an arena in which children first come to understand that one can represent reality one way (e.g., banana as telephone) when in fact it is another (e.g., banana as food) (Kavanaugh, 2006). Although there have been debates about whether young children's understanding of pretense is simply as an action or as a more sophisticated mental representational state (Lillard, 1993, 2007a), preschoolers are capable of creating and discriminating the two worlds of reality and of fantasy, and behaving appropriately in either world without confusion (Golomb & Kuersten, 1996). Lillard (1998) suggests that during metaplay when play partners negotiate what and how they will pretend, they face the challenge of synchronizing diverse conceptualizations and desires. It is vital for children to practice seeing an object or situation from two different perspectives. During enactment, each play partner demonstrates the ability to recognize that the partner may have different beliefs and perceptions about the pretense script such as what are the appropriate character roles for each partner. Play partners also need to respond to each other appropriately with reciprocal and/or complementary actions to the implicit message "this is pretend" embedded in the social interactions (Bretherton, 1989).

Research on children's understanding of mind, known as children's theory of mind (TOM), suggests that children make a transition achieving an understanding of the possibility of false beliefs between ages 3 to 5 (Keenan, 2003). Preschoolers who engage in pretend play more frequently are more likely to pass false-beliefs tasks (see later examples of TOM tasks), even after controlling for their language skills[1] (Astington & Jenkins, 1995; Neilsen & Dissanyake, 2000; Taylor & Carlson, 1997; Youngblade & Dunn, 1995). Intervention studies also demonstrate that pretend play training enhances children's social cognitive skills such as perspective taking (e.g., Harris, 2005; Rubin, Fein, & Vandenberg, 1983). Preschoolers' TOM ability is found to be positively related to joint pretend play with a peer, but not solitary pretend play (Schwebel, Rosen, & Singer, 1999). The present study further examined the association of individual children's TOM ability with their enactment and metaplay during joint pretend play with a same-sex friend.

Although children's TOM systematically improves with age during preschool years, considerable individual differences are found (e.g., Astingon & Jenkins, 1995; Dunn, Brown, Slomkowski, Tesla, & Youngblade, 1991; Wellman, Cross, & Watson, 2001). Social construction theorists (e.g., Carpendale & Lewis, 2004; Dunn, 2004; Dunn & Brophy, 2005; Fonagy, Gergely, & Target, 2007; Hughes & Leekam, 2004; Nelson, 2005; Nelson, Skwerer, Goldman et al., 2003) believe that social influences have a direct impact on children's understanding of people's minds. The knowledge of social understanding is gradually constructed through social interactions between children and social partners. Children derive their understanding of mind from collaborative encounters as they share attention and reciprocate actions (e.g., Carpendale & Lewis, 2004; Tomasello, Carpenter, Call, Behne, & Moll, 2005).

Previous social interaction studies linking pretend play to TOM in children mostly focus on the relationship quality. It is argued that the establishment and maintenance of a shared pretend world depends on the quality of the relationship between the two players (Gottman, 1983). In a series of studies, Dunn and her colleagues (Cutting & Dunn, 2006; Dunn & Cutting, 1999; Dunn & Dale, 1984; Dunn et al., 1991; Youngblade & Dunn, 1995) have demonstrated that shared pretense between preschool friends or siblings is positively correlated with the quality of the relationship and that joint pretend play in both types of relationship is positively related to children's TOM performance. Children who experience collaborative play with their siblings and friends tend to show advanced TOM (Dunn & Brophy, 2005). These findings raise the question about the effect of concordance or discordance between two play partners on their joint pretend play. It is unknown whether playing with a partner at a similar or different level of TOM may alter children's enactment within the pretend play frame and metaplay outside of the pretend play frame.

In sum, this study explored the linkage between pretend play and theory of mind at both individual and dyadic levels. At the individual level, because enactment demands greater social understanding, it was hypothesized that children with advanced TOM abilities would exhibit frequent enactment actions, but not metaplay actions. At the dyadic level, enactment and metaplay by two play partners as a unit were expected to vary according to the concordance or discordance between their TOM abilities. Dyads with matched high and low TOM abilities were expected to engage in prolonged enactment and reduced metaplay. Dyads with mismatched TOM abilities were expected not to show such a pattern.


# METHOD

## Participants

Nineteen 4-year-olds (63% females) were recruited from a university child development lab. The children's mean age was 56 months (range: 50–61 months). Three of the 19 children did not speak English in their homes.


## Procedure

Six months prior to data collection, an additional group of 30 4-year-olds were recruited from the same university child development lab and a Head Start program for testing the appropriateness of toys to be used for play, protocols for the experiment and assessment, and strategies in pairing children. All research assistants to this study were required to spend 15 hours in the classroom for developing a sense of trust with children, training of observation skills, and identifying compatible play partners for children (i.e., friends). For the present study, a pool of 3 same-sex friends was identified for each participating child by the research team on the basis of observations of interactions between children during free play. The play-partner list was then reviewed and confirmed by the full-time classroom teacher.

To reveal the contribution of TOM to children's pretend play, data collection was implemented in three separate phases. During the initial phase, 2 same-sex children identified as friends were invited to play together in an observation room. Initially, the children were curious about the cameras, but within 10 minutes all dyads were attracted to the provided toys and immersed in play. Within 2 weeks of the play session, each child was individually invited to return to the room for the TOM assessment (see details below). A median-split was performed on individual children's TOM scores separately for boys and girls.[2] Based on the children's status in the median classification, 3 groups were formed. The first group (TOM scores Matched Low) consisted of dyads with both play partners ranked below the median. The second group (TOM scores Mismatched) consisted of dyads with one play partner ranked below the median and the other above the median. The last group (TOM scores Matched High) consisted of dyads with both play partners ranked above the median. After categorizing the initial play dyads based on their TOM scores, each group had unequal number of dyads. In order to equalize the number of dyads in each play group, in the final stage the children were re-paired as partners according to TOM scores with another friend. As a result, a total of 15 dyads were observed again for their play; 5 dyads were included in each play group. All play sessions were video-taped.

*Theory of Mind Tasks.* Various false belief tasks have been developed to examine preschoolers' ability to attribute a false belief to themselves or to others. Children's performance on false belief tasks is considered as an indicator of TOM development. A battery of 5 tasks was given to each child resulting in an aggregate of 8 false belief questions. Two tests were variations of Wimmer and Perner's (1983) standard change in location test (i.e., Maxi and the Chocolate. See Appendix A). In both tests the child was asked to predict where the protagonist would look for the item. The Unexpected Contents Test (Perner, Leekman, & Wimmer, 1987) and the Appearance/Reality Test (Flavell, Flavell, & Greene, 1987) were administered to measure the child's ability to recall her/his false belief and to predict the false belief of another. The last test was an explanation and prediction task (Bartsch & Wellman, 1989). The range of scores for the aggregate was 0–8, with a score of "8" indicating all control and test questions were answered correctly.

*Observation of Pretend Play.* During play, children exhibit subtle or explicit verbal and nonverbal behavioral cues to signal that they are playing in a pretend world (Bretherton, 1989; Goncü, 1993). Both individual play actions and dyadic play patterns were observed and coded separately. The preliminary investigation indicated that during the first 10 minutes of a play session children were mostly exploring the room and toys, rather than playing together. Thus, only the second 10 minutes of consecutive playtime was analyzed in this study.

*Individual Play Actions.* Individual children's verbal and nonverbal play actions were coded in separate passes of video viewing to identify enactment and metaplay behaviors. A 20-second continuous time sampling strategy was used, dividing the 10-minute play time into 30 time blocks. Three *enactment* behaviors in the child were classified: (1) *Emotive actions*, including non-verbal acts that emphasize the behavior or attitude of a role being played out (e.g., exaggerated facial expressions to indicate anger or surprise) or coordinated costume articles used to portray a character (e.g., putting on a hat, a purse, and a skirt to play the role of a mother); (2) *Voice modulations* were identified when the child changed her/his voice to represent the voice of a character role (e.g., talking in a deep voice as a superhero) or to give animation to a toy or a non-existent character (e.g., a talking car); (3) *Sequenced actions*, including arrangement and/or integration of toys as props (e.g., setting the table with toy dishes) or temporally sequenced series of two or more actions used to represent an event (e.g., singing a lullaby and swaying cradled empty arms as if rocking a baby to sleep). *Metaplay* included any statement or behavior exhibited by the child to assign a role (e.g., "You be the mommy"), to designate a role (e.g., "What are we going to do now?"), or to negotiate a role (e.g., "I want to be the daddy") (See example in Appendix B). Thirty percent of data from the children were randomly selected and coded independently by a second coder for inter-observer reliability. Percentage of agreement was calculated for each individual behavior which ranged from 82.8% to 95.6%.

*Dyadic Play Patterns*. When playing together, reciprocity of bids and responses occurs between play partners. The continuation of an interactional pattern was indicated either by the verbal response by the play partner or by an evident change in the behavior of the play partner. Using the dyad as the unit of analysis, 4 different play patterns were identified second-by-second from videos: (1) *Enactment*, during which both children were interacting within the pretense play frame. Playing "as if" was identified by the children's conversation, attitude, voice, actions, and/or costumes regarding a mutual theme; (2) *Metaplay*, during which the children stepped out of the pretend play frame to confer over issues regarding the play frame. This was observed explicitly through conversation, such as statements beginning with "let's pretend" or implicitly by actions, such as the selection of costumes or toys to be used as props. The focus of both children was on the onset or eventual continuation of enactment; (3) *Social interaction*, during which dyadic conversation or interaction did not directly pertain to pretense (e.g., discussing the functional use of a toy); and (4) *Other*, during which no explicit or implicit relationship was apparent between the children (e.g., parallel play). Twenty-five percent of the dyads were randomly selected for checking coding reliability. Kappas ranged from .62 to .87 and percentage of agreement ranged from 77% to 92%.

# RESULTS

## Descriptive Analysis

*Individual play actions.* The durations (% of intervals) of four different individual play actions were derived (See Table 7.1 for the descriptive statistics of means and standard deviations).

First, the difference between children's metaplay and each of the three types of enactment actions was examined. Results from three paired-sample t-tests revealed that children engaged in less metaplay than sequenced actions, $t(18) = -1.95$, $p < .05$, and voice modulations, $t(18) = -2.71$, $p < .01$, but more metaplay than emotive actions, $t(18) = 1.96$, $p < .05$. Next, the association between children's metaplay and each type of enactment actions was also explored. Due to the relative small sample size, nonparametric Spearman Rank Correlations were computed. Children's metaplay was positively correlated with voice modulation, $r(18) = .85$, $p < .01$, and emotive actions, $r(18) = .36$, $p < .10$, but not significantly correlated with sequenced actions, $r(18) = .07$, p = *ns*.

*Dyadic play patterns.* Two different measures were derived as indices for dyadic play: total amount (% of play time) and continuation (episode duration in seconds) of dyadic play. The total amount and continuation of play were subject to a one-way repeated-measures ANOVA separately. Three dyadic patterns were compared to reveal the preferential pattern exhibited by two play partners as a unit (See Table 7.1 for means and standard deviations). With respect to the total amount of play, there was no significant difference,

Table 7.1. Descriptive Statistics of Individual Play Actions and Dyadic Play Patterns

| Level | Measure | Pretense Play | Mean (SD) |
|---|---|---|---|
| Individual | Interval | Enactment | |
| | (percentage) | Emotive actions | 11.58 (12.98) |
| | | Sequenced actions | 34.91 (16.00) |
| | | Voice modulations | 29.82 (24.91) |
| | | Metaplay | 21.23 (24.92) |
| Dyad | Total Amount | Enactment | 31.46 (23.09) |
| | (percentage of Play Time) | | |
| | | Metaplay | 20.04 (15.49) |
| | | Social interaction | 18.96 (17.06) |
| | Episode Duration (seconds) | Enactment | 45.75 (27.58) |
| | | Metaplay | 24.53 (22.82) |
| | | Social interaction | 59.20 (70.31) |

Wilks' $\Lambda = .82$, $F(2,13) = 1.45$, $p = ns$, partial $\eta^2 = .18$. Play partners spent similar amount of time in enactment, metaplay, and social interaction. With respect to the continuation of dyadic play episodes, results indicated significant differences, Wilks' $\Lambda = .59$, $F(2,13) = 4.62$, $p < .05$, partial $\eta^2 = .42$. Follow-up pair-wise comparisons revealed that dyads engaged in enactment almost two times longer than in metaplay. No significant difference was found between social interaction and each of the two types of joint pretense play.

## Theory of Mind and Pretend Play

*Theory of mind and individual pretend play actions.* Spearman Rank Correlations were computed to reveal the association strength between children's TOM abilities and their individual play actions. Results revealed significant positive correlations between TOM scores and two individual enactment actions: emotive actions and sequenced actions. The positive correlation between TOM scores and voice modulations was not significant (see Table 7.2).

In addition, as expected, children's individual metaplay was not related to their TOM scores. Together, the correlational analysis suggested that 4-year old children with higher TOM scores were likely to exhibit more frequent enactment actions, but not metaplay actions.

*Theory of Mind and Joint Pretend Play.* To examine the effect of concordance between play partners' TOM on their joint pretense play, two 2 (Dyadic Pretense Play Pattern) x 3 (TOM Concordance/Discordance Group) mixed design ANOVA were performed separately, with the total amount (% of play time) and continuation (episode duration in seconds) of play as the dependent variable.

With respect to the total amount of play time, the three concordance/ discordance groups were not significantly different; dyads with concordant

**Table 7.2.   Correlation between Children's Individual Pretense Play Actions and TOM Scores (n=19)**

| Play Type | Play Actions | Correlation Coefficient |
|---|---|---|
| Enactment | Emotive actions | .47* |
| | Voice modulations | .31+ |
| | Sequenced actions | .50* |
| | Metaplay | .00 |

+$p <.10$     *$p <.05$ (1-tailed)

or discordant TOM abilities spent about the same amount of total time in enactment and metaplay, $F(2,12) = .40$, $p = ns$, partial $\eta^2 = .06$. With respect to the continuation of joint pretense play, results revealed a significant main effect for Dyadic Pretense Play Pattern. Consistent with descriptive analysis, children and their play partners' engaged in significantly longer enactment than metaplay, $F(1,2) = 10.12$, $p < .01$, partial $\eta^2 = .46$. Further, the three groups varying in the concordance between play partners' TOM did not differ significantly in their overall episode duration, $F(2,12) = .67$, $p = ns$, partial $\eta^2 = .06$ (see Table 7.3).

Finally, the results indicated a significant interaction effect for Dyadic Pretense Play Pattern $\times$ TOM Concordance/Discordance Group, $F(2,12) = 4.24$, $p < .05$, partial $\eta^2 = .41$.

To further understand the significant interaction effect, several nonparametric follow-up tests were performed. Wilcoxon Signed Ranks Tests were run to reveal whether each group showed a difference in episode duration between enactment and metaplay. Results demonstrated that the episode durations of enactment and metaplay for dyads in the mismatched group were approximately the same $(Z = 1.095, p = ns)$. By contrast, the episode duration of enactment was significantly longer than that of metaplay for dyads in the matched high concordance group $(Z = 2.02, p < .05)$ and the matched low concordance group $(Z = .00, p < .10)$. Furthermore, nonparametric median tests were performed to compare enactment and metaplay separately among the three groups. Results revealed that although the three groups did not differ in their metaplay, $\chi^2 (2, N=15) = 3.75$, $p = ns$, dyads in the matched high concordance group exhibited significantly greater enactment than those in the matched low concordance group, $\chi^2(2, N=15) = 8.57$, $p < .05$. Together, these results suggested that even though there was no difference in the time distribution (i.e., percentage of play time) of enactment and metaplay among the three groups, there were differential profiles in the continuation of children's joint pretend play. When playing together, children's joint pretend play, specifically, enactment, varied as a function of concordance between their TOM abilities.

**Table 7.3.   Episode Durations (Seconds) of Joint Pretense Play Patterns in Three Different Groups Varying in Concordance between Play Partners' TOM Abilities**

| Play Type | *Concordance between Play Partners' TOM Abilities* | | |
| | *Matched Low* | *Mismatched* | *Matched High* |
|---|---|---|---|
| Enactment | 35.15 (27.59) | 38.38 (32.57) | 63.72 (15.10) |
| Metaplay | 21.73 (25.75) | 36.08 (27.52) | 15.80 (11.45) |

## DISCUSSION

Accumulating evidence indicates that children's understanding of mental states develops within social interaction (e.g., Carpendale & Lewis, 2004; Ensor & Hughes, 2008). Joint pretend play has been identified as an ideal social context for children to develop shared understanding with others. Previous research emphasizes the importance of relationship quality between children and their play partners in children's pretense play (e.g., de Rosnay & Hughes, 2006; Garvey & Kramer, 1989; Goncü & Kessel, 1988; Howes, 1992; Youngblade & Dunn, 1995). Jointly constructed pretend play between peers, but not solitary symbolic play, is found to be related to children's better performance on theory of mind tasks (e.g., Schwebel et al., 1999). However, relatively little is known about whether children's understanding of mind is specifically related to enactment occurring within the pretend play frame or metaplay outside of the pretense play frame. It is also unclear whether the concordance or discordance between two friends' TOM abilities would make a contribution to children's joint pretend play that is beyond the effect of relationship quality. Thus, the present study was designed to address questions concerning the contribution of children's theory of mind to enactment and metaplay in joint pretend play at both individual and dyadic levels.

The descriptive analysis revealed that children engaged in less metaplay actions than enactment actions, specifically, voice modulations and emotive actions. In addition, children's frequent metaplay was related to frequent voice modulations and emotive actions. Together, these findings seem to suggest that 4-year-olds do not rely on extensive metaplay to sustain their enactment during pretend play. However, metaplay can play a supportive role in children's use of paralinguistic signals such as voice and facial expressions during enactment. Explicit communication with a play partner may make children more confident about using implicit messages in reciprocating and complementing their play partners' imaginary transformation of role characters or objects. Although sequenced actions were relatively frequent in children's play, they were not significantly associated with metaplay. Such disassociation may suggest that verbal and nonverbal pretend behaviors enacted in a logically or topically connected sequence may be easy for play partners to recognize. Little or no further communication outside of the play frame is needed.

Our findings demonstrated that children's understanding of mental states was associated with enactment, but not metaplay, at both individual and dyadic level. At the individual level, children with advanced TOM abilities engaged in greater pretense enactment of emotive actions, sequenced actions, and voice modulations. In contrast, individual children's TOM abilities were not associated with their metaplay actions. At the dyadic level, friends with matched TOM abilities tended to engage in longer episodes of enactment than metaplay. The pattern of enactment outweighing metaplay was particularly striking for friends with matched high TOM abilities.

It has been suggested that pretend play may reflect not only sophisticated representational thinking but also social and communication skills in children (e.g., Lillard, 2001, 2007a). Our findings indicate that it is the sustained activity of enactment in joint pretend play that denotes theory of mind proficiency in children. This phenomenon may reflect underlying interpersonal mechanisms such as communication, affect, and language inherently involved in joint pretend play. Lillard (2001, 2007b) has proposed that communication skills such as coordinated joint attention, social referencing, and intentions reading are contributors to pretense understanding. When friends are equally proficient in mental states understanding, it is expected that the play partners may show greater shared attention, send and receive unambiguous signals, and read each other's intentions successfully. The play partners build on and extend each other's ideas effortlessly. The idea of one partner may spark a creative idea in the other, which in turn is elaborated by the first child. These coordinated exchanges speak to the notion of coordinated and synchronous communication between social partners (cf. Harrist & Waugh, 2002).

To continue enactment within the pretend play frame, play partners must coordinate each other's ambiguous symbolic representations for character roles and object transformations. It is plausible that the context of coordinated and elaborated communication in pretense enactment facilitates the construction of shared understanding between play partners, which in turn, fosters their understanding of others' minds. Through coordinating and exchanging contrasting perspectives within the pretend play frame, children come to realize that people not only have mental states such as beliefs, desires, feelings, and/or intentions, but other people's mental states may be different from their own. This social construction explanation is consistent with previous findings that siblings' pretense enactment is associated with their dyadic strategies such as extension and elaborations used to construct shared understandings (Howe, Petrakos, & Rinaldi, 2005) and that mothers' connected turns in communicative acts and semantically connected mental-state references are associated with preschoolers' emotion and mind understanding (Ensor & Hughes, 2008). However, the direction of effects cannot be determined in the present study. It may be the case that children's coordinated and synchronized communication contributes to theory of mind development. Alternatively, it can also be argued that children with relatively mature mind understanding tend to be collaborative play partners who are skillful at complementing and elaborating each other's imaginary actions.

Whereas enactment may reflect the status of "meeting of minds" between friends, in that play partners mutually understand each other and co-construct shared meaning about the plots, roles, and/or actions, metaplay may indicate failed communication or anticipation of errors in communication. When coordination in communication fails, children must think and talk about symbolic representations and other internal mental processes. When partners step out of the "this-is-pretend" play frame and overtly negotiate and discuss rules, plans, actions, or properties of the pretend scenario in order to manage their pretend enactments, their metaplay implies that the "meeting of minds" is yet to be achieved. Negotiation and communication reparation may be characterized by increased negativity. Conflicts may arise during metaplay for dyads with mismatched and matched low TOM abilities because of difficulty in articulating ideas, clarifying role assignments, proposing compromises, and/or revising ideas. For example, Howe, Rinaldi, Jennings, and Petrakos (2002) reported that siblings who engaged in more procedural quarrels were less likely to engage in frequent pretend play. Negative emotions and conflicts may be less conducive to the development of sophisticated theory of mind understanding. Future research is needed to discern the role of affect in altering the relationship between metaplay and understanding of mind.

In addition to communication and affect, language may also be the underlying mechanism that links pretense enactment to children's theory of mind. Children's linguistic abilities are positively associated with their TOM abilities (e.g., Astington, 2003; Astington & Baird, 2005; de Rosnay & Hughes, 2006). Farver (1992) demonstrated that there is a developmental progression in children's use of sophisticated paralinguistic cues (e.g., gaze, voice, gesture) to signify pretense and use of linguistic strategies such as semantically connected turns to expand on a partner's contribution. With age, children also reduce their use of simple repetition, imitation, and/or directive attempts in structuring pretend play. The relationship between language and mind understanding is robust. It has been suggested that the form (i.e., syntax), meaning (i.e., semantics), and function (i.e. pragmatics) of language are essential to children's TOM development (e.g., Astington & Baird, 2005). Even though children in the current study are deemed to be developing normally in their linguistic competence on the basis of a standardized vocabulary assessment, play partners with matched high TOM abilities may be more advanced in one or more aspects of language skills. Greater linguistic competence in syntax, semantics, and pragmatics may not only enhance the effectiveness of play partners' coordinative exchanges in pretense enactment, but also promote the efficacy of discussion and negotiation to achieve a shared understanding in metaplay. By contrast, dyads with mismatched or matched low TOM abilities may have less command in various aspects of language competence. As result, it is challenging for play partners to continue enactment seamlessly by building on and elaborating each other's ideas. It is certainly a challenge for these play partners to repair communication errors and negotiate ground rules for role assignments, prop use, object transformation, and so forth.

Taken together, communication, affect, and language are theorized to be the underlying mechanisms linking TOM to pretend play in children. Reciprocity in communication, positive affect, low frequency of conflict, and sophisticated language are not only indices of individual children's social competence with peers (Denham, McKinley, Couchoud, & Holt, 1990; McCabe, 2005; Schneider & Goldstein, 2008), but also reflections of friendship quality between play partners (Asher & Gazelle, 1999; Berndt, 2002). Socially competent children are more likely to have quality social interaction with their friends, which in turn, may be associated with more advanced pretend play and theory of mind (Doyle & Connolly, 1989; Dunn & Cutting, 1999).

Although we found that metaplay was neither linked to individual children's TOM abilities nor modified by the concordance or discordance between play partners' TOM abilities, metaplay may still serve important developmental functions. For example, metaplay may function as a learning activity for children practicing socio-cognitive skills (Flavell et al., 1987; Rubin et al., 1983). The goal of metaplay is to create a foundation that enables play partners to see and act in coordination with one another and to understand each other in order to play together seamlessly. It is possible that the function of metaplay in the discordant dyads is to provide a platform for the child with low mind understanding to be supported in the negotiations of their pretense scenario by the child with high competency in mind understanding. Whereas the study's operational measurement of enactment required both partners of the dyad to be inside the pretense play frame, the measurement of metaplay required that only one member of the dyad step outside the pretense play frame. Given that children with high TOM abilities demonstrated more enactment pretense play behaviors during the play episode, it is most probable that children with low TOM scores left the pretense play frame for clarification purposes. The process of extended negotiation between the mismatched dyads might function as a mechanism that promotes the development of competency in enactment and/or in mind understanding. Goncü and Kessel (1984) have reported a developmental trend toward greater pretense enactment and less metaplay. Thus, metaplay may be a precursor to enactment. Future research with a longitudinal design is needed to explore the impact of metaplay experience on play partners' enactment.

Finally, it is important to recognize the limitations of this study. The sample size for this study was relatively small. In order to create dyadic groups with the same number of same-sex pairs of friends, several of the children played more than once with a different play partner. The nonsignificant findings may simply reflect an insufficient statistical power in detecting the small effect size. Moreover, the effect of sex difference on the linkage between TOM and joint pretend play profile were not examined, which need to be addressed in future studies. Children in the present study were largely from middle-class families. Future research is needed to further explore whether the significance of concordance between play partners' TOM in pretend play is applicable to children with different socioeconomic backgrounds. Finally, this study only examined the aggregated duration measures in children's enactment and metaplay. Further examination of the sequential patterning in children's dyadic interactions during pretend play may substantially increase our understanding about how TOM abilities are manifested in children's enactment and metaplay.

## NOTES

1. The Peabody Picture Vocabulary Test (PPVT) (Dunn & Dunn, 1997; Williams & Wang, 1997), a widely used standardized vocabulary test, was administered to all children in this study. The three non-English speaking children's percentile ranks ranged between 50–68. No child was one standard deviation below the age norm, indicating normal developing receptive vocabulary abilities. Moreover, the correlation between children's TOM and PPVT scores was not significant. Thus, language skills were not considered further in this study.

2. Because 5 girls scored on the median, based on their scores on the most challenging prediction task (Bartsch & Wellman, 1989), they were placed into different groups.

## REFERENCES

Asher, S. R., & Gazelle, H. (1999). Loneliness, peer relations, and language disorder in childhood. *Topics in Language Disorders, 19*, 16–33.

Astington, J. W. (2003). Sometimes necessary, never sufficient: False-belief understanding and social competence. In B. Repacholi & V. Slaughter (Eds.), *Individual differences in theory of mind: Implications for typical and atypical development* (pp.13–38). New York: Psychological Press.

Astington, J. W., & Baird, J. A. (2005). Introduction: Why language matters. In J. W. Astington & J. A. Baird (Eds.), *Why language matters for theory of mind* (pp. 2–25). London: Oxford University Press.

Astington, J. W., & Jenkins, J. M. (1995). Theory of mind development and social understanding. *Cognition and Emotion, 9*, 151–165.

Auwarter, M. (1986). Development of communicative skills: The construction of fictional reality in children's play. In J. Cook-Gumperz, W. A. Cosaro, & J. Streeck (Eds.), *Children's worlds and children's language* (pp. 205–230). New York: Mouton de Gruyter.

Bartsch, K., & Wellman, H. (1989). Young children's attribution of action to belief and desires. *Child Development, 69*, 946–964.

Berndt, T. J. (2002). Friendship quality and social development. *Current Directions in Psychological Science, 11*, 7–10.

Bretherton, I. (1989). Pretense: The form and function of make-believe play. *Developmental Review, 9*, 383–401.

Carpendale, J. I. M., & Lewis, C. (2004). Constructing an understanding of mind: The development of children's social understanding within social interaction. *Behavioral and Brian Sciences, 27*, 79–151.

Colwell, M. J., & Lindsey, E. W. (2005). Preschool children's pretend and physical play and sex of play partner: Connections to peer competence. *Sex Roles, 52*, 497–509.

Cutting, A., & Dunn, J. (2006). Conversations with siblings and with friends: Links between relationship quality and social understanding. *British Journal of Developmental Psychology, 24*, 73–87.

Denham, S. A., McKinley, M., Couchoud, E. A., & Holt, R. (1990). Emotional and behavioral predictors of peer status in young preschoolers. *Child Development, 61*, 1145–1152.

de Rosnay, M., & Hughes, C. (2006). Conversation and theory of mind: Do children talk their way to socio-cognitive understanding? *British Journal of Developmental Psychology, 24*, 7–37.

Doyle, A., & Connolly, J. (1989). Negotiation and enactment in social pretend play: Relations to social acceptance and social cognition. *Early Childhood Research Quarterly, 4*, 289–302.

Doyle, A., Doehring, P., Tessier, O., de Lorimier, S., & Shapiro, S. (1992). Transitions in children's play: A sequential analysis of states preceding and following social pretense. *Developmental Psychology, 28*, 137–144.

Dunn, J. (2004). The development of individual differences in understanding emotion and mind: Antecedents and sequelae. In A. S. R. Manstead, N. Frijda, A. Fischer (Eds.), *Feelings and emotions: The Amsterdam symposium* (pp. 303–320). New York: Cambridge University Press.

Dunn, J., & Brophy, M. (2005). Communication, relationships, and individual differences in children's understanding of mind. In J. W. Astington & J. A. Baird (Eds.), *Why language matters for theory of mind* (pp. 50–69). London: Oxford University Press.

Dunn, J., Brown, J., Slomkowski, C., Tesla, C. & Youngblade, L. (1991). Young children's understanding of other people's feelings and beliefs: Individual differences and their antecedents. *Child Development, 62*, 1352–1366.

Dunn, J., & Cutting, A. L. (1999). Understanding others, and individual differences in friendship interactions in young children. *Social Development, 8*, 201–219.

Dunn, J., & Dale, N. (1984). I a daddy: 2-year-olds' collaboration in joint pretend play with sibling and with mother. In I. Bretherton (Ed.), *Symbolic play* (pp. 131–158). London: Academic.

Dunn, L. M., & Dunn, L. M. (1997). *Peabody Picture Vocabulary Test* (3rd Ed.). Circle Pines, MN: American Guidance Service.

Ensor, R., & Hughes, C. (2008). Content or connectedness? Mother–child talk and early social understanding. *Child Development, 79*, 201–216.

Farver, J. A. M. (1992). Communicating shared meaning in social pretend play. *Early Childhood Research Quarterly, 7*, 501–516.

Fein, G., & Rivkin, M. (1986). *The young child at play*. Washington, DC: National Association for the Education of Young Children.

Fenson, L. (1984). Developmental trends for action and speech in pretend play. In I. Bretherton (Ed.), *Symbolic play* (pp. 249–270). New York: Academic.

Flavell, J. H., Flavell, E. R., & Green, F. L. (1987). Young children's knowledge about the apparent-real and pretend-real distinctions. *Developmental Psychology, 23*, 816–822.

Fonagy, P., Gergely, G., & Target, M. (2007). The parent–infant dyad and the construction of the subjective self. *Journal of Child Psychology and Psychiatry, 48*, 288–328.

Forbes, D., Katz, M. M., & Paul, B. (1986). "Frame talk": A dramatic analysis of children's fantasy play. In E. C. Mueller & C. R. Cooper (Eds.), *Process and outcome in peer relationships* (pp. 249–266). New York: Academic Press.

Garvey, C. (1982). Communication and the development of social role play. In D. Forbes & M. T. Greenberg (Eds.), *New directions for child development, No. 18. Children's planning strategies* (pp. 81–101). San Francisco, CA: Jossey-Bass.

Garvey, C., & Kramer, T. L. (1989). The language of social pretend play. *Developmental Review, 9*, 383–401.

Giffin, H. (1984). The coordination of meaning in the creation of shared make-belief reality. In I. Bretherton (Ed.), *Symbolic play* (pp. 73–100). New York: Academic Press.

Golomb, C., & Kuersten, R. (1996). On the transition from pretence play to reality: What are the rules of the game? *British Journal of Developmental Psychology, 14*(2), 203–217.

Goncü, A. (1993). Development of intersubjectivity in the dyadic play of preschoolers. *Early Childhood Research Quarterly, 8*, 99–116.

Goncü, A., & Kessel, F. (1988) Preschoolers'collaborative construction in planning and maintaining imaginative play. *International Journal of Behavioral Development, 11* (3), 327–344.

Gottman, J. M., (1983). How children become friends. *Monographs of the Society for Research in Child Development, 48* (2, Serial No. 201).

Harris, P. L. (1991). *The work of the imagination*. In A. Whiten (Ed.), *Natural theories of mind* (pp. 283–304). Oxford, England: Basil Blackwell.

Harris, P. L. (2005). Conversation, pretense, and theory of mind. In J. W. Astington & J. A. Baird (Eds.), *Why language matters for theory of mind* (pp. 70–83). Oxford: Oxford University Press.

Harrist, A. W., & Waugh, R. (2002). Dyadic synchrony: Its structure and function in children's development. *Developmental Review, 22,* 555–592.

Howe, N., Petrakos, H., & Rinaldi, C. M. (2005). "This is a bad dog, You know. . .": Constructing shared meanings during sibling pretend play. *Child Development, 76,* 783–794.

Howe, N., Rinaldi, C. M., Jennings, M., & Petrakos, H. (2002). "No! the lambs can stay out because they got cosies": Constructive and destructive sibling conflict, pretend play, and social understanding. *Child Development, 73,* 1460–1473.

Howes, C. (1992). *The collaborative construction of pretend: Social pretend functions.* Albany, NY: State University of New York Press.

Hughes, C., & Leekam, S. (2004). What are the links between theory of mind and social relations? Review, reflections and new directions for studies of typical and atypical development. *Social Development, 13,* 590–619.

Jarrold, C., Carruthers, P., Smith, P. K., & Boucher, J. (1994). Pretend play: Is it metarepresentational? *Mind and Languages, 9,* 445–468.

Kavanaugh, R. D. (2006). Pretend play and theory of mind. In L. Balter & C. S. Tamis-LeMonda (Eds.), *Child Psychology: A handbook of contemporary issues* (2nd Ed.) (pp. 153–166.). New York: Psychology Press.

Keenan, T. (2003). Individual differences in theory of mind: The preschool years and beyond. In B. Repacholi & V. Slaughter (Eds.), *Individual differences in theory of mind: Implications for typical and atypical development* (pp.121–142). New York: Psychological Press.

Lillard, A. S. (1993). Pretend play skills and the child's theory of mind. *Child Development, 64,* 348–371.

Lillard, A. S. (1998). Playing with a theory of mind. In O. N. Saracho & B. Spodek (Eds.), *Multiple perspectives on play in early childhood education* (pp. 11–33). Albany, NY: State University of New York Press.

Lillard, A. (2001). Pretend play as Twin Earth: A social-cognitive analysis. *Developmental Review, 21,* 495–531.

Lillard, A. (2007a). Pretense play in toddlers. In C. A. Brownell & C. B. Kopp (Eds.), *Socioemotional development in the toddler years: Transitions and transformations* (pp. 149–176). New York: Guilford.

Lillard, A. (2007b). Guided participations: How mothers structure and children understand pretend play. In A. Goncü & S. Gaskins (Eds.), *Play and development: Evolutionary, sociocultural, and functional perspectives* (pp. 131–153). Mahwah, NJ: Lawarence Erlbaum.

McCabe, P. C. (2005). The social and behavioral correlates of preschoolers with specific language impairment. *Psychology in the Schools, 42,* 373–387.

Maccoby, E. E. (1998). *The two sexes.* Cambridge, MA: Harvard University Press.

Nelson, K. (2005). Language pathways into the community of minds. In J. W. Astington & J. A. Baird (Eds.), *Why language matters for theory of mind* (pp. 26–49). Oxford: Oxford University Press.

Nelson, K., Skwerer, D. P., Goldman, S., Henseler, S., Presler, N., & Walkenfeld, F. F. (2003). Entering a community of minds: An experiential approach to 'theory of mind.' *Human Development, 46,* 24–46.

Nielsen, M., & Dissanayake, C. (2000). An investigation of pretend play, mental state terms and false belief understanding: In search of a metarepresentational link. *British Journal of Developmental Psychology, 18*, 609–624.

Perner, J. (1991). *Understanding the representational mind*. Cambridge, MA: MIT Press.

Perner, J., Leekan, S. R., & Wimmer, H. (1987). Three-year-olds' difficulty with false-belief: the case for a conceptual deficit. *British Journal of Developmental Psychology, 5*, 127–35.

Rubin, K. H., Fein, G. G., & Vandenberg, B. (1983). Play. In P. H. Mussen (Series Ed.) & E. M. Hetherington (Vol. Ed.), *Handbook of child psychology: Vol. 4, Socialization, personality, and social development* (pp. 693–774). New York: Wiley.

Sawyer, R. K. (1997). *Pretend play as improvisation: Conversations in the preschool classroom*. Mahwah, NJ: Lawrence Erlbaum.

Schneider, N., & Goldstein, H. (2008). Social competence interventions for young children with communication and language disorders. In W.H. Brown, S.L. Odom, S.R. McConnell, (Eds.), *Social competence of young children: Risk, disability, and intervention* (pp. 233–252). Baltimore, MD: Paul H Brookes Publishing.

Scholl, B. J., & Leslie, A. M. (1999). Modularity, development, and 'theory of mind.' *Mind and Language, 14*, 131–153.

Schwebel, D. C., Rosen, C. S., & Singer, J. L. (1999). Preschoolers' pretend play and theory of mind: The role of jointly constructed pretense. *British Journal of Developmental Psychology, 17*, 333–348.

Slomkowski, C., & Dunn, J. (1996). Young children's understanding of other people's beliefs and feelings and their connected communication with friends. *Developmental Psychology, 32*, 442–447.

Taylor, M. (1996). A theory of mind perspective on social cognitive development. In R. Gelman & T. K. Au (Eds.), *Perceptual and cognitive development* (pp.283–329). New York: Academic Press.

Taylor, M., & Carlson, S. M. (1997). The relation between individual differences in fantasy and theory of mind. *Child Development, 68*, 436–455.

Tomasello, M., Carpenter, M., Call, J., Behne, T., & Moll, H. (2005). Understanding and sharing intentions: The origins of cultural cognition. *Behavioral and Brain Sciences, 28*, 675–735.

Trawick-Smith, J. (1998). A qualitative analysis of metaplay in the preschool years. *Early Childhood Research Quarterly, 13*, 433–452.

Wellman, H. M., Cross, D., & Watson, J. (2001). Meta-analysis of theory-of-mind development: The truth about false belief. *Child Development, 72*, 655–684.

Wimmer, H., & Perner, J. (1983). Beliefs about beliefs: Representation and constraining function of wrong beliefs in young children's understanding of deception. *Cognition, 13*, 103–128.

Williams, K. T., & Wang, J. J. (1997). *Technical references to the Peabody Picture Vocabulary Test—3rd Edition*. Circle Pines, MN: American Guidance Service.

Youngblade, L. M., & Dunn, J. (1995). Individual differences in young children's pretend play with mother and sibling: Links to relationships and understanding of other people's feelings and beliefs. *Child Development, 66*, 1472–1492.

## APPENDIX A

In the original false belief task (Wimmer & Perner, 1983), children are shown two dolls: a mother and her son, Maxi. The mother and son dolls have just returned from shopping in which they purchased chocolate. Maxi places the chocolate in a cupboard A and leaves the room. While Maxi is out of the room, the mother moves the chocolate from cupboard A to cupboard B. When Maxi returns to the room, Maxi will look for the chocolate. The child is asked, "Where will Maxi look for the chocolate?" To answer successfully, the child must recognize that Maxi is unaware of the transfer of the chocolate from cupboard A to cupboard B and that Maxi will act upon his own false belief (i.e., the chocolate is in cupboard A) and give the answer that Maxi will look in cupboard A.

## APPENDIX B

Two girls, Sarah and Linda, are playing in the center of the room. Sarah is sweeping the floor with a toy broom and Linda is standing next to her holding a baby doll. During the enactment (lines 1–6, 15–21), Sarah plays the mother and directs the scenario, while Linda responds in character as the daughter. Two girls transition from enactment into metaplay to negotiate character role names (lines 7–14), after which they continue with enactment.

1: Sarah: "Honey, now let me sweep right here. I'm going on a date, Honey."
2: Linda: "OK."
3: Sarah: "And I have to use this and take care of doggie. Um, I mean take care of"
4: Linda: "Baby"
5: Sarah: "Baby, and doggie's going to go with me, so be a good girl."
6: Linda: "She will. She will mom. She will."
7: Sarah: "And pretend that your name was"
8: Linda: "Emily"
9: Sarah: "Emily. And my name is Sholby."
10: Linda: "Noo, how 'bout"
11: Sarah: "I know"
12: Linda: "Cheetah? How bout my names be Cheetah, and your name be Rose. OK?"
13: Sarah: "No. Alright. My name bees Rose and your name bees Chia."
14: Linda: "Cheetah"

15: Sarah: "Chia. Alright, Cheetah. I have to go on a date."
16: Linda: "OK."
17: Sarah: "Be a good girl, big sister. I'm going on a date while you baby-sit."
18: Linda: "The baby"
19: Sarah: "The baby"
20: Linda: "I'll put her to bed. I make sure she'll go to bed."
21: Sarah: "Alright, rub her back."

*Part III*

# TEACHER SUPPORT FOR PLAY IN EDUCATIONAL SETTINGS

*Chapter Eight*

# Rough and Tumble Play in Early Childhood Settings: Challenges for Personnel Training

Michelle Tannock

Young children engage in varied forms of play as they seek to explore their world and understand its contexts. Children need to have meaningful experiences and opportunities to explore within play. When children are afforded opportunities to play freely, they are able to express themselves, build social networks, and develop fundamental skills which will last through their adulthood years. Thus, play holds an important role in early childhood development.

Young children gain the most from their play with support from those around them. However, support for some forms of play, such as rough and tumble play, can be difficult as educators remain uncertain of the role this form of play holds within early childhood settings resulting in unique needs for personnel training and policy development. The purpose of this article is to review our current knowledge of rough and tumble play with application to the context of early childhood education and examine several early childhood texts to explore their presentation of this topic for educators. Two areas are included that rarely receive attention in the research literature on rough and tumble play—the notion of an episode of such play as a dynamic process rather than a static event and the need to consider individual sensory-motor preferences in the management of rough and tumble play. Recommendations will be given for pre-professional and professional training to support such play behaviors in the early childhood setting.

The domain of play has been a topic of consideration of philosophers throughout history; the writings of Rousseau (1963) and Pestalozzi (1973) are just two examples. The social nature of play has been widely considered by researchers in the 20th century such as Parten (1932), Bowlby (1969), Piaget (1951), and Vygotsky (1978). Clearly, the social elements of the play of young children have not only held the interest of philosophers and researchers, but are of interest to a wide range of scholars including historians, psychologists, sociologists, educators, anthropologists and zoologists.

The history of scholarly interest in the play of preschool age children has addressed general and specific areas of interest such as gender differences (Evans, 1998), creativity (Singer & Singer, 1985), pretend play (Paley, 1988), and play group entry techniques (Trawick-Smith, 1988) but less attention has been given to some aspects and elements of play including rough and tumble play in the early childhood setting.

## PLAY, LEARNING AND SENSORY MOTOR DEVELOPMENT

Rousseau's (1963) image of children often enveloped play. Particularly for young children, prior to entry into elementary school, play serves not only as an enjoyable experience, but also as a vehicle for learning. The play of children can occur in almost any setting such as the playground, backyard, preschool or the backseat of a car. Within these vastly differing environments, a wide range of learning occurs. Different developmental domains that are impacted include social-emotional development and the recognition of emotions in others, physical abilities, social skills, and language. Physical and social learning occurs, for example, when children chase each other. They discover how their bodies move, how their playmates might respond to shifts in the development of the game, how to problem solve if their playmates want to change the rules or accidentally fall down, and how to use language to express their reactions and opinions to others (Tannock, 2008).

Sutton-Smith (1997) recognized that play is often viewed as developmental activity for children. The play of children serves as the initial avenue for the development, practice, and mastery of many skills including sensory motor development. Physical or gross motor skills are developed, practiced, and mastered through rough and tumble play, also known as rough housing, playful rough behavior, play fighting, and physical activity play. As children run, climb, and test their strength with one another they are practicing and mastering large motor skills. Neurologically, rough play encourages development of the sensory system (Kranowitz & Miller, 2006). Physical contact also may support tactile/kinesthetic and proprioceptive sensory development and meet a need in some children for increased feelings of deep pressure to muscles, joints, and skin. Children vary in their individual needs and preferences for types and amounts of activity; physical contact with others such as touch and pressure; degree of proximity and a need for personal space in relation to familiar and less familiar others; and sensitivity to texture, sounds, light. Much of our knowledge about individual variation in typical children comes from clinical findings with children who are atypical (Kranowitz & Miller,

2006). In addition to physiological including neurologically-based variations in children, other factors that impact individual differences include gender, temperament, early child-rearing experiences and related relationships, and cultural factors. Cultures have been grouped into contact and non-contact cultures (Remland, Jones, and Brinkman, 1995). For example, some cultures discourage extensive physical contact or loud laughter that are common in contact rough and tumble play such as wrestling versus non contact rough and tumble play such as chasing.

## SOCIAL-COGNITIVE DEVELOPMENT AND PLAY

As children move into the preschool years, social interaction and learning through play takes on an increasingly encompassing role. Children are entering into preschool classes, daycare programs, and a multitude of community adventures such as sports, art, or music. With each venture, most children gain additional independence from the family. Young children are developing an increased awareness of peers and are able to enter into a series of social play experiences with children of similar age. Interactions with peers may take place in formal settings such as the preschool or daycare or the interactions may occur within informal settings such as the local neighborhood or at a playground.

Early peer interactions serve not only as sources of enjoyment and learning, but may also be necessary for learning. Children learn about their world and the social expectations of others through play with peers. Peers play an important role as children interact within fairly egalitarian relationships unlike their relationships with adults. The peer relationships offer opportunities to explore a variety of social behaviours such as disagreement, cooperation, competition, and aggression that might not be experienced in the same way as in relationships with adults (Hartup & Moore, 1990).

Piaget (1951) identified the importance of play in the cognitive development of children. While Piaget recognized that limits in the cognitive abilities of young children may restrict the extent of play, play also serves as a medium for practicing those skills that have been learned. This process of cognitive development, for Piaget, is defined in specific stages of development. The first is the sensory motor stage for children up to about age two; the second is the preoperational stage for about ages two to seven; followed by the third stage of concrete operations from about age seven to eleven. Piaget (1951) identified the preoperational stage as the stage of symbolism and representation that begins at approximately age one or two and lasts until age seven. During this stage of play children are practicing skills that will become elements of their concrete operational play that leads to the development of games with rules. Fischer (1980) expanded upon Piaget's (1951) theory by stressing the importance of experience in cognitive development. For Fischer, gaining a cognitive understanding of the social system within the home is supported as children gain an understanding of the social system within a peer's home. This type of learning is sustained when children engage in play that is a reflection of home environments (e.g., playing house, or assigning family roles in pretending to be a family of puppies). Thus, play can serve to provide many practical experiences which enhance learning including developing an understanding of social rules and expectations.

Vygotsky (1962) placed even greater importance on the role of the environment in cognitive development than did Piaget. Where Piaget considered cognitive development to take the form of a maturational process, Vygotsky placed the emphasis for cognitive development on the environment and the social interactions of the individual. Both Piaget and Vygotsky support the view that children are learning through their play as they act on their environments. For example, children learn about mathematics when they determine who has the most blocks; they learn about reading when they look at books or tell a story; they gain understanding of their environment when caring for a doll as they imitate their parents; and they expand their language when they talk with each other and construct meaningful sentences in order to convey their ideas. The cognitive abilities of children serve as a foundation for the social elements of play. Children interact with objects and individuals within their environment when they engage in play. The manipulation of objects and understanding of others enhances their cognitive skills. Rough play has social benefits in the development of such social skills as give and take, taking turns, cause and effect, and playing by the rules (Kranowitz & Miller, 2006).

## ROUGH AND TUMBLE PLAY IN CHILD RESEARCH

Sutton-Smith and Rosenberg (1961) examined the popularity of children's games over a 60 year period from 1898 to 1959. The results of their review indicated that one game that was continuously popular throughout this period was the game of wrestling. The physical nature of play has been explored in research primarily in terms of aggression (Goldstein, 1995). With the connection between rough and tumble play and aggression, educators of young children may find themselves uncertain of how to interpret or manage the play. The roles of positive physical contact within play, that of rough and tumble play, present challenges for educators seeking to understand this form of play.

Rough and tumble (R&T) play has been considered a "neglected aspect of play" (Pellegrini & Smith, 1998, p. 577). While R&T play has recently become a topic of growing interest to more researchers, further consideration in terms of how this form of play is interpreted by educators is needed in order to specifically address the challenges that the play holds in early childhood settings. As detailed by Reed (2005), "research of day care and school personnel's attitudes and values toward R&T play need to be assessed" (p. 69). The research on R&T play which has been undertaken has primarily involved elementary school aged children with primarily boys as participants (Pellegrini & Smith, 1998; Reed & Brown, 2000). As a result, Reed (2005) noted the need to understand the rough and tumble play behaviours of both young boys and girls. While there is an obvious gap in the research literature on the perspectives of educators and how they interpret and respond to rough and tumble play, it is a logical conclusion that the extent to which R&T play is encouraged or discouraged in early childhood settings is dependent upon how educators interpret the R&T play of children, both boys and girls.

## ROUGH AND TUMBLE PLAY IN ANIMAL RESEARCH

The term 'rough and tumble play' originated from animal research related to Harlow and Harlow's (1965) investigation of the social development of Rhesus monkeys. R&T play in this research included the initial identification of the play face in connection with play. The play face was described as an open mouth expression showing teeth which looks aggressive but is actually non-aggressive and playful. This research by Harlow and Harlow was connected with the play of young children when their *play face* display and delightful expressions mimic that of the Rhesus monkeys. The identification of the play face in research confirms that while R&T play is physical in nature and may mimic aggression, no intentional violence or aggression is involved (Power, 2000; Reed & Brown, 2000).

There are two main similarities between R&T play in animals and children. First, animals are more anxious to engage in R&T play after being kept separated for long periods of time from other animals (Scott & Panksepp, 2003). This same phenomenon occurs among children who are confined to classrooms for extended periods of time. Children who spend extensive time frames in learning environments engage in play with increased excitement once they were outside of the classroom (Scott & Panksepp, 2003). In order to investigate this concept, Pellis and Pellis (2007) conducted a study of the impact of a lack of R&T play among young rats in connection with the development of social cognition. This research highlights a need for rough and tumble play in normal development. The lack of such play resulted in organizational changes in the brains of young rats that were denied opportunities for R&T social play experiences. Pellis and Pellis (2007) recognized, in relating their findings to young children, that "it may not be the case that the more socially competent children engage in more play fighting, but rather that the play fighting may promote the development of social competency" (Pellis & Pellis, 2007, p. 97).

A second similarity was noted in the study of rats that engage in rough and tumble play, predominantly at 32 and 40 days of age (Scott & Panksepp, 2003). Children are most active R & T players at the age of seven years (Humphreys & Smith, 1984) and within lifespan adjusted time frames, this would be approximately equivalent to the age of the rats. Through exploration of animal behavior, researchers are able to see such similarities and expand our current understanding of young children's R&T play (Power, 2000).

## CONCEPTUALIZING ROUGH AND TUMBLE PLAY

According to King (1992), children view play as self-chosen, preferred, and gratifying. There are multiple definitions of R&T play and they include a variety of behaviors. R&T play is defined as fun, social-interactive behavior that includes running, climbing, pouncing, chasing and fleeing, wrestling, kicking, open-handed slapping, falling, and other forms of physical and verbal play fighting (Freeman & Brown, 2004; Pellegrini & Smith, 1998). The elements of R&T play have also been similarly categorized by Reed and Brown (2000) to include fleeing, wrestling, falling, and open-handed slaps, running play fighting, and chasing. Freeman & Brown (2004) and Lagacé-Séguin & d'Entremont (2006) divide rough and tumble play into two forms, "contact forms (play fighting) and non-contact forms (chasing)" (p. 464).

R&T play has been hypothesized as an evolution of the exercise play, or physical activity play, of very young children. McCune (1998) explains,

> The peak of exercise play at 4 or 5, the age by which children perfect such skills as running, skipping, and jumping, suggests that the playful occurrence of these activities is related to their recent or ongoing mastery. Subsequently these actions are incorporated into everyday life—hurrying to keep up with mom, jumping over a puddle—and into organized physical sports. Rough-and-tumble play integrates exercise play with social pretend play (p. 602).

This physical mastery of skills is incorporated into the social interactions of the young child during the development of R&T play.

The line between aggression and play is, at times, ambiguous but Scott & Panksepp (2003) claimed that R&T play is a unique set of behaviors that can be reliably distinguished from aggression and other childhood activities. These distinguishing features include *reciprocity, mutuality, evidence of companionship rather than intended dominance, eye contact,* and *shared positive affect.* One common element of recent descriptions and definitions of R&T play related to affect is the inclusion of a *play face* where participants are smiling and laughing (Reed & Brown, 2000) and show an open mouth "active" smile. This play face, as previously described in the discussion of animal research, is an important characteristic since it distinguishes R&T play from aggression. According to Reed and Brown, aggressive behavior involves anger and a determination to cause harm to another, unlike the playful nature of R&T play. Reed and Brown (2000) describe the *play faces* of children engaged in R&T play as smiling expressions coupled with open-handed touches rather than the angry facial expressions coupled with closed fists during physical contact in aggression. These emotional expressions and actions are part of the indicators of intent to playfully interact versus dominate or be aggressive. DiPietro's research (1981) also supports the importance of intent in R&T play. She states, "aggressive actions were distinguished from playful ones on the basis of their perceived intent to inflict injury, as well as the recipient's perception of the intent. This judgment was based on the facial qualities of both children . . . and their verbalizations" (p. 55).

Using these descriptors as a working definition, R&T play can be recognized within the play of young children in a variety of early childhood settings. While the play may be recognized as R&T, the settings in which the children are at play may be vastly different. Each educational setting is unique and the background and characteristics of the children different thereby presenting varying challenges for educators as they develop a curriculum to guide the activities and program. The philosophies and training of the educators also will impact different curriculum designs and their support across early childhood settings. As educators seek to develop curriculum that reflects the interests of the children, they need to develop a level of acceptance and understanding of all elements of play. One of the elements in need of consideration within the social domain of play is R&T play. It may be that R&T play within early childhood settings has not been fully understood because R&T play has been viewed as a predominantly male form of play (Pellegrini & Smith, 1998). Early childhood educators are predominantly women, which may lead to a lack of awareness of male patterns of play. With increased understanding of various patterns of play, educators may be better able to distinguish among play behaviors.

## IS ROUGH AND TUMBLE PLAY REALLY PLAY?

Rough and tumble behaviors are considered to be play behaviors (Pellegrini & Smith, 1998; Reed & Brown, 2000) and yet they also may be described as non-play behaviors. As stated by McCune (1998), "Play has been difficult to define because it occurs as an aspect of many activities rather than being limited to a specific kind of activity; thus it rarely occurs in isolation" (p. 601). R&T play has not yet been accepted universally as a form of play, although the majority of research appears to support its inclusion as a form of play (McBride-Chang & Jacklin, 1993; Pellegrini, 1989). Further, the identification of R&T play as behaviour manifested cross-culturally (Whiting & Edwards, 1973) supports the view of R&T as a form of play.

Pellegrini and Smith's (1998) comprehensive literature review of R&T play is of importance because it is one of a very few scholarly literature reviews of R&T play. Within the review, Pellegrini and Smith identified age and gender trends, the functions of physical play, and proposed suggestions for further research that include a need for more descriptive data on the forms of physical activity play and their age trends through childhood and adolescence" and, "more data on gender differences in exercise play" (p.589).The review illustrated that, "forms of physical activity play are quite common in childhood" (p. 579).

A qualitative study by Reed and Brown (2000) included observing the R&T play of seven boys aged six to nine years with a focus on expressions of care displayed within the play. The researchers also interviewed the boys about their R&T play. The boys commented on, "where and when it was appropriate to express care and intimacy for one another, which often is contrary to traditional ideas about play and recess" (p. 104). Reed and Brown also identified a need for educators and administrators to reconsider the importance of R&T as "one way boys express care, fondness, and friendships toward each other" (p. 104). This need for educators and administrators to recognize the importance of R&T play is supported by Pellegrini and Perlmutter (1988) who recommended that R&T play be provided for in elementary schools.

## THE DEVELOPMENT AND FREQUENCY
## OF ROUGH AND TUMBLE PLAY

Three to five percent of the play of preschool children can be considered to be R&T play (Pellegrini, 1984). Pellegrini and Smith (1998) discussed the emergence of R&T play as represented by an inverted-U shape and reported that "Rough-and-tumble increases during the late preschool and early primary school years, accounting for about 5% of observed recess behavior, peaks in later primary years at around 10%, and then declines during early adolescence, accounting for less than 5% of play" (p. 580). R&T play is frequently present for portions of playtime ( Humphreys & Smith, 1984; Pellegrini, 1984; Pellegrini & Smith, 1998). The inverted U-shaped distribution of time may reflect a sensitive period in development during which the performance of motor acts alters brain development especially in the fine control of motor output (Byers, 1998).

## FUNCTIONS OF ROUGH AND TUMBLE PLAY

There are multiple possible functions of R&T play and they include the health and cognitive benefits of exercise, socialization of adult-like behaviors, and development of friendships and bonding with others. Pellegrini and Smith (1998) presented two opposing perspectives. First, that "children engage in play to learn and practice those skills necessary to be functioning adult members of society". Second, that "play may be viewed not as an incomplete or imperfect version of adult behavior, but as having immediate benefits during childhood" (p. 581). Pellegrini and Smith (1998) identified the need for exercise as another possible function of rough and tumble play as, "during the preschool/primary school years children engage in substantial amounts of exercise play" (p.579) with health benefits for those who regularly engage in vigorous games and sports. The development of endurance and strength may be a benefit of rough and tumble play in two ways. First, the play can lead to heightened arousal and second, "exercise play might, by breaking up cognitive tasks, provide spaced or distributed practice rather than massed practice." (Pellegrini and Smith, 1998, p. 584). This distributed practice might, according to Pellegrini and Smith, help children to attend to cognitive tasks. If children are given opportunities to exercise during a mid-point in a period of completing cognitive tasks, the contention is that their ability to attend to these cognitive tasks is improved.

When children engage in rough and tumble play, it superficially may appear that they fight and are aggressive towards their friends. However, Reed and Brown (2000) recognized that R&T play is also a venue for the physical expression of caring and friendship amongst players. R&T play is not only a form of physical activity, but also a means through which boys can express emotional connections in a socially acceptable manner often through physical contact. The expression of caring behaviors amongst children does vary by gender and boys and girls have different perspectives on close relationships and how care is expressed in such relationships (Reed & Brown, 2000). R&T play may be one of the few socially acceptable ways for males to express care and intimacy for another male with reciprocity and mutual consent distinguishing R&T play from real fighting, out of control aggression, or bullying (Freeman & Brown, 2004).

## GENDER DIFFERENCES IN ROUGH AND TUMBLE PLAY

Scott and Panksepp (2003) suggested two central differences between boys and girls in rough and tumble play. First, based on their research, they found that boys had more physical contact when engaging in R&T play than girls and were rougher than girls. Second, females engaged in more rough and tumble play which was non-contact such as rolling, when compared to males. In addition, males tend to engage in exercise play at higher rates than females in all cultures where exercise play has been investigated. Smith and Lewis (1985) researched the role of rough and tumble play, fighting, and chasing in 145 R&T play episodes in early childhood settings and found that 84 involved only boys, 22 only girls, and 39 involved both genders. While not all boys like or engage in R&T play, and some girls do engage in such behaviors, the strong gender difference in the frequency of R&T play may be influenced by socialization. Pellegrini and Smith (1998) argued that boys and girls are socialized into different, and often segregated, worlds. Girls are more closely supervised by parents and educators so vigorous physical behavior is discouraged and verbal skills rather than physical skills are promoted to facilitate relationships and resources.

## EARLY CHILDHOOD EDUCATORS AND ROUGH AND TUMBLE PLAY

Several factors can impact attitudes to and management of R&T play in early childhood settings. Based on interviews and discussions with hundreds of early childhood and elementary teachers, Reed, Brown and Roth (2000) concluded that teachers found R&T play to be an ongoing concern and a behavior that continued to exist despite efforts to eliminate it. The main factors impacting negative attitudes to R&T play include the preponderance of female staff, concerns about injury, difficulty distinguishing R&T play from aggression, and attitudes to types of play from a gender and educational perspective.

Such concerns are likely to continue based on increased caution related to liability issues and child injury within educational settings; concerns about the impact of popular child media as promoting child aggression and the practice of such role play in schools (Sherburne et al 1988; Reed, Brown & Roth,

2000) and the promotion of techniques for managing challenging behaviors in the classroom (Powell, Dunlap, & Fox, 2006).

## Educator Gender Bias in Attitudes to Rough and Tumble Play

Rough and tumble play is predominantly a male form of play that in an early childhood setting occurs within an environment traditionally dominated by females. Freeman and Brown (2004) discuss the dilemma for early childhood educators who want to support individualized opportunities for self development and want to avoid perpetuating gender-biased stereotypes that only boys enjoy R&T or that such play is inappropriate for girls. One factor related to such a dilemma is that female and male educators differ in the form and function of the play in which they engage with children. Sandberg and Pramling-Samuelson (2005) recognized that male preschool educators are more willing to play with children especially a participation in physical play. They also have a greater understanding and recognition based on their own experiences. It would be expected that female educators, who have not been exposed to this form of play either as players or through training, would discourage such play and view R&T within a framework of aggressive behavior.

Sandberg and Pramling-Samuelson (2005) found that male preschool educators and female preschool educators view child development differently. Male educators focused on physical development while female educators focused on social development. In their study they noted that the males described how boys used games with rules whereas the females described how girls used role-play. Another finding was that female educators and male educators differed in their willingness to play with children. Females were identified as less enthusiastic in their play with the children compared with male educators. In addition, male educators also spend greater periods of time at play with children in order to enhance their relationships with children.

It is the frequent lack of fundamental understanding of this predominantly male form of play that warrants consideration as educators seek opportunities to authentically support all children (Tannock, 2008). In a study by Cooney and Bittner (2001), male early childhood educators discussed the gender bias they encountered while in training. This study reported that men acknowledged bias in their college classes, in the choice of adapted course texts, in discussion directions, and in the content chosen for inclusion in early childhood training programs. Reed and Brown (2000) recognized that research on R&T play has been dominated by a focus on the play of boys and that this form of play tends to be misunderstood by females. As a result, males engaging in rough and tumble play in early childhood settings stand a greater risk of being reprimanded for engaging in the activity. This is not a malicious act on the part of the female educators; rather, according to Reed and Brown (2000), it is an action based on misunderstanding. Just as there are different parenting styles, educators have different styles of teaching and coaching and concerns about liability in the care of the children they teach. For example, Lagacé-Séguin and d'Entremont (2006) conducted a study in which parenting styles that were recognized in connection with R&T play included emotion coaching, emotion dismissing, authoritative parenting style, authoritarian parenting style, and permissive parenting style. They concluded that an emotion coaching parenting style acts as an additional *protective* factor to prevent children from engaging in R&T play (Lagacé-Séguin & d'Entremont, 2006). The researchers, in this case, viewed R&T play as a negative expression among children related to ineffective parenting styles.

## Preoccupation with Any Risk of Injury

The positive benefits of rough and tumble play may be recognized by some educators but the question of injury within play is often a concern (Dockett & Tegel, 1996). There is frequently a connection drawn between R&T play and children being injured or a fear that the rough-housing may escalate or lead to aggression. Recent teacher concern includes observations of the number of children who want to re-enact superhero play or war and fighting events from movies, television programs, and computer games (Reed, Brown, & Roth, 2000).

R&T play can occur as brief episodes such as affectionate nudging or pushing back and forth, to much longer episodes such as rolling and wrestling down a grassy slope. Any such episode has an initiation by one or more of the interactive partners, a development of activities and behaviors, and an eventual cessation or conclusion. During the development of such play episodes the nature of the physical and verbal interaction may change with new physical activities introduced, other participants added, and the conversation or vocal accompaniments being modified. R&T play episodes are, therefore, not static events but a dynamic process; that is, any given episode changes over time. Concerns by educators appear to be two-fold. Firstly, that any type of R&T play may promote aggression in children and immediately result in physical injury. Secondly, that the R&T play, if initially tolerated, may escalate into physical injury later. That even a small risk may result in one incident, that could be catastrophic, pervades the current climate of over-protectiveness by parents and schools and has given rise to the introduction of preventive programs (Schwebel et al, 2006).

Humphreys and Smith (1984), when seeking schools in which to conduct their study on R&T play, found strong differences in the beliefs and attitudes of educators: "Some [educators] saw such activity as harmless fun, and were happy to let it carry on provided nobody was in danger of getting hurt, while at the other extreme, some saw all such behavior as aggressively motivated and forbade it" (p. 253). Humphreys and Smith's research focus was on R&T play behaviors not teacher attitudes but their observations in obtaining suitable research sites illustrate an important fact that many educators do not realize that their perception that R & T play leads to aggression is largely unfounded (Pellegrini & Perlmutter, 1988). The lack of clarity and understanding among educators on the role of R&T play, including how to distinguish it from aggression was considered by Schafer and Smith (1996). This study demonstrated that while educators are exposed to R&T play on a daily basis, they experience difficulty when attempting to distinguish what is aggressive and what is playful. As in other studies, participants in this study also related common concerns that playful fighting could lead to aggression. Such concern for play becoming harmful for young children often results in R&T play being presented as a behavior needing supervision or elimination.

There is a need to fully understand how educators in early childhood settings recognize and interpret R&T play before determining how they manage such types of play in children and their opinions about behavior management. If educators also do not know how to appropriately manage or govern R&T play, this will remain an ongoing challenge. Some qualitative research into the area of educator perceptions has been conducted (Tannock, 2008) but additional research is needed to fully understand educator perspectives.

## The Early Childhood Environment

Young children spend increasing amounts of time outside their homes as they attend childcare programs including daycare and preschools. This early connection with formal programming may impact play opportunities with other children. Hewes (2007) found that children who attend early childhood programs spend less time at play compared to children who do not attend such programs. Hewes argued that early childhood education programs focus more on academic educational opportunities and less time on recreational activities including physical play. In order to benefit from time and settings dedicated to free and spontaneous play with others, children need opportunities, adequate time, and wide open space to play outside of the classroom (Reed & Brown, 2000).

Preschool and elementary educators have an important role in supporting young children's involvement in play, including R&T play, by providing multiple opportunities within multiple contexts for young children at play (Reed & Brown, 2000). Early childhood educators influence young children's play through their support or discouragement of different forms of play. For children to become proficient players the support and agreement of both parents and educators is needed.

Scott and Panksepp (2003) stated, as discussed earlier in this chapter, that R&T play encourages children to learn and to develop pro-social behaviors. When educators understand that R&T play does not involve aggression, it may be that they will develop a more positive perspective on this type of play. They need to be able to identify R&T play, know how to respond to it, and how to set limits that do not discourage the play and are child-directed and child-centered. The provision of adequate education and training on R&T may be the key to reversing the previously described current attitudes and beliefs of many educators.

## Educator Materials and Training

Early childhood educators participate in training programs as part of the process to become licensed to work with young children in licensed settings. Training programs may utilize a variety of supportive materials, such as text books, for the purpose of conveying information about early childhood education and care. These textbooks reflect not only current trends and "best practices" but also incorporate research literature into a functional format which educators can utilize in their daily interactions with young children.

A review of early childhood education text books was undertaken by this author to determine the degree to which rough and tumble play is included. Eight common early childhood education textbooks were included in the review (Craig, Kermis, & Digdon, 1998; Eliason & Jenkins, 2003; Frost, Wortham & Reifel, 2008; Hendrick, 2001; Johnson, Christie, & Wardle, 2005; Kaiser & Rasminsky, 2003; Prochner & Howe, 2000; Reynolds, 2001). The text by Craig, Kermis, and Digdon (1998) includes a small section on rough and tumble play. The authors recognize that R&T play is, at times, mis-interpreted and in need of clarification as a valued form of play unique from actual aggression. This focus on clarifying R&T play is also demonstrated in the text by Frost, Wortham and Reifel (2008). Here R&T play is included and clearly identified as separate and different from aggression. In two of the reviewed texts R&T play is placed within sections on supervision. The Kaiser and Rasminsky (2003) text places R&T play in a chapter on bullying. The half-page of information details the role of R&T play as, "a normal activity that at one time probably helped to develop fighting skills and now perhaps plays a part in working out the dominance relationships in a group" (p. 244). Another text, by Reynolds (2001), highlights the need to supervise R&T play while also stating that R&T play is often forbidden in child care centers. Reynolds suggests that the female-dominated environments are not designed to allow for R&T play. This supports the position of Reed and Brown (2000) that R&T play is typically limited in environments that are female dominant such as early childhood settings. The Hendrick (2001) text includes a chapter on managing aggression. The statement, "It's difficult sometimes to decide when it's rough-and-tumble and when someone's likely to get hurt" (p.307) is placed under a photo of two boys engaging in what may be interpreted as R&T play or aggression; the facial expressions are not visible in the photo. The Johnson, Christie, and Wardle (2005) text includes a section on the relationship between R&T play and social cognitive ability within a framework of supporting development through play. This text includes some distinctions between R&T play and aggression in the form of basic details on what constitutes each form of behavior.

While some early childhood education textbooks included limited discussions of R&T play, early childhood websites included less information. A review of websites for the *National Association for the Education of Young Children*, the *Association for Childhood Education International*, and the *International Play Association* including the *American Association for the Child's Right to Play* revealed little information on R&T play. Although formal early childhood organizations have few resources available to support an understanding the role of R&T play, parenting and education sites are beginning to discuss this form of play. For example, *Education.com* includes information from the Committee for Children titled "Guidelines for Distinguishing Aggression From Play Fighting" which highlights the distinctions recorded in research such the play face, role exchange, and consideration for other players to determine level of strength or force used in the play. At some sites such as *Parenting.com* notation is made on how R&T play is considered a boy form of play but fathers should be encouraged to also engage in such play with daughters. This reflects the predominant focus of R&T play on parenting and educator websites where it is accorded very little attention whereas discouragement of aggressive physical behavior is a dominant topic.

This review of selected early childhood education texts and some well-known US websites demonstrates a general lack of discussion on R&T play. It appears that R&T play, in texts or web-based informational sites, is a neglected aspect of play and requires increased attention from the education and psychology experts in the field of play in order to enhance the dissemination of information for the public and professionals (Pellegrini and Smith, 1998).

## Recommendations for Pre-professional and In-Service Training of Early Childhood Personnel

Reed, Brown and Roth (2000) list 10 topics of concern on R&T play that should be included in pre-professional and in-service training for educators.

Freeman and Brown (2004) suggest 6 areas of concern that, if addressed, could support a change of views and attitudes on R&T play. The combined recommendations can be summarized as the provision and adaptation of play spaces or playgrounds with a section dedicated to R&T play; training of adults and children to recognize and identify emotions in others; training of educators on the role of R&T play in developing caring relationships and friendships; the encouragement of teacher self reflection on gender differences and gender stereotypes; the involvement of children in decisions about where and when to allow R&T play; the education of children about R&T play, the process of creating explicit rules, and respect for others; and the need to continue to promote research on this type of play.

Children can learn to use language and/or signs or gestures to indicate how to be part of or cease the R&T play. They can develop rules such as when either child or the teacher says "stop" the R&T play will cease. These rules could include no kicking, scratching, pinching, or biting, and no hitting or attacking anyone's head or private parts. In addition this author would add recommendations as discussed in this chapter, that teacher education is needed on knowledge of cultural differences on contact and non-contact play, the role of individual sensory motor needs, and training in the ability to understand changes in the interpersonal dynamics within R&T play episodes.

Educators need to distinguish between negative aggressive and bullying behaviors and R&T play and therefore R&T play may be a topic that also can be included in training on the management of challenging behaviors in young children. Teacher training is needed in not just observation but also listening (when the children's conversations can be heard) to support skills needed to recognize the meaning of simultaneously occurring (language, affect, and action) behaviors. Table 8.1 presents a checklist that can be adapted to groups of more than 2 children. It can be used to discuss the concept and practice of R&T play, as a tool to conduct actual observations to assist in the differential recognition of R&T play, or to make decisions on management of the behavior.

The checklist focuses on the main areas of physical behaviors, affect, language, the relationship/friendship, individual preferences, and prior history. *Physical behaviors* may be a combination of contact or no contact. *Affect*, especially as shown through facial expressions, are a continuously changing signal and can rapidly shift from positive to, for example, confused or frustrated. *Language* such as name-calling, teasing, whispering, are an integral part of play and may indicate intent and mutual enjoyment. Language, in the form of narratives, will also indicate if the R&T play is part of enactment of super hero play (Jarvis, 2007). Teacher knowledge of the individual children

**Table 8.1.   Checklist for Positive Reciprocity in Dyadic Assessment of Rough and Tumble Play**

|  | Child 1 | Child 2 | Comments |
|---|---|---|---|
| Physical behaviors (contact)<br>Are they engaged in reciprocal and similar behaviors e.g. pulling-pushing? | | | |
| Physical behaviors (non contact)<br>Are they engaged in reciprocal and similar behaviors e.g. running/chasing? | | | |
| Facial affect- Slight smile or active smile/play face.<br>Does each child show smiling and appear positive about the experience? | | | |
| Facial affect-Negative<br>Does either child show evidence of fear indicative of potential aggression or bullying? | | | |
| Vocal Affect-Laughter<br>Are the children producing sounds that are positive—laughter squeals, laughter screams, chuckling, giggling or laughing? | | | |
| Language-Gestures<br>Are the children producing similar gestures such as pointing, waving, beckoning, that are positive or neutral rather than negative or rude such as aggressively shaking a fist? | | | |
| Language-Vocal<br>Are the sounds the children produce such as shouts, exclamations, animal or vehicle sounds, and exertion sounds non-threatening? | | | |
| Language-Verbal interaction<br>Is their language to each other positive and not argumentative? Is any teasing good natured and not negatively provocative? | | | |
| Language-Types of Play<br>Does the language suggest R & T is part of superhero play or other pretend play that could include aggression? | | | |
| | | | *(continued)* |

**Table 8.1.    (*continued*)**

|  | Child 1 | Child 2 | Comments |
|---|---|---|---|
| Friendship status<br>Are they friends with each other and<br>play with each other often? |  |  |  |
| Sensory motor preferences<br>Do these children typically engage in<br>R & T play with no previous history of<br>physical fighting and aggression with<br>each other? |  |  |  |
| Personal history<br>Any previous history of bullying any<br>other child? |  |  |  |
| Evidence of negative intent<br>Is there any intent to harm as indicated by<br>nonverbal or verbal behaviors? |  |  |  |

under their supervision is important because it contributes to understanding *individual preferences,* such as which children seek out physical contact with others, or need additional opportunities for physical activity. Knowledge of the children's *prior history* is helpful because R&T play has been found more among popular children with leadership qualities than children who are rejected (Reed, Brown, & Roth, 2000). Additional considerations are 1. What is the *setting*: indoors, outdoors and is this appropriate for the type of play? For example, chasing on a wet surface around a swimming pool may reflect suitable R&T play but in a potentially dangerous setting. 2. What are the *teacher expectations* and have these been verbalized to the children? For example, if the children have been asked to walk in a single line to transition from outdoors to indoors, physical play between two children violates the teacher given directions. 3. How many *participants* and who are they? Is this a large or small group or dyadic interaction only? 4. Do the children have *rules* about what is acceptable physical activity and contact and how to satisfactorily conclude R&T play? Communication between some friends may be easier for some children than others, such as when their partner invites the other to play, and the ability to listen to and respect when one child says they have had enough of a given behavior. 5. Are there *routines and rituals* of R&T play between certain children in particular settings? Children enjoy repetition of enjoyable activities and may associate R&T play with similar predictable behaviors as a regular routine each time they are in the same setting.

# CONCLUSION

Early childhood educators encounter a variety of play forms amongst young children. Some play behaviors are more readily interpreted and understood by educators while others, including R&T play, are in need of further consideration. The disdain for R&T play may be due in part to the gender division between female educators and the boys in their care who are engaging in the play. It also may be due to a lack of understanding of the developmental role of physical interaction, the role of contact in the context of bonding and friendships, and the individual sensory motor needs of children. While the importance of R&T play has been identified within animal research, the findings and value for this form of play have not filtered down to educator training levels. Scholars and early childhood textbook authors need to include comprehensive discussions of R&T play within the context of normative child development to encourage educators in the field to interpret the play in a manner which could be considered best practice and adopted as standard practice for educators working with young children. We need continued research to provide evidence-based best practice in early childhood settings.

# REFERENCES

Bowlby, J. (1969). *Attachment and loss: Vol. 1. Attachment.* New York: Basic Books.

Byers, J. A. (1998). The biology of human play. *Child Development, 69*(3), 599–600.

Committee for Children. (2007). *Guidelines for distinguishing aggression from play fighting.* Retrieved http://www.education.com/reference/article/Ref_Distinguishing/.

Cooney, M. H. & Bittner, M. T. (2001). Men in early childhood education: Their emergent issues. *Early Childhood Education Journal, 29*(2), 77–82.

Craig, G. J., Kermis, M. D., & Digdon, N. L. (1998). *Children Today: Canadian edition.* Scarborough, ONT: Prentice-Hall.

DiPietro, J. A. (1981). Rough and tumble play: A function of gender. *Developmental Psychology, 17*(1), 50–58.

Dockett, S., & Tegel, K. (1996). Identifying Dilemmas for Early Childhood Educators. *Australian Research in Early Childhood Education, 1,* 20–28.

Eliason, C. & Jenkins, L. (2003). *A practical guide to early childhood curriculum* (7th ed.). Upper Saddle River, NJ: Merrill Prentice Hall.

Evans, K. S. (1998). Combating gender disparity in education: Guidelines for early childhood educators. *Early Childhood Education Journal, 26,* 83–88.

Fischer, K. (1980). A theory of cognitive development: The control and construction of hierarchies of skills. *Psychological Review, 87,* 477–531.

Freeman, Nancy K. and Brown, M. H. (2004). Reconceptualizing rough and tumble play. Ban the banning. In S. Reifel and M. H. Brown (Eds.) *Social contexts of early education, and reconceptualizing play,* Vol II. Advances in early education and day care, *13,* 219–234. New York: Elsevier.

Frost, J. L., Wortham, S. C., and Reifel, S. (2008). *Play and child development* (3rd ed.). Upper Saddle River, NJ: Pearson.

Goldstein, J. (1995). Aggressive toy play. In A. D. Pellegrini (Ed.), *The future of play theory* (pp. 127–147). New York: State of New York University Press.

Harlow, H.F. & Harlow, M.K. (1962). Social deprivation in monkeys. *Scientific American, 207*(5), 136–146.

Hartup, W. W., & Moore, S. G. (1990). Early peer relations: Developmental significance and prognostic implications. *Early Childhood Research Quarterly, 5,* 1–17.

Hendrick, J. (2001). *The whole child: Developmental education for the early years* (7th ed.). Upper Saddle River, NJ: Prentice-Hall.

Hewes, J. (2007). The value of play in early learning: Towards a pedagogy. In Jambor, T., & Gils, J. V. (Eds.), *Several Perspectives on Children's Play: Scientific Reflections for Practitioners* (pp. 119–132). Belgium: Garant.

Humphreys, A. P. & Smith, P. K. (1984). Rough-and-tumble in preschool and playground. In P. K. Smith (Ed.), *Play in animals and humans* (pp. 241–266). Oxford: Basil Blackwell.

Jarvis, P. (2007). Monsters, magic and Mr. Psycho: A biocultural approach to rough and tumble play. *Early Years, 27*(2), 171–188.

Johnson, J. E., Christie, J. F., & Wardle, F. (2005). *Play, Development, and Early Education.* Boston, MA: Pearson.

Kaiser, B. & Rasminsky, J. S. (2003). *Challenging behavior in young children: Understanding, preventing, and responding effectively.* Boston, MA: Pearson.

King, N. R. (1992). The impact of context on the play of young children. In S. A. Kessler and B. B. Swadener (Eds.) *Reconceptualizing the early childhood curriculum: Beginning the dialogue* (pp. 43–61). New York: Teachers College Press.

Kranowitz, C. S. & Miller, L. J. (2006). The out of sync child. Recognizing and coping with sensory processing disorder. New York: Penguin.

Lagacé-Séguin, D. G., & d'Entremont, M-R. L. (2006). The role of child negative affect in the relations between parenting styles and play. *Early Childhood Development and Care, 176,* 461–477.

McBride-Chang, C., & Jacklin, C. N. (1993). Early play arousal, sex-typed play, and activity level as precursors to later rough-and-tumble play. *Early Education and Development, 4*(2), 99–108.

McCune, L. (1998). Immediate and ultimate functions of physical activity play. *Child Development, 69*(3), 601–603.

Paley, V. G. (1988). *Bad guys don't have birthdays: Fantasy play at four.* Chicago: University of Chicago Press.

Parenting.com. (2009). Retrieved http://www.parenting.com/.

Parten, M. B. (1932). Social participation among pre-school children. *Journal of Abnormal and Social Psychology, 27,* 243–269.

Pellegrini, A. D. (1984). The social cognitive ecology of preschool classrooms. *International Journal of Behavioral Development, 7*, 321–332.

Pellegrini, A. D. (1989). What is a category? The case of rough-and-tumble play. *Ethology and Sociobiology, 10*, 331–341.

Pellegrini, A. D., & Perlmutter, J. C. (1988). Rough-and-tumble play on the elementary school playground. *Young Children, 43*(2), 14–17.

Pellegrini, A. D., & Smith, P. K. (1998). Physical activity play: The nature and function of a neglected aspect of play. *Child Development, 69*(3), 577–598.

Pellis, S. M. and Pellis, V. C. (2007). Rough-and-tumble play and the development of the social brain. *Current Directions in Psychological Science, 16*(2), 95–98.

Pestalozzi, J. H. (1973). *How Gertrude teaches her children* (L. E. Holland & F. C. Turner, Trans.). New York: Gordon Press. (Original work published 1894).

Piaget, J. (1951). *Play, dreams, and imitation in childhood*. New York: Norton.

Powell, D., Dunlap, G. & Fox, L. (2006). Prevention and intervention for the challenging behaviors of toddlers and preschoolers. *Infants and Young Children,* 19(1), 25–35.

Power, T. G. (2000). *Play and exploration in children and animals*. Mahwah, NJ: Lawrence Erlbaum.

Prochner, L. & Howe, N. (Eds.) (2000). *Early childhood care and education in Canada*. Toronto: UBC Press.

Reed, T. L. (2005). A qualitative approach to boys rough and tumble play: There is more than meets the eye. In F. F. McMahon, D. E. Lytle, and B. Sutton-Smith (Eds.) *Play: An interdisciplinary synthesis* (pp. 53–71). Lanham, MD: University Press of America.

Reed, T., & Brown, M. (2000). The expression of care in the rough and tumble play of boys. *Journal of Research in Childhood Education, 15*(1), 104–116.

Reed, T., Brown, M. & Roth, S. A. (2000). Friendship formation and boys' rough and tumble play: Implications for teacher education programs. *Journal of Early Childhood Teacher Education, 21*(3), 331–336.

Remland, M. S., Jones, T. S., & Brinkman, H. (1995). Interpersonal distance, body orientation and touch: Effects of culture, gender, and age. *The Journal of Social Psychology, 135*(30), 281–297.

Reynolds, E. (2001). *Guiding young children: A problem-solving approach*. Toronto: Mayfield.

Rousseau, J. J. (1963). *Emile* (B. Foxley, Trans.). London: J. M. Dent & Sons. (Original work published 1762).

Sandberg, A., & Pramling-Samuelson, I. (2005). An interview study of gender differences in preschool teachers' attitudes toward children's play. *Early Childhood Education Journal, 32*, 297–305.

Schafer, M. and Smith, P. K. (1996). Teachers' perceptions of play fighting and real fighting in primary school. *Educational Research, 38*(2), 173–181.

Schwebel, D. C, Summerline, A. L., Bounds, M. L., & Morrongiello. B. A. (2006). The stamp-in safety program. *Journal of Pediatric Psychology, 31*(2), 152–162.

Scott, E., & Panksepp, J. (2003). Rough and tumble play in human children. *Aggressive Behavior, 29*, 539–551.

Sherburne, S., Utley, B., McConnell, S. M., & Gannon, J. (1988). Decreasing violent or aggressive theme play among preschool children with behavior disorders. *Exceptional Children, 55*(2), 166–172.

Singer, J. L., & Singer, D. G. (1985). *Make believe: Games and activities to foster imaginative play in young children.* Glenview, IL: Scott, Foresman.

Smith, P. K. & Lewis, K. (1985). Rough-and-tumble play, fighting, and chasing in nursery school children. *Ethology and Sociobiology, 6*(3), 175–181.

Sutton-Smith, B. (1997). *The ambiguity of play.* Cambridge, MA: Harvard University Press.

Sutton-Smith, B. & Rosenberg, B.G. (1961). Sixty years of historical change in the game preferences of American children. *The Journal of American Folklore, 74*(291), 17–46.

Tannock, M.T. (2008). Rough and tumble play: An investigation of the perceptions of educators and young children. *Early Childhood Education Journal, 35*(4), 357–361.

Trawick-Smith, J. (1988). "Let's say you're the baby, OK?" Play leadership and following behavior of young children. *Young Children, 43*(5), 51–58.

Vygotsky, L. S. (1962). *Thought and language.* Cambridge, MA: MIT Press.

Vygotsky, L. S. (1978). *Mind in society: The development of higher psychological processes.* Cambridge, MA: Harvard University Press.

Whiting, B., & Edwards, C. (1973). A cross-cultural analysis of sex-differences in the behavior of children age three through 11. *Journal of Social Psychology, 91*, 171–188.

## Chapter Nine

# The Teacher's Role in Enhancing Sociodramatic Play in Early Childhood Classrooms: A Study in Head Start Classrooms

## Mira Tetkowski Berkley and Kate Mahoney

A substantial body of research supports the importance of dramatic and sociodramatic play in early childhood settings (e.g., Bergen, 1988, 2002; Fein & Rivkin, 1986; Klugman, 1995; Singer, 1973; Smilansky, 1968). Benefits that have been identified include cognitive (Bergen, 2002; Piaget, 1962; Vygotsky, 1933/1976) and psychosocial gains (Erikson, 1950/1963; Isaacs, 1933/1967; Parten, 1932). However, these benefits are seldom realized. This is partly because teachers are rarely actively and consciously involved in enhancing opportunities for play, especially sociodramatic play (Benham, Miller & Kontos, 1988; Bennett, Wood & Rogers, 1997; Berke, 1996; Charlesworth et al., 1993; Kemple, 1996; Smilansky & Shefatya, 1990; VanderVen et al, 1995).

Sociodramatic play is a form of symbolic play and the most mature form of dramatic play (Shefatya, 1995; Smilansky, 1968; Smilansky & Shefatya, 1990). It is what children know as playing pretend. Sociodramatic play occurs when children adopt different roles and interact based on a scenario they spontaneously create together. Action and language express children's existing knowledge of their world experience including people, situations, and objects. For the purpose of this paper we use Smilansky and Shefatya's (1990) definitions of dramatic and sociodramatic play. Dramatic play includes four elements (imitative role-play, make-believe with regard to objects, verbal make-believe with regard to actions and situations, and persistence in role-play) whereas sociodramatic play includes two additional elements (interaction between at least two players and verbal communication). Thus sociodramatic play has the greatest learning potential due to rich opportunities for children's construction of knowledge through collaborative discourse. Through sociodramatic play, children mobilize and combine cognitive, language, and social skills (Shefatya, 1995).

When questioned, most preschool teachers state that they value sociodramatic play. In practice, however, there is little evidence that sociodramatic play is provided as a conscious part of the early childhood curriculum planning process and even less evidence that teachers attempt to optimize its occurrence (Bennett, Wood, & Rogers, 1997; Berke, 1996; Charlesworth, et al., 1993; Kemple, 1996). This may be due, in part, to the early childhood tradition of non-involvement of adults in children's play (e.g., Klugman & Smilansky, 1990; Read, 1971; Roskos & Neuman, 1993). As such, early childhood teacher preparation programs may include few, if any, specific strategies for enhancing sociodramatic play as part of early childhood education curriculum. Consequently, the typical approach to sociodramatic play in preschool classrooms is to include a dramatic play area, typically a housekeeping area including dress-up clothes and props. Children are often left alone by teachers when playing in these areas, unless conflicts arise.

Few studies have addressed the roles of teachers during play and the individual differences among teachers in their involvement with children in play activities (Kontos, 1999). The ability of preschool teachers to provide developmental support for children in play is impacted by their training and expertise. The majority of individuals serving preschool children in early childhood programs (including Head Start and child care) do not have baccalaureate degrees in early childhood or a related area (Powell & Dunn, 1990). Typically these teachers or caregivers are, at most, minimally trained in early childhood care and education while providers of care in more informal settings are likely to have even less, if any, training (Children's Defense Fund, 2005).

In order to examine the roles and activities of teachers related to sociodramatic play, this research explored the following questions: What was the level of sociodramatic play that existed in each classroom? What was the level of teacher involvement in children's sociodramatic play? What barriers might exist that impede sociodramatic play opportunities for children and teacher involvement in their play? An additional goal of this study was to use the findings to suggest, within the context of any barriers, how early childhood educators can be helped to provide more opportunities for increasing the frequency and quality of sociodramatic play.

## METHOD

### Ethnographic Research Design

This study was conducted primarily with an ethnographic approach (Goetz & LeCompte, 1984). The goal of ethnography is not prediction, but understanding (Ayers, 1989). In this case, the goal was to better understand sociodramatic play. Many prominent researchers support the use of qualitative methods in research on early childhood education (e.g. Ayers, 1989; Silin, 1987; Trawick-Smith, 1998; Walsh, Tobin, & Graue, 1993). The recognized complexity of the teaching/learning situation can more effectively be understood by using or including a qualitative design. Ethnographic designs may include strategies to elicit data that accurately represent the world view of the participants being studied. The strategies used in the current study are empirical and naturalistic, and use an ethnographic, holistic, and eclectic approach (Goetz & LeCompte, 1984).

The first author was a participant observer (Spradley, 1980) in two early childhood settings during regularly scheduled free play. In participant observation, the researcher "observes what people do, listens to what they say, and participates in their activities whenever possible" (Stainback & Stainback, 1988, p.48). According to Spradley (1980), ethnographers do not merely make observations, they also participate. Spradley promotes the idea that participation allows researchers to experience activities directly, to get the feel of what events are like, and to record their own perceptions. At the same time, Spradley recognizes that an ethnographer can hardly ever become a complete participant in a social situation. By participating in the range of teacher roles in play--including stage manager, mediator, player, scribe, assessor and communicator, and planner (Jones & Reynolds, 1992)--the teacher's role in sociodramatic play was expected to be better understood. During this study, 57 hours were spent in one classroom and 27 hours in another classroom, meetings were held with teaching staff on six separate occasions, and 13 hours of formal interviews were recorded. All participant observations occurred over a time span of 8 months.

## Setting and Participants

Two Head Start classrooms in a rural county in Western New York were selected as a convenience sample for this study. Human subjects review was completed at the university level and all teachers consented to participate in this study. All children and their parents, except for one, consented to participate. Head Start, the largest federal early childhood program, serves a large number of preschool children from lower SES backgrounds. Most Head Start teachers have only entry-level training. The participating teachers in this study were at level II (entry-level) of early childhood professional development as defined by the National Association for the Education of Young Children (Willer, 1994), having completed either the CDA credential, Associate degree, or an early childhood certificate program. Many Head Start teachers and teaching assistants have received on the job early childhood training through the Child Development Associate (CDA) program, earning the CDA credential. Head Start has traditionally held a strong commitment to on-going in-service training for all staff, even after credentials have been earned. More specifically, of the four teachers in this study, two had completed the CDA credential while employed as Head Start teaching assistants. The other two had completed their Associate of Applied Science (A.A.S.) degree in Human Services with a concentration in early childhood, which included completion of an Early Childhood Certificate (a 30 credit credential) from the local community college. These four individuals were representative of Head Start teaching staff in this area.

The first classroom (classroom A) had seventeen 4 year old children, 8 girls and 9 boys. Nine children were European American (4 girls, 5 boys); five were Hispanic (2 girls, 3 boys); and three were African American (2 girls, 1 boy). Three of the seventeen children were in foster care, two lived with grandparents, one lived with a single father, nine lived with single mothers, and two lived with mothers and step-fathers. One child, reported to be living with just her mother, had daily contact with both of her parents. None of the children lived with both biological parents. This classroom was a full-day, year-round classroom.

The second classroom (classroom B) was a half-day afternoon program meeting four days each week, Monday-Thursday. The classroom staff shared the classroom with a morning team. There were 18 children enrolled in the class including 15 who were enrolled for the duration of the study. Fourteen of these children were participants including 9 children who were European American (5 girls and 4 boys) and 5 who were African American (2 girls and 3 boys). Half of the children lived with a single mother, one lived with her grandmother, and the other six lived with both parents.

## Data Collection

*Classroom observations.* At first, classroom observations were conducted to measure the level of sociodramatic play and the level of teacher involvement in the play. For the first observations, recordings were done with field notes and a small audio tape recorder. In addition, each session was videotaped. Initially, observations were focused on sociodramatic play. Then the focus shifted to the role of the adult, including the researcher's, in play.

*Smilansky Scale.* The Smilansky Scale for Evaluation of Dramatic and Sociodramatic Play (Smilansky & Shefatya, 1990) was used to assess the quality of identified play episodes. Using the six play elements (see Table

**Table 9.1.  Six Elements of Play According to the Smilansky Scale**

Dramatic Play

| | |
|---|---|
| 1. Takes on a role | The child transforms into something or someone that he or she is not during play |
| 2. Makes believe with objects | The child pretends objects are something they aren't during play |
| 3. Makes believe with actions or situations | The child pretends he or she is in a situation that isn't really happening during play |
| 4. Persistence | The child begins to play the same game for at least five minutes |

Sociodramatic play (1-4 plus 5-6)

| | |
|---|---|
| 5. Interaction | The child is playing with another person and collaborating with him or her |
| 6. Verbalization | The child is using words to add meaning and context to the play |

9.1), 22 five-minute segments of play, selected because they were identified as episodes of dramatic play, were assessed using the Scale.

The Smilansky Scale is a criterion-referenced assessment tool that has been established as reliable and valid in structured research settings and to be effective for diagnosing play behavior in non-structured settings as well. High inter-rater reliability has been established in both the Hebrew and English versions (Smilansky & Shefatya, 1990).

During the observations, all six of the criteria were rated based on a scale from 0–3. Zero on the scale was given to the criteria that were not present at all during the five minute play interval. A score of one was given to the criteria that were present during the play, but to a limited degree. For instance, the child demonstrates the criterion once or twice during play. A score of two was given to the criteria if the element was present during the play to a moderate degree; i.e., the criterion was present in the play and seen more than twice, but was not consistent throughout the five minute interval. A score of three was given to the criteria if the element was consistent and seen many times during the five minute interval. Once each episode was rated, the scores were added together and then divided by three to get the average. The average produced one overall play quality score. The higher the score, the higher quality aspects were shown within the play episode.

*Interviews.* Formal and informal interviews occurred throughout the study with the teachers and teacher-aides focusing on the research questions listed previously. Formal interviews took place away from the children. Informal interviews, those opportunities for additional conversations, occurred with the teachers occasionally. Thirteen hours of interviews (seven with staff

from classroom A and six from classroom B) were audio-recorded and transcribed.

*Questionnaires and surveys.* The Teacher Belief and Instructional Activities Scale, Preschool Version (Hart et al., 1990) was administered to the
teaching staff. This scale is used to establish the consistency between teacher
beliefs, specifically relating to developmentally appropriate practices, and
their classroom practice. Data from the Scale also provided further background information about the participants.

*Memos.* Reflection was an important part of reviewing field notes and
tapes. Additional notes in the form of memos (Strauss & Corbin, 1990) were
kept throughout the process as relevant themes began to emerge. These were
used to assist in the explanation of phenomena observed.


## Validity Considerations

Maxwell (1992) considers descriptive, interpretive, and theoretical validity
to be appropriate validity considerations for most qualitative research. To
increase descriptive validity, the process of documentation included video-
taping, audio taping, field notes, and memos to record observations instantly
or almost instantly and relied as little as possible on memory of events.
Methodological triangulation was used to address interpretive validity. As
described previously, multiple methods of data collection were administered
to increase accuracy in interpretation. In addition, a dense amount of data was
collected to allow multiple opportunities at capturing trends through multiple
observation opportunities. Theoretical validity was established by embedding
the research questions for this study on the six well grounded elements that
characterize dramatic and sociodramatic play (Smilansky & Shefatya, 1990),
and by the use of two established and published criterion instruments (Smilansky & Shefatya, 1990; Hart et al., 1990) of which validity and reliability in
similar contexts have been well established.

Inter-observer reliability was established to reduce threats to internal validity using strategies recommended by Goetz and LeCompte (1984). First,
data were recorded mechanically to reduce the dependence of the observer on
writing. Second, verbatim accounts of interviews (low-inference descriptors)
with the key participants and of many classroom play episodes were recorded.
Third, peer examination was accomplished by corroboration with two early
childhood colleagues, one doctoral student and one assistant professor. Both
colleagues examined samples of videotaped play episodes and checked tran-
scriptions for accuracy, adding increased reflection and reliability to data
interpretation.

## RESULTS

### The Teachers

In classroom A, Alice was the head teacher and Barbara the assistant teacher (all names are pseudonyms). This was a full-day, year round classroom. In classroom B, a half-day afternoon program, Judy was the head teacher and Karen the assistant teacher. The Teacher Belief and Instructional Activities Scale (Hart et al., 1990) was administered to them, indicating that all four held beliefs consistent with the philosophy of developmentally appropriate practices (Bredekamp & Copple, 1997) including agreement on the importance of children's participation in dramatic play. (Please note the use of the term "dramatic play" here is consistent with the instrumentation used.)

Alice had completed her CDA credential as an assistant teacher several years earlier. At the time of the study, she was one of the most experienced teachers working in this Head Start program, in her eighth year. She was selected for the first full-day classroom because of her experience and high regard by the program administrators.

Alice was perceived by the researcher as a warm and nurturing person who almost always smiled. She frequently greeted children with hugs. During free play time, when not preparing materials, cleaning or conversing with other adults, she positioned herself on her knees in strategic locations to be near groups of children. Her chosen position placed her at the children's eye level where interactions were frequent.

After initial observations in classroom A, it became evident that Alice was the anchor, the stable presence in this classroom. Her relationships with the children were especially close. The nature of this full-day classroom led to the composition of this class that included many children with social-emotional and developmental needs. To be eligible for this classroom, parents had to meet the income guidelines and to be working or in school full-time. In fact, most of the parents had been working or in school full-time since their children were born. Most of these children had been in multiple settings for child care, as many as fifteen or more during fewer than five years of life. This surfaced as being particularly critical in recognizing the importance of Alice's "anchor" role.

Barbara was the teaching assistant in classroom A. Barbara had a background typical of many Head Start staff, in that she had been a Head Start parent before continuing her education and becoming a staff member. Through her initial contact with the program as a parent volunteer, Barbara decided to enroll in the local community college. At the time of the study, Barbara was in her second year. Although her A.A.S. credential exceeded Alice's CDA, Barbara remained the assistant to Alice's strong presence, looking up to Alice for leadership. During free play time, Barbara assumed most of the responsibility for cleaning up after breakfast and for supervising brushing teeth, custodial and maintenance activities. She would interact with children while doing these activities, but only positioned herself to really focus on the children and their activities when those tasks were done.

Judy was the head teacher in classroom B. She was in her second year at Head Start and also was a former Head Start parent with an A.A.S. degree. Her presence was that of a calm, warm and nurturing adult, nearly always with a smile and a twinkle in her eye. Although she wouldn't often enter into children's play, her interactions with the children were playful. This often occurred during clean-up times. Judy definitely valued children's free play and allowed long, uninterrupted time for play every afternoon. Her responses to the children's play were often very supportive and seemed intuitive. That is, she was not able to explain reasons for her methods or the importance of supporting their play other than knowing that it was beneficial.

Karen was the assistant teacher in classroom B. She was in her fifth year at Head Start. Karen had earned her CDA credential. She and Judy worked as a strong team, functioning more as co-teachers than teacher and assistant. This was their second year working together. Karen's presence was very calm, nurturing, gentle and playful. Her tone of voice was quiet and respectful, giving individual children her undivided attention, with sustained eye contact at their level. She was thoughtful, and the most reflective, in her responses to children. She often challenged them, in a playful way, to think and solve problems on their own.

## Participant Observer

The participant observer role within the classroom varied during the course of the study. It was easier to become more integrated into classroom A than classroom B, mostly due to logistics of time and schedule. In both classrooms, I (I refers to the first author who was responsible for all data collection) was eager to implement teacher roles as recommended by Smilansky and Shefatya (1990) and others (e.g., Jones & Reynolds, 1992; Monighan-Nourot, Scales, VanHoorn, & Almy, 1987; Paley, 1984). I intended to become directly involved in children's sociodramatic play, though this was new to me. Like many early childhood teachers, I had not focused my attention on sociodramatic play during my fifteen years teaching young children. My involvement within children's play had been more intuitive than intentional, always as the head teacher with responsibility to oversee the entire classroom. I became familiar with both classrooms by taking my lead from the children. In classroom A, I was quickly incorporated into play episodes by the children. I was increasingly aware of the number of administrative and other demands placed on teaching staff, even more than when I was in the classroom less than a decade earlier. These demands make it very difficult for the classroom teachers to provide sustained attention to specific play episodes.

During the study, recommendations drawn from the studies of Smilansky and Shefatya (1990) were used to provide children with enriching experiences and evocative materials. For example, after a few weeks, I met with Alice and Barbara to plan for a specific dramatic play area: the pet shop. This was based upon the children's interest in animals. I arranged for a visit from a pet store owner and a real dog. I introduced props to inspire pretend play to care for pets. Later we planned a clinic theme and I encouraged the teachers to arrange for the children to visit the nurses in their building. These were meaningful and comprehensible experiences intended to be supplemented by the adults' involvement in the play (Smilansky & Shefatya, 1990). We also worked together to address other aspects of the classroom such as strategies for transitions and clean-up and assigning clean-up and maintenance tasks to volunteers in order to free the teachers for more active interaction with children's play.

As I became more familiar to the children in both classrooms, I assumed new teacher roles to better understand and support children's pretend play, such as deliberately talking with them about their play and joining in as a player. I also wrote stories and drew pictures of their play, particularly of their block structures. I tried to be intentional in my interactions that I had with the children's play in both settings, incorporating reflection throughout. Reviewing the videotapes was particularly helpful in identifying and reflecting on specific examples of adult involvement with children, particularly in and for their play.

## Other Classroom Adults

There were many other adults who were present in the classrooms, with varied roles. The sheer number of adults became an interest and concern as the study proceeded. These included foster grandparents, therapists, volunteers, special education itinerant teachers, college students, other Head Start staff, and one-on-one aides for one child. Interestingly, almost no parents were present during the study. Some of these adults performed purely custodial duties, particularly tidying up the classroom. Others became engaged in children's activities, including play.

## Sociodramatic Play

At the beginning of the study, only very low level dramatic play episodes, as defined by the Smilansky Scale, were evident, not actual sociodramatic play, as illustrated below (Example 1) in an interaction between two children playing at the sand table. This was typical of most of the observed episodes of dramatic play, with only one child very briefly making believe.

**Example 1.   Low Levels of Dramatic Play between Child 1 and Child 2**
Child 1          I'm making some cornbread
Child 2          It's sand
Researcher    He's pretending
(Child 1 agree with the researcher and described the sugar he was adding)
(Child 1 continued to cook and serve and eat for about three minutes interacting
with the researcher. Child 2 gave sand to the researcher but never joined in play
with Child 1)

Throughout the study, in classroom A there was no evidence of any sociodramatic play during 15 of the 32 visits. In classroom B, there were frequent episodes of dramatic play, children pretending alone, with a few episodes of sociodramatic play. Using the Smilansky Scale for Evaluation of Dramatic and Sociodramatic Play (Smilansky & Shefatya, 1990), the quality of 22 five-minute segments of recorded play was assessed and found to be low quality and limited. This was due especially to limited persistence in role play with a partner, often with only one of the other components. The longest and most involved play episodes occurred after the introduction of brand new materials and from direct adult involvement.

For instance, props were added to support a pet shop theme to supplement the dramatic play area in classroom A in January. These included stuffed animals, a pet food dish, books about pets, and unstructured loose parts such as rubber gaskets, bottle caps and empty containers. Bottle caps and gaskets became food for stuffed dogs. Two children spent nearly an hour feeding a stuffed dog, the longest example of children sustained in play together observed during the study.

A few weeks later, Alice was sitting near three of the boys who had spread out a cloth. Alice offered prompts that initiated a picnic play episode as shown below (Example 2).

**Example 2.   Teacher's Role in Sociodramatic Play**
Teacher    What kind of food are we going to eat on our picnic? Can you think of
                something you want to eat?
(Two children approach)
Teacher    Crystal, what are you having on our picnic? Can you make me
                something? What are going to make me?
Child 1    I'm pretty hungry.

(The teacher continued to narrate and converse with the two children as the children pretended to eat at this picnic for six minutes.

The importance of Alice's presence and engagement to sustain this play became clear when the special education coordinator entered the room to ask her a question. He crouched down to where Alice was sitting. This adult exchange lasted less than one minute, during which time interaction between the children stopped. The pretend picnic that was occurring between teacher and children disengaged after this brief interruption even though Alice didn't even move.

## Teacher Roles during Free Play

Had their training prepared them to be successful play facilitators? None of the teachers felt they had received specific preparation for sociodramatic play. Alice suggested that she learned more about sociodramatic play just from all the years of teaching, especially bringing things in to the classroom and seeing how the children use different materials. Judy suggested that her best preparation for sociodramatic play came from parenting.

Focusing particularly on any episodes of pretend play during free play time, I observed that the teachers were not significantly involved. They were, however, always busy. The following eight categories of teacher roles were observed, often occurring simultaneously: maintaining safety and responding to emergencies; performing maintenance and custodial duties; creating the classroom atmosphere; preparing and supervising creative activities; observing and watching; being directly involved with adults such as parents and volunteers; having direct interaction with children, and administrative activities. Their administrative activities included completing paper work, attending meetings, and fulfilling other program demands (for instance, arranging for substitutes and making and answering telephone calls). Teachers were directly involved with children in several ways: enforcing rules; mediating conflicts; assisting in turn-taking; comforting; including children in routines; assisting children with materials, equipment or clothing; talking with children; and finally, playing with children. Self-reflection memos informed the above observations. A memo written in April reflected that

> You can't look at sociodramatic play in isolation. This means that things like room arrangement and routines (including transitions) all impact the socio-dramatic play possibilities. The teacher's role is impacted greatly by all the demands which are placed on her. She prioritizes—almost in a triage-style.

The major focus in both classrooms was *safety*. Teachers followed high activity and positioned themselves to prevent potential danger. *Maintenance and custodial duties*, particularly with routines during and following mealtimes (cleaning tables and floors, putting away food, hand washing and tooth brushing) took a lot of time. Although there are opportunities for a teacher to relate to children during these necessary (and important) times, opportunities for richer interactions and for teachers to engage directly in children's meaningful play activities were minimal. This was particularly true for classroom B where the sinks were outside of the classroom. Yet, in each classroom, teachers were successful in creating a classroom atmosphere that was conducive to play and creative activities. When sociodramatic play did occur, it was enhanced by two factors present in both classrooms: allowing *free use of materials* and providing *extensive time for free play*, at least an hour every day.

One morning, after playing the game Candyland with the foster Grandpa, Andrea and Jessica gathered all of the special picture cards from the game and placed them in a small purse. As they walked across the room to the area that had been set up to be a store, Jessica stopped to say, "I'm playin' go down to the movie with my friend Andrea!" and she invited me to join them. The girls sat at a desk where the toy cash register had been placed, holding the purse filled with the Candyland cards. Andrea took out a card, placed it in the drawer of the cash register, turned the handle (so pictures moved). Andrea then explained how I could see a movie and directed me to a card to place in the drawer. As we watched, she said, "This is a sad one." The cash register was being used as a VCR, with the Candyland cards representing the cassettes.

In a memo written following this episode I wrote about,

> the importance for these children to have permission to use materials in creative ways. Many people wouldn't want to risk losing parts of a game. I'm not sure I would have! This whole episode was inspired by using the cards from Candyland in a totally different way.

Fulfilling the teacher's role of "stage manager" (Jones & Reynolds, 1997), I began to regularly bring things into the classroom that I thought the children might use creatively as props for make-believe, mostly found materials. There was no preconceived idea of how these materials would be used. Having observed how many ways the gaskets and bottle caps were freely used (such as pet food and coins), I wrote in a memo,

> One point, as simple as it may sound, is for teachers to not have preconceived ideas about the use of materials in the environment and to encourage children's

creative use of things. I continue to see the value in stuff—particularly stuff we have no known use for.

The teachers in both classrooms were intentional in planning and supervising creative art activities and sensory experiences. During free play time, these were the activities most often directly supervised by the teachers. On the contrary, permanent areas in the classroom, including the dramatic play and block areas, were not attended to specifically by the teachers on a daily basis.

Because verbal make-believe with regard to actions and situations and verbal communication are two of the six elements in good sociodramatic play (Smilansky & Shefatya, 1990), and because of the importance of vocabulary development, direct talk between teachers and children during play became a focus of the study. In high quality play, children use oral language by engaging in conversations, expanding vocabulary, presenting play scenarios and providing audiences for one another. They test predictions, essential later to the process of reading, as they develop oral scripts together (Fromberg, 2002). But these children were rarely using language this way in their play.

I became intentional in providing children with vocabulary to support their activity. For instance, when the dramatic play area had a clinic theme, I deliberately used the terms otoscope and stethoscope to describe those props that had been added. Another use of language was to narrate the children's play. Such narration often served to clarify the roles children were playing as new players joined the play. Through reviewing transcripts, other examples of less productive adult language emerged. In a memo I wrote,

> Be more patient and observe a lot—so language can relate more specifically to what child is doing. Use information from observing to formulate meaningful questions—or statements—regarding the children's activities.

Adult play with children within sociodramatic play occurred very rarely and when it did, hardly lasted more than a few minutes. Yet the times when adults were involved were the times when the play was most likely to be sustained and to be richer in quality. Some of the longest play episodes over the course of the study were with adults, but not the teaching staff. As stated above, the teachers rarely had the opportunity (or took the opportunity) to become involved in children's play. When they did, they were very often interrupted, as described during the picnic play episode in Example 2. It became evident that even brief interruptions of this sort seriously disrupted what were very fragile play situations.

The one adult who entered children's play with undivided attention was the foster Grandpa who was present in classroom A on Fridays. Once he sat in the play car in the play yard, driving with children for most of the hour. During the play, he offered suggestions for destinations to add to the children's ideas. He also played in the clinic, following the children's role suggestions. One morning, as he left for a coffee break, he told me that while playing with the children he had "delivered" three babies that morning!

As a participant observer in this study, I was involved in longer play episodes and was able to devote my attention to sustaining the play. With this attention, children's play did increase in quality through greater complexity of play and increased language use, particularly as I was able to scaffold their play by modeling language, pretending, problem solving and including more players.

## Teacher Roles and Responsibilities Related to Play

In addition to the roles that were directly observed during free play, the teachers had many other roles and responsibilities related to play. Those that most directly supported the enhancement of sociodramatic play were *planning and preparing the classroom environment*. Both classrooms were organized into areas or centers including designated areas for creative art, blocks, dramatic play, sensory experiences, books, manipulatives, and two computers in each room. Children's cubbies and space for circle time also existed. The basic design arrangement in both classrooms was completed at the beginning of the school year. There were few opportunities for the staff to attend to planning and arranging the classroom environment during their paid working hours. Alice and Barbara either came to school early or stayed late on the occasions when the room was rearranged.

Although Judy and Karen were interested in arranging the classroom to support their plans for children's play, they faced additional challenges because the classroom was shared with a morning class and staff. There were some philosophical differences between the two teams; the morning staff was much more rigid in their expectation of how materials were to be used by children. When Judy wanted to do a transportation unit and begin with many cardboard boxes (to inspire making cars, trains and a bus), the morning staff created a specific train station made from single-use props, saying that the boxes were too messy. In discussing the shared room, both Judy and Karen stated strongly that if they had their own classroom, it would be completely different, with many more opportunities for children's exploration and creativity.

Other challenges were maximizing the opportunities for observation and methods of observation; monitoring of children's movement and safety; and the organization of materials within the classroom. The teachers watched the children carefully but the written observations were limited to activities in which individual children were involved. These were kept in children's permanent records. Closely related to the difference between watching and observing is the difference between following high levels of activity and redirecting children. Teachers watched particularly for children's safety. One of the main ways this was done was to follow the children who were particularly active and perceived as potentially dangerous. A priority became keeping these children busy (with age appropriate activities), but not necessarily with consideration to their individual interests, strengths and/or needs. While focusing on high activity, teachers often missed quiet children whose play experiences could have been enhanced with adult attention.

Finally, materials were not organized in a way that enabled children to know where to access everything and how to put things away. Specific places for props and toys were hardly evident during my observations. Instead, adults in these classrooms were often involved in picking up toys and materials that they placed randomly on shelves and in bins. This may not be the optimal way to support children's play.

## The Children

The children in this study had emotionally, socially, and environmentally challenging backgrounds and circumstances and the primary role of the teacher was to meet their unique and basic needs including their attachment to and relationships with others. Children who have had secure emotional ties with caregivers will be prepared to explore and become involved in more sophisticated play, the type of play necessary for optimal development (Bowlby, 1988; Creasy, Jarvis & Berk, 1998; Kontos & Wilcox-Herzog, 1997) and the lack of such experiences may have impacted the infrequency of sociodramatic play in these children. Many of the children, especially in classroom A, appeared to be seeking emotional ties, primarily with Alice and this nurturing role appeared to supersede her other roles.

## DISCUSSION

### Sociodramatic Play in Each Classroom

There was little sociodramatic play occurring in either classroom. However, all four teachers valued and respected children and their play and were playful themselves in their interactions with children. Their beliefs were consistent with developmentally appropriate practice as was reflected in the Teacher

Belief Scale (Charlesworth, et al., 1993; Hart, et al., 1990). Children benefit-ted from being allowed at least an hour for free play every day (Christie & Wardle, 1992; Paley, 1984; Tegano & Burdette, 1991; Wien, 1996). These four teachers were very flexible in their expectations of how children could use materials within the classroom.

## Teacher Involvement in Children's Sociodramatic Play

Despite multiple demands on their time, the teachers were able to support play to some extent. This was made possible through long free play times, a respectful atmosphere that was conducive to using materials freely and creatively, and occasionally giving children undivided attention while they played. The three main areas previously described as challenges in the sup-port of sociodramatic play—use of observation, focus on very active children and their safety, and organization of materials could be changed to enhance teacher involvement.

Watching for children to be safe is vital for good care. Observing children to determine their developmental strengths and needs also is critical for qual-ity education. Observation includes watching, but also involves listening and then reflecting on the meaning of what has been observed (Jablon, Dombro & Dichtelmiller, 2007). As Jones (1999) says, "observing *is* teaching" (p. 16). Trained observers of children in play recognize opportunities to offer chal-lenges as they continue to grow, thus using observation for program planning. Additional training in observational assessment and related skills might have helped these teachers to maximize their observational opportunities.

The management of the most active children, while still engaging the less active and quieter children, and the organization of the environment to allow physical play, without major safety risk, may be two areas that need to be addressed in pre-service and in-service training.

Restoring order to provide children with opportunities for educational ex-periences is deliberate and is a form of learning and support (Berk & Winsler, 1995). It is at a higher intellectual level than just putting away toys. Truly restoring order helps to clarify the figure-ground relationship in the environ-ment (Jones & Reynolds, 1992) making possibilities clear to children. For instance, in the dramatic play area, props should be presented in a logical order, separated from each other in a way that will make sense to the children. If the classrooms themselves were organized more intentionally as learning environments, more opportunities for higher quality play may have been realized. When tidying the play areas includes putting toys and materials in clearly designated spaces, the learning environment is then prepared for its next use by the children.

## Barriers to Sociodramatic Play and Teacher Involvement

The demands on the teachers were many and frequently required them to attend to tasks that were not directly supporting children's play. The demands limited their ability to interact with the children and created barriers that impeded sociodramatic play opportunities. For the full intellectual benefits of sociodramatic play, verbal interaction with adults needs to be deliberate and articulate. Bennett et al. (1997) described a mismatch between teacher assumptions and outcomes, particularly in situations where the children's learning through play is not supported by the appropriate language to assist concept formation and cognitive processes.

In considering teacher education, both pre-service and in-service training need to be considered. Knowledge and skills about play can be a primary focus or embedded in other educational and developmental training. Early childhood textbooks and websites often contain professional jargon such as the use of the terms "support", "facilitate", or "enhance" play. The meaning of these words must be defined and made explicit. Other terms and concepts such as a "prepared environment" also may not be understood by pre-service teachers. In addition to understanding the terminology associated with play, pre-service teachers need to be taught specific skills and strategies. Many of the useful resources that are available to teachers for the enhancement of sociodramatic play do not appear to be used by practicing teachers (e.g., Berk, 2001; Bodrova & Leong, 2003; Cooper & Dever, 2001; Jones & Reynolds, 1992; Owocki, 1999; Reynolds & Jones, 1997; Singer, Golinkoff & Hirsch-Pasek, 2006).

## SUGGESTIONS FOR PRESCHOOL TEACHER TRAINING

Some practical ideas emerged from this study in the form of recommendations for early childhood teachers (see Table 9.2). Although there are often program requirements and constraints that may limit individual teacher's autonomy, most early childhood classroom teachers should have the flexibility to apply the following suggestions. Support from program administrators could guarantee their implementation.

## Future Directions

It is impossible to consider sociodramatic play in isolation without considering the impact of teaching roles, teacher-child factors, environment, and other factors. In order to promote changes within this context, mentor teachers might

**Table 9.2.    Recommendations to Increase Sociodramatic Play Opportunities**

- Extend play time to an hour or more.
- Allow free use of classroom materials and the opportunity to combine different materials during play.
- Divide classroom adult responsibilities, placing a high priority on one teacher sustaining play.
- Observe for opportunities to support learning and development through play.
- Enrich or complicate children's play. This may be through adding props, providing experiences or entering into play.
- Avoid interruptions to play. Plan an alternative way for teachers to receive messages when they are engaged with children.
- Provide props that will inspire specific sociodramatic play themes.
- Provide props with no predetermined use (loose parts and found materials) as well as theme-specific props.

work within the classroom, alongside the teachers, to model our recommendations, including preparation of the classroom environment and use of supportive materials. The development of model play-based classrooms in a variety of early childhood programs, and resource centers with play materials and play related library resources for lending to teachers, would provide additional support.

Teachers also should be prepared to defend the importance of play for children's learning, social skills and general development. Teachers may need further training to be able to articulate to parents, administrators and others the value of play experiences they are providing in preschool settings. By learning to become reflective about the work they do with children, teachers can provide evidence when they defend professional decisions such as allowing a long time for play and requesting additional funding and resources.

Many societal changes have impacted children's lives and perceptions of early childhood education. Most notable is the No Child Left Behind legislation. This legislation has emphasized content standards, assessments, and accountability, resulting in more teacher-directed, prepared curriculum models, focusing on academic achievement with fewer and fewer opportunities for children to play (Stipek, 2006). Play is endangered in Head Start as programs are under increased pressure to demonstrate children's progress in narrowly defined ways. Play experts are concerned that play appears to be disappearing from children's lives (e.g., Frost, 2007; Isenberg & Quisenberry, 2002; Zigler & Bishop-Josef, 2006). Never has it been more important to continue research and teacher training that demonstrates the importance of sociodramatic play, to support advocacy efforts to maintain and increase sociodramatic play opportunities for young children, and to give teachers the training they need to implement evidence-based best practices in child play.

# REFERENCES

Ayers, W. (1989). *The good preschool teacher.* New York: Teachers College Press.

Benham, N., Miller, T. & Kontos, S. (1988). Pinpointing staff training needs in child care centers. *Young Children, 43*(4), 9–16.

Bennett, N., Wood, L. & Rogers, S. (1997). *Teaching through play: Teachers thinking and classroom practice.* Philadelphia, PA: Open University Press.

Bergen, D. (Ed.). (1988). *Play as a medium for learning and development.* Portsmouth, NH: Heinemann Educational Books.

Bergen, D. (2002). The role of pretend play in children's cognitive development. *Early Childhood Research & Practice, 4*(1). Retrieved http://ecrp.uiuc.edu/v4n1/bergen.html.

Berk, L. E. (2001). *Awakening children's minds: How parents and teachers can make a difference.* New York: Oxford University Press.

Berk, L. E. & Winsler, A. (1995). *Scaffolding children's learning: Vygotsky and early childhood education.* Washington, DC: NAEYC.

Berke, J. E. (1996). *The effect of prenatal and postnatal cigarette smoke exposure on the developmental readiness of preschool children.* Unpublished doctoral dissertation, State University of New York at Buffalo.

Bodrova, E. & Leong, D. J. (2003). Chopsticks and counting chips. *Young Children, 58*(3), 10–17.

Bowlby, J. (1988). *A secure base: Parent-child attachment and healthy human development.* New York: Basic Books.

Bredekamp, S. & Copple, C. (Eds.). (1997). *Developmentally appropriate practice in early childhood programs.* Washington, DC: NAEYC.

Charlesworth, R., Hart, C. H., Burts, D. C., Thomasson, R. H., Mosley, J., Fleege, P. O. (1993). Measuring the developmental appropriateness of kindergarten teachers' beliefs and practices. *Early Childhood Research Quarterly, 8,* 255–276.

Children's Defense Fund. (2005). *The state of America's children 2005.* Washington, DC: Children's Defense Fund.

Christie, J. F. & Wardle, F. (1992). How much time is needed for play? *Young Children, 47*(3), 28–32.

Cooper, J. L. & Dever, M. T. (2001). Sociodramatic play as a vehicle for curriculum integration in first grade. *Young Children, 56*(3), 58–63.

Creasy, G. L., Jarvis, P.A., & Berk, L. (1998). Play and social competence. In O.N. Saracho & B. Spodek (Eds.), *Multiple perspectives on play in early childhood education* (pp. 116–143). Albany, NY: State University of New York Press.

Erikson, E. H. (1950/1963). *Childhood and Society.* New York: W. W. Norton.

Fein, G. & Rivkin, M. (Eds.) (1986). *The young child at play: Reviews of Research* (Vol. 4). Washington, DC: NAEYC.

Fromberg, D. (2002). *Play and meaning in early childhood education.* Boston, MA: Allyn & Bacon.

Frost, J. L. (2007). The changing culture of childhood: A perfect storm. *Childhood Education, 83*(4), 225–230.

Goetz, J. P. & LeCompte, M. D. (1984). *Ethnography and qualitative design in educational research.* San Diego, CA: Academic Press.

Hart, C., Burts, D., Charlesworth, R., Fleege, P., Ickes, M. & Durland, M. (1990). *Teacher beliefs scale: Preschool version.* Baton Rouge, LA: Louisiana State University.

Isaacs, S. (1933/1967). *Social development in young children.* London: Lowe & Brydone.

Isenberg, J. & Quisenberry, N. L. (2002). Play: Essential for all children: A position paper of the Association for Childhood Education International. *Childhood Education, 79*(1), 33–39.

Jablon, J. R., Dombro, A. L., & Dichtelmiller, M. L. (2007). *The power of observation for birth through eight.* Washington, DC: Teaching Strategies.

Jones, E. (1999). An emergent curriculum expert offers this afterthought. *Young Children, 54*(4), 16.

Jones, E. & Reynolds, G. (1992). *The play's the thing: Teachers' roles in children's play.* New York: Teachers College Press.

Kemple, K. M. (1996). Teachers' beliefs and reported practices concerning sociodramatic play. *Journal of Early Childhood Teacher Education, 17*(2). 19–31.

Klugman, E. (1995). Adding the play dimension to teacher education: One model. In E. Klugman (Ed.), *Play, policy & practice* (pp. 71–85). St. Paul, MN: Redleaf Press.

Klugman, E. & Smilansky, S. (Eds.). (1990). Where do we go from here? In E. Klugman & S. Smilansky (Eds.), *Children's play and learning: Perspectives and policy implications.* New York: Teachers College Press.

Kontos, S. (1999). Preschool teachers' talk, roles, and activity settings during free play: why are they so important? *Early Childhood Research Quarterly, 52*(2), 4–12.

Kontos, S. & Wilcox-Herzog, A. (1997). Teachers' interactions with children: Why are they so important? *Young Children, 52*(2), 4–12.

Maxwell, J. A. (1992). Understanding validity in qualitative research. *Harvard Educational Review, 62*, 279–300.

Monighan-Nourot, P., Scales, B., VanHoorn, J., & Almy, M. (1987). *Looking at children's play: A bridge between theory and practice.* New York: Teachers College Press.

Owocki, G. (1999). *Literacy through play.* Portsmouth, NH: Heinemann.

Paley, V. G. (1984). *Boys and girls.* Chicago, IL: The University of Chicago Press.

Parten, M. D. (1932). Social participation among preschool children. *Journal of Abnormal and Social Psychology, 27*, 243–269.

Piaget, J. (1962). *Play, dreams and imitation in childhood.* New York: W.W. Norton & Company.

Powell, D. R. & Dunn, L. (1990). Non-baccalaureate teacher education in early childhood education. In B. Spodek & O. Saracho (Eds.), *Early childhood teacher preparation* (pp. 45–66). New York: Teachers College Press.

Read, K. (1971). *The nursery school: A human relationships laboratory.* Philadelphia: W. B. Saunders.

Reynolds, G. & Jones, E. (1997). *Master players: Learning from children at play.* New York: Teachers College Press.

Roskos, K. & Neuman, S. B. (1993). Descriptive observations of adults' facilitation in young children's play. *Early Childhood Research Quarterly, 8,* 77–97.

Shefatya, L. (1995). The assessment of dramatic and sociodramatic play: goals, tools, criteria, and conceptual frameworks. In E. Klugman (Ed.), *Play, policy & practice* (pp. 97–116). St. Paul, MN: Redleaf Press.

Silin, J. G. (1987). The early childhood educator's knowledge base: A reconsideration. In L. Katz (Ed.), *Current topics in early childhood education, Volume VII* (pp. 17–31). Norwood, NJ: Ablex.

Singer, J. (1973). *The child's world of make-believe.* New York: Academic Press.

Singer, D., Golinkoff, R., & Hirsch-Pasek, K. (2006). *Play = Learning: How play motivates and enhances children's cognitive and social-emotional growth.* New York: Oxford University Press.

Smilansky, S. (1968). *The effects of sociodramatic play on disadvantaged preschool children.* New York: John Wiley & Sons.

Smilansky, S. & Shefatya, L. (1990). *Facilitating play: A medium for promoting cognitive, socio-emotional and academic development in young children.* Gaithersburg, MD: Psychosocial & Educational Publications.

Spradley, J. P. (1980). *Participant observation.* New York: Holt, Rinehart & Winston.

Stainback, S. & Stainback, W. (1988). *Understanding and conducting qualitative research.* Dubuque, IA: Kendall/Hunt.

Stipek, D. (2006). No Child Left Behind comes to preschool. *The Elementary School Journal, 106*(5), 455–465.

Strauss, A. & Corbin, J. (1990). *Basics of qualitative research: grounded theory procedures and techniques.* Thousand Oaks, CA: Sage.

Tegano, D. W. & Burdette, M. P. (1991). Length of activity periods and play behaviors of preschool children. *Journal of Research in Childhood Education, 5,* 93–99.

Trawick-Smith, J. (1998). Why play training works: An integrated model for play intervention. *Journal of Research in Childhood Education, 12,* 117–129.

VanderVen, K., McIntyre, K., Schomburg, R. & Tittnich, E. (1995). Enhancing children's sociodramatic lay through teacher instruction: The play training collaboration. In E. Klugman (Ed.), *Play, policy & practice* (pp. 21–36). St. Paul, MN: Redleaf Press.

Vygotsky, L. S. (1933/1976). Play and its role in the mental development of the child. In J. Bruner, A. Jolly & K. Sylva (Eds.), *Play* (pp. 537–554). New York: Basic Books.

Walsh, D.J., Tobin, J.J., & Graue, M.E. (1993). The interpretive voice: Qualitative research in early childhood education. In B. Spodek (Ed.), *Handbook of research on the education of young children* (pp. 464–476). New York: Macmillan.

Wien, C. A. (1996). Time, work, and developmentally appropriate practice. *Early Childhood Research Quarterly, 11,* 377–403.

Willer, B. (Ed.). (1994). A conceptual framework for early childhood professional development. In J. Johnson & J. B. McCracken (Eds.), *The early childhood career lattice: Perspectives on professional development* (pp. 4–23). Washington, DC: NAEYC.

Zigler, E.F. & Bishop-Josef, S.J. (2006). The cognitive child versus the whole child: Lessons from 40 years of Head Start. In D.G. Singer, R. M. Golinkoff & K. Hirsh-Pasek (Eds.), *Play=learning* (pp.15–35). New York: Oxford University Press.

*Part IV*

# REFLECTIONS ON THE
# NATURE OF PLAY

## Chapter Ten

# Play as Ascending Meaning Revisited: Four Types of Assertive Play

### Thomas S. Henricks

In the academic world, the phenomenon of play tends to be a "floater," one of those vague filaments that comes across a person's field of vision and then, just as mysteriously, passes away. In the brightest of lights, that curious assemblage of lines and dots presents itself to consciousness and can be observed with some clarity. Much more commonly, floaters are merely accompaniments to our way of seeing. We "edit them out" or otherwise incorporate them into our more general approaches to the world. In any case, such shadowy patterns are only curiosities or distractions, idiosyncratic formations that stand between consciousness and the more fundamental matters of our lives.

In other writings, the author (Henricks, 1999; 2006) has argued against this view of play-as-floater. However unusual or mysterious playful experiences seem, play itself should not be seen as some elusive phenomenon that flits across ordinary experience. Even more pointedly, play should not be held up as an activity that is somehow exceptional or "special," something that is set against all other sorts of activity combined. Play is just as ordinary—and just as important—as the other things that people do.

The current essay attempts to provide a general model of play by comparing that activity to three other kinds of activity—ritual, work, and communitas. Play, the author argues, is one of the fundamental (and quite ordinary) modes of human relating. In that context, the first part of the essay describes how play is similar to—and different from—the three other activities mentioned above. To accomplish that end, the author reprises certain elements from his (Henricks, 1999) view of play as "ascending meaning." The second part of the essay confronts the question of whether such a general model can really account for the great variety of theories about play's nature and implications (see Millar, 1968; Ellis, 1973; Levy, 1978; Spariosu, 1989; Sutton-Smith, 1997). Drawing upon the theories of some prominent play theorists, the author presents four different patterns of play—manipulation, dialogue, rebellion, and exploration—and shows how these patterns are characteristic responses to four different kinds of "situations" that players confront. In such ways, this essay revisits and modifies the earlier model.

## DEFINING PLAY BY COMPARING IT TO OTHER KINDS OF ACTIVITY

As indicated above, it is the author's view that researchers must not set play *apart* but rather set it *beside* other kinds of activity as a way of appreciating both what play has in common with these other forms and what makes it different. This project—of re-connecting play to the ordinary matters of the world—may seem a bit like lassoing a butterfly and tying it to a stake in the yard. However, the field of play studies has long enough been marked by what might be called an "ideology of exoticism," in which play is held to be a province unique unto itself. One version of this ideology—the so-called "idealization" of play—has been identified and then criticized by Sutton-Smith & Kelly-Byrne (1984a). In their view, play has too often been idealized as a place of wonder, innocence, and industry—where people can (and will) be their best selves. In that idyllic viewpoint, the play world is a kind of magic circle where burdens are set aside, creativity is indulged, and the imagination runs in thoroughly worthy directions.

For his part, the author has no wish to dispute the proposition that play is one of the great laboratories of human possibility (see Lin & Reifel, 1999) where wonderful experiences routinely are produced. Historically, play has indeed functioned as a reservoir of personal freedom, both the freedom "from" external constraint and consequence and the freedom "to" take on the world in new (and old) ways. Play has long served as a bulwark against the controlling impulses of adults and tyrants of every other description. However, anyone who has inhabited a schoolyard knows that much mischief and misery also occurs under the name of play. Play can exemplify our noblest ideals, but it can also be mean-spirited and morally "bad" (see Pellegrini, 1995). Players themselves may exhibit generous and cooperative qualities: they can also be self-centered and fiercely competitive. Sometimes, they pursue their ambitions in entirely independent ways; sometimes they allow themselves to be "organized" by others. Players bring into being wonderful new things; just as frequently they dissemble and destroy. As Huizinga (1955) explains in the last sentences of *Homo Ludens*, play in the final analysis is not a moral affair. It is an engine that spews effects of many types and must be guided by conscientious souls.

If play is in such ways ordinary—or at least subject to the same infirmities as other activities—how is it to be distinguished from these other patterns? In the author's view, play can be compared profitably to three other patterns of human expression: work, ritual, and communitas. All four patterns—which are identified below—are considered here to be largely voluntary or *willful* forms of action; that is, in every case, actors think about the situations they are in and plan their behaviors accordingly. There are of course other sorts of behavior that are largely adaptive or even involuntary reactions to events that "happen" to us. Behaviors we have very little control over—falling down stairs, sleepwalking, jumping out of the way of a speeding car, psychological compulsions, and other unthinking responses—are not addressed in the current essay. Play and the other three patterns are instead said to be "minded" activities, when people think about how they wish to engage the world.

Notably, all four forms of willful activity are at times expressed as "routine" behaviors (i.e., as elements of everyday living) and at other times are cut away from such routines and developed as distinctive or "bounded" events. Although Huizinga (1955) emphasized how play may be disconnected from ordinary affairs by distinctive settings, rules, clothing, paraphernalia, skills, regimes of time, and so forth, such separating mechanisms are also used by the other three forms of behavior. That is, people commonly put on special clothing, enter circumscribed environments, and adopt distinctive mannerisms when they go to work, attend a church service, or gather at a public festival just as they do when they go off to play. To acknowledge this is to broaden Bateson's (1971) well-known dictum that animals (and humans) typically express to one another that "this" (the world they are about to enter) "is play." Creatures also let one another know when they are about to fight, have sex, back away fearfully, settle down to rest, and so forth. That is, while the author agrees with Bateson that players routinely indicate to one another that they are about to enter a limited, specialized world, he also emphasizes that other activities often get "narrowed" in these same ways.

More problematic is the issue of whether play activities share qualities found in the other three forms of behavior. For example, players commonly exhibit the creativity and entrepreneurial spirit typically associated with workers just as they exhibit the love of excitement and desire for fun that characterize forms of communitas like public festivals, spectator events, and parades. Even more curiously perhaps, play is sometimes "ritualized"; that is, the activity exhibits repetitive or predictable patterns rather than moments of spontaneity and uncertainty that people frequently associate with play. In the author's view then, play is to be identified less by its possession of *entirely* unique traits (separating it from all other activities) than by the distinctive way in which it *combines* traits also found in those other activities. For the same reasons, the author emphasizes that concrete behaviors and events in the world can only be more or less "playful" (as opposed to the other three types) or that some "aspects" of any concrete event may seem playful while other aspects are not.


## PLAY AS ACTIVITY THAT IS BOTH
## TRANSFORMATIVE AND CONSUMMATORY

The author contends that playful behavior is distinguished by a combination of two qualities: transformation and consummation. These qualities, it is argued, are pertinent to all activities commonly considered playful, including puns, riddles, and tongue twisters, sports and games, feats of pleasurable imagination, dramatic improvisation, gambling, artistic and musical creation, teasing, jokes and rhymes, adventures in balance and endurance, and rough-and-tumble behaviors. Such activities are *transformative* in the sense that they represent efforts by people to assert themselves against the elements of the world, to alter those elements, and in so doing to learn about the nature of reality and about their own powers to operate in those settings (see Schwartzman, 1978). Said most directly, play is ultimately a project of comprehension and control.

This way of defining play as a confrontational activity opposes those theories that emphasize play as an act of joining together, cooperating, forming a common identity, and so forth (see Sutton-Smith, 1997: 91–111). All scholars of play, including the current author, know that these themes are tremendously important aspects of human festivity. This author, however, departs from other views in that he defines these ways of entering into transcendent form (that is, giving oneself to or accepting external, unifying patterns) by two other terms: "communitas" and "ritual". In the author's view, to play is to engage the world in a teasing, testing way and to encounter the vicissitudes of experience that accompany such manipulations. Even in a largely cooperative activities—such as square dance or quilting bee—the specially "playful" elements are the various assertive behaviors that result when one tries to discover if he or she can move the body through difficult circumstances, respond assertively to another's jest, "create" a beautiful design from stray pieces of cloth, and so forth. That active component is recognized when we tell another person, "It's your play," and they in turn deal a card, shoot a ball or "bust a move" on a dance floor.

Furthermore, although play (in its more game-like forms) is typically rule-bound or even ritualistic, such regularity is not its essence. After all, most activities conform to rules. To follow a set of rules in a single-minded way is not to "play," or at least not to play in the spirited way that most people associate with that term. Instead, rules are presented in this essay as essentially the vehicles that allow people to focus their confrontations with one another or other objects of their play (see Caillois, 1961). The true spirit of play is the burst of creative expression, the awareness that subjectivity can re-make the world in patterns of its choosing. Following rules is not a distinctively playful act; manipulating, circumventing, or otherwise "tweaking" those rules for one's own pleasure is.

In such ways, the author reorganizes the vision of play that is presented in Huizinga's (1955) classic *Homo Ludens*. Huizinga's own effort was to identify (and revivify) a playful approach to the world against the grim, work-like orientation that he associated with the industrialization and bureaucratization of the nineteenth and early twentieth centuries. However, Huizinga was (for the most part) content to mix play with other activities in what he (1955: 31) called the "play-festival-rite" complex, a pattern of formalized public gathering that was especially prominent in societies of the past. Although the current author acknowledges that these forms continue to be linked in important ways, he seeks to separate them analytically in this essay as a way of distilling what is essential to play.

Although play emphasizes transformative behavior, play is not the only one of the four forms to do so. Like Marx's (1964; 1999) idealized pre-capitalist laborer, people at "work" manipulate material (and symbolic) forms and by that process discover themselves in those "mirrors" of their creation. They are driven forward in this process by ideas about what is needed in the world; in that sense, reality is re-cast in human terms. However, unlike play, work is *instrumental* in character. Workers juggle means and ends that are distant to one another; the experience of the process is less important than the product that arises. For such reasons, workers focus on the future; frequently unpleasant activities are undertaken for rewards to come. Significantly, work—as in Marx's view—is not to be understood simply as economic activity that (in the modern version of that idea) people get "paid" for. Much more generally, people "work" when they mow the lawn, wash dishes, exercise on treadmill, drive their kids to soccer games, and so forth.

In sharp contrast, players tend to operate in the present, or more precisely, inside the boundaries of space and time that mark the play occasion. To such degrees, play is *consummatory* rather than instrumental; Players are preoccupied with the quality of their experiences in such events. Even when they are pushing themselves ahead in ways that are not particularly enjoyable, they are focusing primarily on goals that lie within the event itself (as in the case of games). Success or satisfaction is judged in those terms. In other words, although play-like activities may be difficult to distinguish at a distance from work-like activities (for example, whether one is playing or working when she "practices" the piano), play is separated from work by the fact that the principal *rationale* for play is found inside the event itself. In other words, players celebrate the moment; the only thing that matters to players is what they are doing with one another *now*. This is the meaning of "consummation" that applies here: one is fulfilled or completed within the boundaries of the event.

Quite different are the two patterns of *conformitive* (rather than transformative) behavior: ritual and communitas. In both these latter cases, human behavior is an act of compliance or adjustment to the forms and forces of the "external" world. At such moments, we do not seek to control events through our own schemes as must much as we try to "fit into" or accommodate ourselves in the required ways. In both forms, behavior is an act of willful self-adjustment.

Opposite to play is ritual. As the anthropologist Turner (1969) argues, rituals are activities that direct and even change the self. Moreover, rituals—like work—are essentially instrumental occasions. That is, rituals are symbolically guided events that carry us from the past into the future, from one moment to the next. We enter these forms because we wish to move ahead in stipulated ways, to free our minds for more creative exploits, to comply with the requirements of others, and so forth. Weddings, baptisms, puberty ceremonies, funerals, and the seemingly endless routines of home and office come to mind. Oddly perhaps, rituals can be personal as well as social and cultural affairs. When we give ourselves willingly to our own psychic habits and proclivities, the parameters of consciousness are narrowed dramatically. At any rate, in rituals of every type subjectivity accepts the terms set by pre-established "external" patterns.

Play is not alone in its emphasis on consummation; this theme is also central to communitas. Although this latter word is not in common currency (see Goodman & Goodman, 1947; Turner, 1969 for somewhat different uses), it is presented here to express the ways in which people find satisfaction in—and even luxuriate in—external form. For this author, communitas refers to a host of activities that many other writers consider "playful"—such as parades, festivals, picnics, public dramas, parties, pageants, musical performances, dance club raves, and spectatorship at sporting events (see McMahon, 2007). At such times, people allow themselves to be "taken in" by or become part of events that are determined largely by forces beyond their control. We do this not because (as in the case of ritual) we have something enduring to gain by our involvement but because we enjoy the process of participation . We enjoy being "moved" by a wonderful concert, an exciting sports event, or even a great party. As noted above, Huizinga tended to describe such participative activity as "festival."

The author elsewhere (Henricks, 2006) has presented graphically the relationship between these four themes. For the purposes of this essay, it is enough to list the characteristics of the four types as: play (transformative, consummatory behavior), work (transformative, instrumental behavior), communitas (conformitive, consummatory behavior), and ritual (conformitive, instrumental behavior). The author is well aware that the complicated, ever-changing behaviors that all of us produce are not easily shoved into these four "boxes." For that reason, the four categories are introduced here as ideal types that can help observers identify relevant qualities of behavior or, more precisely, indicate which aspects of that behavior seem to show which of those qualities.

Similarly, the author acknowledges that play (and the other three types) always has an important subjective or interpretive component; that is, play draws (at least part of) its character from the orientations of its participants. In one sense, this suggests the importance of asking those participants how they feel about their activity, including the reasons they are doing it and the experiences they are having while they are doing it (see Csikszentmihalyi, 1975). In another sense, it suggests the ways in which the judgments of the managers (and observers) of play also "frame" the activity. Adults routinely judge children to be "at play" because they see no consequences for the activity beyond the event itself; play managers declare activities to be "play" or "fun" regardless of the participants' experiences.

Such difficulties of interpretation can be illustrated by the example used above, playing the piano. Arguably, playing the piano may feature all four behavioral types described above; and the same practice session may move from one pattern of experience to another as the person continues to play. To be specific, we may "tinkle the ivories" in ways of our choosing because it give us pleasure to do so; that pattern of expressive manipulation is defined here as play. Differently, we may grind our way ahead (with results that perhaps sound identical to a listener) because we need—or have been told we need—to get better. Such is work. Differently again, we can focus on the pleasure we obtain by conforming to the directions on the score and by otherwise immersing ourselves in the "music." That pattern of immersion has been described above as communitas. Finally, we may immerse ourselves in those same musical forms and traditions because we wish to become a "proper" musician. That future-oriented approach to one's identity has been termed ritual. These preceding remarks seem to suggest that play is an elusive experience that suddenly morphs from one pattern to another when (in the example used above) the music teacher tells us to "straighten up" or when we feel ourselves suddenly transported by the sounds we are producing. The fluidity and potentiality of human experience is acknowledged here; but it is also emphasized that this fluidity is checked or narrowed by various personal, social, cultural, bodily, and environmental constraints. Those organizing principles—such as the distinctive *rationales* for activity noted by the author—need to be studied. More generally, the challenge for play scholars is to break apart the idea of play as an exotic, seamless unity, to identify play's various elements, and to show how those elements operate in real-life events.

## PLAY AS ASCENDING MEANING

Play scholars may note that this approach—or at least the elements that relate to play—is quite similar to Piaget's (1962) theory, in which he describes play as behavior that features relatively "pure assimilation." For Piaget, human development features the creation and maintenance of "schemas," psychologically supported patterns for thought and action. Somewhat like scientists, children (and the rest of us) try to build frameworks that make sense of the world. As we mature, we establish much more complicated and externally validated cognitive structures to help us recognize and direct our behaviors toward the tremendously variable objects we encounter. Life is a process then of trying out and attempting to manage the world in terms of these personal schemas and, alternately, of adjusting or modifying our thoughts and behaviors to those external patterns. In Piaget's view, play features a dominance of the former pattern (i.e., assimilation) over the latter (what he termed "accommodation"). More extremely, play features almost "pure" assimilation, the tendency of the ego to administer the world for the sake of its own personal satisfaction and without regard for the external consequences of those encounters.

The current approach differs from Piaget's in that the author tries to locate play in its relationship to the three other patterns described above. Moreover, the author focuses on the polarity between transformation-conformity (or Piaget's assimilation-accommodation) in terms of a more general theory of meaning that he calls the "ascending-descending meaning" perspective. That perspective will not be discussed in detail here (see instead Henricks, 1999). However, the central premise of that approach is that human beings locate themselves in vast realms of order—patterns of relationship that exist within the psyche, society, culture, organism, and physical environment. Establishing the "reality" of the patterns that "exist" in those different fields—for example, that people "have" psychological orientations that influence how they behave, that groups in society exist and have identifiable characteristics, that there are cultural patterns in societies, and so forth—has been the historic work of the social sciences. The reality of physical forms and relationships—that there are patterns that go on within our bodies and within the vast physical environment in which we live—has been the legacy of the physical sciences. Most generally then, the theory argues that there are objects in the world (and patterns of movement by those objects) that present themselves to consciousness. Human experience is basically a "sense-making" operation (both affective and cognitive) in which people try to "locate" themselves and act amidst these pre-existing patterns. Many times, we are able to manage experience along the lines of our own personal frameworks or patterns (and construct experience according to what the author calls "ascending" meaning). Alternately, we adjust to externally based patterns that we recognize but do not control (and thereby understand our position in terms of "descending" meaning). The transformative activities listed above—play and work—are claimed to be exercises in ascending meaning, that is, times when people attempt to impose their will on the world and construct their understandings of that world (and of themselves) in those personal terms. By contrast, ritual and communitas—the conformitive modes of behavior—are said to illustrate descending meaning. That is, they are occasions when people understand themselves and their activity in largely external terms. Most of the daily activities of life—including our relationships with other people—exhibit a continual tension or tug-of-war between these different "frames" of interpretation (see Goffman, 1974); reality becomes "constructed" in these two different ways.

Furthermore, play—as an act of assertion or transformation—occurs on two quite different planes represented by physical and symbolic "meaning." Some play is largely a physical act in which players set themselves against the objects and patterns of the world. Players make their bodies move in response to their own psychic demands, but they also use those bodies to manipulate the external object world. That is, we force the physical world to respond to us—for example, by making our bodies jump high in the air so that we may come down on a puddle of water and make a terrific splash. Moreover, we may even try to control our own bio-psychic demands, as when we try to hold our breath for as long as we can or keep running onward in a race when our body is screaming for us to stop. To that extent, play is the attempt of consciousness—the momentary awareness of the circumstances of existence—to control or manipulate external objects and patterns of every type. Those objects and patterns also include symbolic forms, that is, publicly communicable ideas. People play symbolically when they confront the idea systems of other people, established cultural forms, or even their own "schemas" (to use Piaget's terms). People play with words and images—those that occur in the world and those that appear only in our minds—just as they play with other objects. Again, play represents the attempts of consciousness to confront, interrupt, and manipulate both physical and symbolic forms. Other elements of the theory—including the rationale for how meaning either "ascends" or "descends"—are described in the source noted (Henricks, 1999).

## FOUR PATTERNS OF ASSERTIVE PLAY

However well intentioned the above formulations, there is—in the author's own estimation—something unsatisfactory about them. If play is a project in comprehension and control, shouldn't play be marked by a careful, plotting—even, plodding—quality? Shouldn't tennis and bridge players always choose opponents they can beat rather than those who can give them a "good game"? Shouldn't players "quit when they're ahead" instead of continuing to seek the excitement that comes from resistance, uncertainty, and challenge?

Such difficulties are also apparent in Piaget's view of play as *assimilation*. In Piaget's case, the play world appears to be ceded to the mentally industrious child, busy bees or beavers that try (often in a rather solitary way) to expand their own powers. For such reasons, Piaget's portraits of childhood play seem more like exercises and practices than adventures in hilarity, creativity, and surprise. By discovering practices that work, children are strengthened and reassured. Similarly, Piaget's (1965) account of moral development portrays youthful game players as moral claimants and negotiators, who wish to set terms for and then administer their social interactions. In either case, play is ultimately an order-seeking enterprise and a utilitarian ethic prevails.

However legitimate this approach, Piaget's theory does not account well for the qualities of novelty and fun that most people associate with play. Likewise, his emphasis on the purely psychological (even solitary) aspects of play perhaps causes him to neglect the more dynamic, relational aspects of this phenomenon. As the author (2006) has argued elsewhere, play is a pattern of *interaction* as much as it is a private *orientation* or *behavior*, a back-and-forth *interplay* as much as straight-forward manipulation of the object-world. Children do not jump into a giant mud puddle simply to experience the pleasure the controlling their bodies; they jump because they want to see what the water will do in response to that jump. That is, players wish to do more than reassure themselves about their own powers; they wish to know what the world will do when it is provoked.

Still, it would be foolish to declare Piaget's great studies wrong and other (more process-oriented or dialectical) descriptions right. In this author's view, Piaget's theory is well suited for the kinds of play-objects he chooses to describe in his studies. However, different kinds of play-objects (and playmates) tend to produce different patterns of playful *interaction*. When those play-objects are more powerful and dynamic, the player is required to devise new strategies instead of straight-ahead manipulation. By saying this, the author does not wish to violate his own principle that play is a project of assimilation, assertion, or ascending meaning. Instead, he argues that there are different styles of playful assertion that are linked to the "situations" or "relationships" in which play occurs.

In the following, attention is given to four different patterns of relationship: *privilege, subordination, engagement*, and *marginality*. Those four patterns express varying degrees to which a subject (such as the player of a game) is able to control the objects of his or her world (different play-objects, other players, and so forth). Consistently with the ascending-descending meaning perspective described above, the author views relationships between people and the world as featuring attempts by such people to direct the course of their own action or, alternately, recognitions that they must comply with the directions of otherness (such as other people or other forceful elements of the world). In that sense, human relationships always feature a "balancing of claims," in which participants call upon and seek to direct others. Sometimes, we are able to control the other (or object) without much resistance on its part. We secure compliance without having to comply ourselves. That (relatively imbalanced) relationship between subject and object is termed here "privilege." At other times, we find ourselves confronting forces that are much more powerful than we are. When people are placed in situations with powerful others, that relationship is called (from the subject's point of view) "subordination."

Different again are more "balanced" relationships, when both participants are able to make claims of more or less equal strength that the other must recognize. When both parties are able to make relatively high or strong claims on one another—that is, when there is a reciprocal or give-and-take pattern of relationship, that situation is termed here "engagement." Finally—and perhaps most interesting—is the situation where neither party makes effective claims on the other. In relationships of this type, participants are oriented to or interested in one another but are unable (or unwilling) to engage the other. This relationship—in which people consider otherness "at a distance"—is termed here "marginality."

To summarize, four different patterns of relationship are of special interest to scholars of play studies (or of human studies more generally). These are relationships featuring high claims by subject and low claims by object (privilege), low claims by subject and high claims by object (subordination), high claims by both subject and object (engagement), and low claims by both subject and object (marginality). To use a metaphor, people's connections to the world are similar to a handshake. That grasp may exhibit high pressure from one side and low pressure from the other, high pressure from both sides, or low pressure from both sides. Arguably, she who controls the grasp effectively controls the "relationship." Arguably also, a grip that features high pressure from both sides is the most committed and dynamically engaged.

Each of these patterns of relationship, it is argued here, breeds its own style of play. If play, as defined above, is a transformative mode of human encounter, then players must consider how they can transform objects that have differing abilities to control or resist them. To be sure, there are times when people choose to conform to or comply with the forms of otherness (actions that have been described as ritual and communitas) and there are times when people choose to ignore those forms or otherwise not be engaged. Players, by contrast, are always interested in "making something" out of a situation, in trying to make their mark upon it. Because situations vary, styles of play vary. The following describes four of these styles and the situations to which they correspond—manipulation (privilege), rebellion (subordination), dialogue (engagement), and exploration (marginality).

## Play as Manipulation

As stated above, manipulation is the style of play that most clearly expresses standings of privilege.

To be privileged is to be able to "claim" or control the activity of others without being controlled by them. For sociologists, people who have superior access to the valued resources of their societies—that is, to wealth, power, prestige, and knowledge—are commonly described as being socially privileged; however, the term "privilege" can be used more generally to denote a "superordinate" or dominant standing in relationships of any type. To use the author's terminology, positions of privilege maximize ascending meaning (the ability to control others) and minimize descending meaning (the prospect of being controlled by those others). At any rate, to be privileged to be able to control the elements of the world—whether those elements be a rock, one's own hand, a bucket of sand, the flow of a stream, and so forth—without having to adjust substantially to those elements.

Play for superordinates often takes the shape of privately directed manipulations. Because the world cannot "give us trouble" (or so we think), the privileged player is free to move it about, put its elements together, and subsequently take them apart. Play, to return to Piaget's model, is largely an act of self-guided movement and construction. As Piaget (1962, p. 89) himself describes the matter, "Play, on the contrary, proceeds by relaxation of the effort at adaptation and by maintenance or exercise of activities for the mere pleasure of mastering them and acquiring thereby a feeling of virtuosity or power." Play is a case of applying or trying out pre-established ideas, images, and behavioral orientations on the world.

The reader perhaps will have considered already that this view of play seems most applicable for our relationships with inert or passive objects, or at least with those over which we have much control. As the author (1999, pp. 264–265) has argued elsewhere, the "freedom" of play is attributable largely to our ability to enter and leave the play setting at will, to start and stop action sequences, to control the course of the action as it occurs, or even to improvise in interruptive ways that are thought be "spontaneous." Clearly, we are able to control—and take pleasure from the control of—some objects more than others. Most accessible to us are those personal possessions that William James (1952) called the "self," especially our bodies and minds. Play can be seen as an act of getting ourselves to do things. We can make ourselves stand on one foot, hop about, puff our cheeks out, repeat silly words, hold our breath for as long as possible, and so forth. As we practice these behaviors, we become better at them. Whatever the official "reasons," "motivations," or 'functions" of play, one effect of that activity is to shore up our understandings of the limits of will, to comprehend what we can do to ourselves.

More expansively, we can take on the external objects of the world. For the energetic player, there is much to be done. Blocks are to be put in a pile, flowers to be painted on a piece of paper, stones to be thrown, shoes to be scuffed on newly polished floors, and (in the author's case) words to be mashed out on a computer keyboard. We can perform these functions as well as we do because, in the examples given, the objects in question are relatively compliant in the face of those advances. Even people—both those who are relatively powerless and those who pretend to powerlessness (as in the case of a congenial parent)—may allow themselves to be "played with" in this way. Little children grab their adoring parents' noses, make "raspberries" on their cheeks, pull their hair, and so forth. In such ways, children learn about their rightful province in the world, which actions give pleasure to themselves, which actions gives pleasure to others, and which ones are hurtful or even destroy the objects they manipulate.

As many scholars (see, e.g., Groos, 1976; Hall, 1917: Freud, 1967) have noted, manipulative play tends to have a repetitive quality, as if something is being exercised or practiced. A piece of behavior is started, stopped, and begun again. If quality of self-satisfaction is what instigates and then sustains the behavior, then such activities are pursued only as long as they provide that satisfaction. However, continual, unmodified repetitions at some point suggest personal compulsion rather than conscious direction, the need to forestall dissatisfaction rather than the desire to attain its opposite. Even as repetitions, play behaviors are rarely smooth, orderly affairs. As Fagen (1995) argues, animal play commonly features exaggerated gestures, jerky movements, grotesque play faces, and light and fast movements, what Miller (1973) calls "galumphing." In other words, play typically involves a *stretching* of behavioral capabilities. Even these exaggerations are not pursued endlessly. Rather play seems to be an act of self-stimulation, in which the external world (be that world the body or other, more remote objects) is used as a sounding board for private capabilities. To that extent, even repetitive play pursues an "optimal" level of stimulation (see Berlyne, 1960), a psychological territory that exists between the extremes of boredom and anxiety (see Csikszentmihalyi, 1975).

## PLAY AS REBELLION

However much people aspire to positions of privilege in the world, that lofty station is not their customary lot. To be sure, most of us have opportunities to control the movements of our bodies and the character of our thoughts, and we can manipulate objects that are small, inert, or otherwise powerless. Manipulative play allows us, if only for a few moments, to wear the mantle of the gods. However, most of human existence is an entanglement in various realms of order too powerful for us to control or even comprehend. The broader patterns of society, culture, and the natural environment stand beyond day-to-day occurrences and cannot be altered by individuals in any significant way. Even psychic and organismic patterns (the workings of our minds and bodies) proceed in ways that the inhabitants typically do not (and often cannot) consciously control.

Much of life then is an act of compliance or *accommodation* (to use Piaget's term) to these external patterns. When we give ourselves willingly to the forms and forces we recognize, those acts of subordination (as described by this author) take the shape of ritual and communitas. However, few scholars see play as an act of conciliation, concession, or obedience. Players try to assert themselves against external realities; they de-form and then re-form what they encounter. With the matter so defined, how can play be said to occur when one addresses the great forces of the world, patterns that are indifferent to our willful interventions? How does the surfer test the largest wave, the climber the steepest hill?

Clearly, many aspects of the physical world are too vast or too powerful to be played "with." We cannot change the laws of gravity, eliminate our need for air and water, endure extreme temperatures, extend our lifespan indefinitely, and so forth. Under such circumstances, play usually involves an attempt to place these matters into much narrower situations over which individuals can exercise some measure of control. That is, although we cannot change the laws of gravity, we can see how far *we* can jump or bounce on a trampoline or rise in a hot air balloon. Similarly, we may try to defy our need for oxygen by holding our breath for as long as possible, by swimming underwater with the aid of an aqualung, and so forth. In such cases, players transcribe profound realities into manageable, concrete forms.

Just as individuals cannot control the outlines of the physical world, so they cannot (without the assistance of huge numbers of others) re-shape the vast, publicly accessible patterns known as culture. This point of view, it should be noted, is central to postmodernism (see Rosenau, 1992; Spariosu, 1989; Henricks, 2001). Although postmodernists tend to stand against the (modernist) thesis that the world is ultimately orderly, principled and systematic and that humans can comprehend these principles, postmodernists do see the human predicament as an (ever-shifting) location within vast forms and forces over which individuals themselves have relatively little control. Having given up the quest to realize universal, transcendental "truth," contemporary people reconcile themselves to living in smaller, more intimate ways amidst swirling, often unpredictable relationships. In that sense, people are "in play" as much as they "play with" the world. To use a metaphor, we humans are swimmers in a wide ocean whose boundaries we cannot perceive. We feel ourselves being shifted about and encounter an ever-changing assortment of material and symbolic forms. Such fluid, uncertain circumstances demand alertness, flexibility, and readiness of response. Deprived of any clear vantage point from which to comprehend all these comings and goings, little "glimpses" of the world is perhaps all we will ever have (see Heidegger, 1962).

For the postmodernist, being cast about in this way is not a cause for sorrow. Instead people must face up to those circumstances by living in ways that honor the reality of the world's concreteness, transience, fragmentation, and uncertainty. Even though they are "in play," people can be players as well as play objects (see Hans, 1981). To do this, as in the examples of physical play used above, one must redefine experience as a *participation* in transient, concrete forms. Control *can* be exerted though the choices one makes — a new pair of shoes, tonight's television viewing, an appetizing meal, an interesting photograph or magazine article, and so forth. Focusing each moment in this way, we can design our lives as a personalized, ever-changing collage. To the extent that these constructions conform to our own transient desires, life itself becomes play.

The preceding comments suggest the extent to which people (especially in their roles as players) can "make something" out of their subordination. While we cannot control the broader realities in which we live, we can at least translate those issues into smaller, concrete settings where we can perform modest acts of control. For such reasons, the author (Henricks, 2009) has argued that play is sometimes an act of "regression" expressed as a series of cognitive, emotional, and socio-moral simplifications. However, many times a person is unable to define a situation as he or she wishes. Indeed, it is the essence of subordination that one is unable to do so. Commonly, we are controlled by "otherness" in concrete, closely confined ways. In the face of authoritative people or rule systems that make specific demands on us, how is it possible to play?

In the author's view, play is a "rebellion of consciousness" against the forces of the world. In ordinary parlance, rebellions are acts or shows of defiance directed at some authority figure or established convention. One form of rebellion is to evade or escape the powerful figure, to move (as children do in certain societies) toward independence. As described above, play is often a form of withdrawal, a movement of reality into a more manageable sphere that the player can control. A different level of rebellion occurs when people "take on" their rulers in more direct ways, try to upset the prevailing hierarchy, or even "take it over" themselves. In other words, play not infrequently takes the shape of outright defiance or defilement, publicly observable attempts to oppose, humiliate, and transfigure the regimes of the powerful.

The view of play as "anti-structure" is developed most fully in folklore and cultural anthropology (see Turner, 1969). Because folklore (see Opie & Opie, 1969; Sutton-Smith et al., 1995) tends to study children in settings that the children themselves control (that is, away from adult-dominated classrooms and homes), that discipline presents a rather different side of child life than is shown in psychological or educational studies of "human development." For folklorists, childhood is a bubbling pot of dreams and desires that spill out in ways that can be socially awkward, hurtful, and even outrageous. Children's songs, stories, poems, street games, and so forth are attempts to "name" the issues (and anxieties) of life and to give people opportunities to work through the behavioral and emotional possibilities of a world that has been so named. Some of this is a wondering about the nature and functions of the changing body (and the curious adult physiognomy that awaits these children). Other portions are devoted to the social or symbolic worlds of adulthood and how children can assert themselves in such settings (see Fine, 1983).

As both anthropologists and folklorists emphasize then, children are not simply industrious, docile workers who solve math puzzles and practice their reading skills. When they gather together, they do not simply transcribe adult practices but instead modify those patterns or even create their own (see Ottenberg, 2005). Playful children can be petulant, boisterous, careless with the feelings of others, and downright "mean." They are fond of "showing off " and "grossing out" one another. They are hungry for the peer-based status that comes from demonstrating their defiance of adult rules. Like Halloween pranksters, children take a certain pleasure in misbehavior (see Clark, 2007). Players curse, spit, gossip maliciously, tell off-color jokes, share "dirty" pictures, and so forth in full knowledge that these activities are, at official levels, wrong. We adults fancy ourselves superior to these misbehaving children. However, much of that superiority stems from the fact that we have greater power to direct our own behaviors and a greater stake in the maintenance of society's rules. Nevertheless, under the right circumstances, playful adults can be just as undisciplined, rancorous, and obscene.

This latter theme has been developed by social anthropologists and by sociologists like Goffman (1961), who have been influenced by anthropological perspectives (see Lancy and Tindall, 1976; Roopnarine, Johnson, & Hooper, 1994; Handelman, 1998). In traditional societies, social norms and hierarchies are often protected from direct criticism and change. Because of that, some societies build in opportunities for publicly regulated tension-release, "immorality" of certain types, and even status-inversion. Such displays are effectively social counterpoints, public "reaction-formations" (to use Freudian language) that are not simply *escapes from* the world but rather *confrontations with* or *reversals of* its guiding themes. In this light, perhaps the best known description continues to be Geertz's (1972) account of the Balinese cockfight, in which he argues that the wild betting and licentiousness of the cockpit in that society somehow counters the emphases on social harmony and personal control that are the more typical features of Balinese life. In such ways, play is an act of resistance and rebellion.

## Play as Dialogue

Different again are circumstances in which the participants are relatively balanced in their abilities to "claim" or influence one another's behavior. In what the author; following Csikszentmihalyi (1990), terms "engagement," people commonly give themselves to situations whose challenges or requirements approximate their own abilities to control those situations. Interaction in such contexts is sustained by acceptable levels of tension or uncertainty and by recognitions of mutual need or reciprocity. At such times, a person "gives as good as he gets." To return to Piaget's terms once again, adaptation in such settings features a balancing of assimilation (i.e., subjective control) and accommodation (i.e., adjustment to external demands).

It is argued here that play under the conditions of engagement exhibits a character different from the other forms of assertive play. To illustrate this point, consider the examples of a person playing with three different kinds of animals: a slow-moving beetle, a tiger, and a large dog. In the first instance, the play is likely to be a form of *manipulation*. With a stick or finger, the player blocks the beetle's path or makes it move ahead. Inevitably the beetle ends up on its back and the player tries to set it aright. In such play events, one learns about his or her own ability to control the movements of a small creature and, to a lesser extent, about the qualities of that creature. Much different is the quality of *rebelliousness* or fearlessness that is exhibited by playing with a tiger. Animal "tamers" are celebrated for their apparent abilities to defy the great beasts. They enter the caged unarmed, make their charges jump through hoops, and even put their heads in the animals' jaws! This display of the trainer's "powers" is, of course, a carefully regulated event. Other humans who are interested in playing with tigers must resort to much more modest forms of defiance—jumping up and down outside the tiger's cage, making silly faces, calling out, and otherwise demonstrating their own simian heritage. Typically such acts of false bravado in the face of the powerful garner what they deserve: sublime indifference.

Playing with a dog can be located between these extremes. A dog, if energetic and socially responsive, will beg you to take it for a walk or to throw a stick. Dogs usually respond to "commands" but sometimes they do not. Moreover, they try to control their human companions. They may not chase the stick with appropriate enthusiasm each time or surrender it when asked; they jump up on their human playmates or pull on their clothing. When the spirit moves a large dog, it runs under its owner's legs and knocks him down. Whatever the merits and demerits of such behavior, most people would surely grant that the last style of play is a more balanced and thoroughly interactive exchange.

Sutton-Smith's scholarship speaks to many of the types of play that have been presented above. However, his work is especially an understanding of the interactive or dialogical qualities of play (Sutton-Smith, 1977; 1997). In that view, play is commonly lively, unpredictable and contentious. Players are not simply "satisfied" with their accomplishments but often baffled, delighted, and energized by what occurs. Play is an encounter between the expected and the unexpected. Indeed, play is fascinating to the degree that the activity is equilibrating (that is, order-seeking) and disequilibrating (disorder-seeking) at the same time (Sutton-Smith & Kelly-Byrne, 1984b). In that regard, his (Sutton-Smith, 1966) critique of Piaget's "manipulative" view of play is instructive. If play is only an expression of previously developed schemas—i.e., an application or strengthening of what one already knows, how does play promote "development"? In other words, play must also involve a series of responses to the challenges of a changing world. Those reactions and reinventions are fundamental to the play experience.

Moreover, the play world is filled with many different kinds of meaning converging all at once. As his (1997) *The Ambiguity of Play* amply demonstrates, different scholars have emphasized selectively different complexes of meaning. However, it should be noted that ordinary people in their play seize different aspects of the experience as well. Play events—or somewhat differently, moments of the same play event—can be about (to name some of Sutton-Smith's "rhetorics" or "ideologies") the experiences of *power,* the *self,* or *community identity.* Play can be a reconnoitering with *fate,* a wandering of the *imagination,* an explosion of *frivolity,* or even a self-guided tour of Piagetian *progress.* Because play events can be many things at one time, play can seem multivalent or even paradoxical. The same play activity can be both good and bad, hard and easy, selfish and communitarian, assimilative and accommodative, and so forth.

This richness and complexity of play events is perhaps shown best under the terms of what the current author calls here "engagement." That is, the improbability and complexity of an event are maximized when "claims" on the player are coming from a number of different directions. As Simmel (1950) argues, two-person relationships are more complicated than solitary activity; adding another person—or another—to the mix increases that complexity dramatically. As he notes in his (Simmel, 1950, pp. 40–57) great essay on "sociability," festive gatherings are attempts to honor the interests (and satisfactions) of many different people at once. Because the sociable event fills up quickly with such tremendous human possibility, an affair like a party must have "rules" that narrow these private enthusiasms and even guest lists that keep the heterogeneity of attendees within bounds. For similar reasons, people in groups often play "games" (i.e., featuring formats of descending meaning) rather than pursue the less bounded, more psychologically generated forms of play. To help focus and simply matters further, games commonly have only two sides.

Nevertheless, writers like Bakhtin (1981) have emphasized the more effulgent, carnival-like qualities of modern life. In such accounts, experience is a meeting place or convergence of many kinds of things at once. Such encounters are emotional as well as cognitive and moral affairs. Inside the heads of participants thought becomes a kind of "dialogue" of the imagination that parallels the myriads of interchanges that happen between actors and their objects. He compares the sense of possibility that pervades the festival grounds of ancient societies to the public life of contemporary societies. In the current author's view, parties and festivals (as described by Simmel and Bakhtin) are perhaps better understood as examples of *communitas*—that is, as immersions into public form—than as species of playful transformation. However, clearly, events of this type feature both the sense that people can in these settings create new possibilities for themselves—that is, play—as well as the sense that they have entered a realm of order that transcends them and orchestrates their possibilities—that is, communitas (see McMahon, 1999). And the emphasis can shift from one pole to other, or even back and forth, as the event (and one's awareness of that event) moves along. Such themes have been developed recently by Edmiston (2008), who emphasizes how relatively equal others co-partner, negotiate, and live within the symbolic worlds that they create.

Of special pertinence is the question of whether relatively balanced, dialogical events open up or close down the awareness of participants. Again, in the author's own view, scholars like Bakhtin and Sutton-Smith tend to emphasize the burgeoning of possibility that occurs in play. However, Csikszentmihalyi (1990) takes an opposite line of approach. For that scholar, play (and work) sometimes produces a highly unusual centering of awareness. That quality of awareness Csikszentmihalyi terms "flow." Much like Goffman (1961), Csikszentmihalyi is interested in what factors encourage people to focus on a chosen line of action rather than to become distracted by thoughts about how the self, the other, or the situation in its broadest implications is "doing." In that light, flow signifies a condition in which the participant is deeply embedded in his or her activity, when external concerns and ideas of time melt away, when differences between subjective and objective realms blur into a sense of intimate connection. Csikszenmihalyi's belief in the prospects of participative intimacy is much stronger than that of Goffman, but both writers share the view that focused engagement is encouraged by situations where the *capabilities* of the actor match the *levels of challenge* represented by the environments of their quest. Thus, mountain climbers are most engaged by climbs of appropriate challenge, tennis players by equally skilled others, surgeons by pathologies of sufficient difficulty, and so forth. To be confronted by tasks that are too easy or too difficult is to invite the excursions of consciousness known, respectively, as boredom and anxiety.

As Csikszentmihalyi (1990, p. 29) himself emphasizes, human consciousness is capable of flitting from one issue to another in mere fractions of a second. For that scholar then, the problem is to understand how people stay focused on largely *technical* challenges (i.e., how to move one's knight in a game of chess or place one's foot in climbing a hill). For Goffman, the mysteries to be explained are largely *social* challenges; that is, how people are able to stay focused on one another in a joint line of action. Sutton-Smith and Bakhtin choose to not limit the focus of players so narrowly. Play is always about many kinds of meanings converging at once. Engagement is less a moment of focused intimacy than it is receptivity to the fact that many interesting things are about to happen and that the players should make themselves ready for such contingencies now.

## Play as Exploration

In many ways, the most interesting of the four standings is the one that is probably the least studied: marginality. In the social sciences, marginality is usually considered to be a "negative" concept (see Stonequist, 1937). That is, marginal people are presented as those who wish to be *more* involved in the situations to which they are oriented but are prevented from doing so by other people who oppose them or by additional factors beyond their control. Many people, it is presumed here, have gazed through the windows of an expensive restaurant or club and felt the sense that inside is a world to which they will never belong. If society is a restricted club, then marginality is the status accorded to those would-be participants who are kept at its edges, allowed to enter and participate only as menials, or—like Simmel's (1950, pp. 402–409) "stranger"—accepted in limited or superficial ways. In that regard, sociological studies of race, class, and gender are as much about marginality—the simultaneous experiences of inclusion and exclusion—as they are about subordination.

Studies of undesired marginality—on topics like race relations, poverty, and so forth—have been critical in the social and behavioral sciences, but those studies hardly exhaust the meaning of this topic. Of most importance then is the fact that people not infrequently *choose* to stand on the edges of their relationships with others. As nearly every sociologist would point out, people orient themselves to other people—and to social forms like roles, relationships, groups, and so forth—in negative as well as positive ways. In other words, many identities or circumstances—being labeled as a criminal, incorrectly connected to a political party we detest, associated with old companions or family members that now embarrass us, and so forth—we actively reject. Under such conditions, "alienation" becomes a personal preference; we voluntarily marginalize ourselves from unwanted identities even as they threaten to engulf us. Somewhat defiantly, we claim ourselves to be "in" that world but not "of" it.

In an even more complicated way, most human encounters feature different degrees and forms of marginality. That is, although we consider ourselves to be oriented to persons and events, often are engaged with those events in only half-hearted or distant ways. Indeed, only a small portion of the time do we actually "interact" with other people, if interaction means talking and listening to them, moving our bodies in response to their movements, and so forth. A good bit of the time we are just semi-interested bystanders during our own social encounters (see Goffman, 1961). In other words, even though we appear to be interacting with others, we are actually thinking about the personal traits of the speaker instead of what they are saying, the situation we are jointly in, or even our own qualities and aspirations. More extremely, we find ourselves daydreaming about entirely unrelated things while they are talking. We muse about interactions that have been completed and fantasize about things we should have said or done or will say or do when we see those same people again. However earnestly we commit ourselves to our interactions with the object-world, many of those interactions are only partial involvements.

A reader patient enough to grant this expanded view of human marginality still may wish to know: what has marginality to do with play? After all, marginality has been presented above as a circumstance of diminished involvement, a kind of "middle-land" where people feel both the attraction to something and the separation from it. Isn't play, by contrast, the project of being actively engaged with those circumstances—of seizing and then trying to control aspects of the world?

To be sure, the three patterns of assertive play presented above emphasize people's active participation in concrete circumstances. *Privileged* players focus on and actively manipulate the object world. They throw balls, build with blocks, pluck the strings of musical instruments, and so forth in patterns of their own choosing. *Subordinate* players rebel against the unwanted intrusions of powerful others. The scene of their behavior is frequently a tumult; the air is filled with defiant voices and gestures. *Engaged* players are so captured in the give-and-take of their own circumstances that there may have little time for pause or reflection. To be in dialogue is to live deeply in the moment. Shouts of surprise and glee abound. Surely play in these more energetic, demonstrative, and passionate forms is the "true" version of that activity.

It is argued here that play also appears in less confrontational, more provisional ways. As Simmel (see Levine, 1971) argued, there is always a certain difference or "distance" that exists between our subjective selves (the sphere of what we know and feel) and the concrete realities of the world (including society's expectations for us). That distance—effectively the groundwork of human freedom—provides us with opportunities for creative exploration. People feel themselves set apart or different from the context of their lives. That sense of otherness or "alienation" (that concept having been purged of its typically negative connotations) is the vantage point from which we are able to select elements of the world and bring them close to us so that we may inspect their features.

Although such a viewpoint may not be welcomed by social scientists who emphasize observable behaviors rather than the interior (and therefore unobservable) thoughts of their subjects, Simmel's general argument here should be familiar enough to most play scholars. As the psychologist Jerome Singer (1992, 1995) has emphasized, play is often a pattern of semi-engagement with the world, a taking of objects into our minds and considering them there. Said differently, play is quite frequently a musing, "hypothetical" sort of activity. Although many play events are direct, intimate encounters that keep people firmly rooted to the present, many others explore life in a "subjunctive" tense. That is, players routinely play out the possibilities of life in their minds; at such times a "what-if" mentality prevails. In that light, we imagine what it would be like to be a king or queen, a football hero, a rock star, and so forth and act out the implications of those roles. Occasionally, those enactments are public dramas, moments of pretense we perform for others. Perhaps more of the time, the fabulous coronations, mad touchdown dashes, sold-out concerts, and so forth are award-winning performances seen only by ourselves. More frequently yet, we play out these fabulous visions only in our minds. Players dream of things that never were and never will be—and let those dreams live only in their minds. As every play scholar knows, play is somehow about the power of the imagination to disturb the world.

It may be imagined then that play, in this guise at least, is simply a flight from reality. When we cannot manage our play in more active or heroic ways, we move matters "indoors," where our transformations can take the shape of entirely private fantasies. This "privatist" view of imagination (and of play) was opposed strongly by the sociologist George Herbert Mead. In Mead's (1964) view, human thought is to a large extent the act of imaginative role taking, a process of sorting out the implications of behavior in our minds before we act. At such times, we judge the world against our own mental ideas (essentially already established expectations about what is likely to occur). However, our ideas are not simply private formulations. Quite the opposite, our musings are *socially* grounded both as remnants of our trial-and-error experiences with others and as pre-established *symbols*, publicly shared meanings about such behaviors, persons, and situations. Other people's behaviors are "meaningful" to us to the degree that we can place them into these systems of symbolic representation. For the same reason, we can make our own intentions understandable to others. Neither for Mead nor for Singer is the imagination simply a withdrawal into the private recesses of mind. It is instead an internal processing of publicly traded ideas and images, an energetic (and often anxious) reflection on how social behaviors will occur, have occurred, and are occurring now.

To be sure, Mead's view of reflective and imaginary thinking as an "internalized conversation" of culturally defined gestures is not a complete explanation of this matter. Thought is not always so "pragmatic" or so socially responsible. At times, our imaginations run away from effective and civilized lines of behavior to indulge forbidden fears and desires. As Freud (1952) held, the psyche is fed from many sources; only some of these are socially approved ideas or morals. More pointedly, Fein (1987) describes how children's fantasies and narrative accounts are driven more by vivid, unexpected, or disturbing events than by cognitive consistencies and inconsistencies. As Singer

(1992) argues, "make-believe" play is an activity that helps people simplify and render harmless the complexities of the world; as such it provides a place to comprehend the differences between reality and fantasy.

The nature and implications of human imagining is beyond the scope of this essay. However, the author wishes to make two points: 1) that imaginative play can be more or less connected to (or conversely, "distant" from) the objects of the world and 2) that there are different pathways or types of imaginative play. To make the first point is simply to claim that purely interior transformations—expressed in dreams, daydreams, or other more consciously directed fantasies—are somewhat different from play that involves concrete objects (see Sawyers and Carrick, 2003). The latter case—which includes play with dolls or other representative objects—represents activities that are intermediary to purely imaginative exploits and the three other, more activist styles of play described in the preceding pages. In that sense, doll play is perhaps more about the *ideas* that those symbolic figures are able to bring into our minds than about the *actual manipulation* of the dolls as concrete objects.

It is important to emphasize, following Piaget (1962), that play is not equivalent to all forms of imagination, to dreams, or to imitative styles of behavior. Play is not usually made equivalent to events that happen to people and therefore evade their conscious control. In that light, even some of our fantasies—for example, imagining oneself as being trapped or injured—are not usually deemed playful. And behaviors dominated by processes of adjustment (Piaget's accommodation or the author's descending meaning) seem more like acts of imitation than playful exploit. Departing from Piaget, this author claims that intra-psychic play of the imaginative type is less an application of pre-existing "schemas" than an act of subjective resistance to (and manipulation of) those very schemas. In imaginative play, we take the world inside us and subject those now-personalized ideas and images to the same kinds of transformations that we perpetuate on external objects.

The second point is that imaginative or exploratory play follows three different pathways that parallel the three styles of play developed above. In that sense, imaginative play sometimes explores visions of *privilege*. When children (or adults) play in this way they consider what it would mean to be bigger, smarter, or more powerful. Not uncommonly those fantasies are exercises in excess. That is, in our imaginations we are not simply football players, dancers, or movie stars; we are the greatest, the most talented, the most beautiful, and so forth of these types. Alternately, we ponder over-powering situations dominated by persons we despise or fear. If in real life, we cannot address the prospect of our own *subordination*, at least we can take on our demons in our minds. In that light, children's fantasies are often attempts to confront and process our deepest concerns. However, play is not capitulation. Instead, in imaginative play we give these fears concrete shapes in our minds, attempt to control the emotions that seize us as we confront those images, and then envision strategies that help us live with these uncertainties. If in the first instance, imaginary play is a pattern of psychic indulgence, in the latter it is a pitched battle.

Commonly of course, our imaginations runs in both directions at the same time or rather feature alternating confrontations with images that are powerful and with those that are weak. We can also imagine our *engagement* with equally matched or otherwise worthy others. We picture ourselves in a swordfight with some dastardly prince: we "woolgather" about being sexually involved with some significant other. However we imagine those energetic dialogues, it is submitted here that players focus primarily on their own subjective skills and experiences and not on the equivalent experiences of the other. That is, play is typically an exploration of our own standings in the world, standings that we attain through our own efforts.

## SUMMARY

To summarize, the author in this essay has attempted to modify his own theory of play as "transformative behavior" or "ascending meaning." How people play is not simply a self-styled behavior but also a pattern of interaction based on the character of the play objects to which the player is oriented. Types of play—manipulation, rebellion, and dialogue—have been connected to distinctive patterns of relationship—privilege, subordination, and engagement. Finally, the author has focused on a fourth style of play that is encouraged by experiences of marginality, what he terms "exploratory" play. Whether playful transformation exhibits purely mental images (as in the play of the imagination), real-world objects that are laden with cognitive and emotional meaning (as in doll play), or less symbolically charged objects (as in play with blocks or balls), the message of the activity is largely the same: play is the assertive response of organisms to their standings in the world.

## REFERENCES

Bakhtin, M. (1981). *The dialogic imagination.* Austin: University of Texas Press.
Bateson, G. (1971). The message: This is play. In R. E. Herron and B. Sutton-Smith (Eds.), *Child's play* (pp. 261–269). New York: Wiley.
Berlyne, D. (1960). *Conflict, arousal, and curiosity.* New York: McGraw-Hill.

Bogardus, E. (1959). *Social distance.* Los Angeles, CA:

Caillois, R. (1961). *Man, play, and games.* New York: Free Press.

Clark, C. (2007). Role play on parade: Child, costume, and ceremonial exchange at Halloween. In D. Sluss & O. Jarrett (Ed.). *Investigating play in the 21st century: Play and Culture Studies, Vol 7* (pp. 287–306). New York: University Press of America.

Csikszentmihalyi, M. (1975). *Beyond boredom and anxiety.* San Francisco: Jossey-Bass.

Csikszentmihalyi, M. (1990). *Flow: The psychology of optimal experience.* New York: Harper and Row.

Edmiston, B. (2008). *Forming Ethical Identities in Early Childhood Play.* New York: Routledge.

Ellis, M. (1973). *Why people play.* Englewood Cliffs, NJ: Prentice-Hall.

Fagen, B. (1995). Animal Play, Games of Angels, Biology, and Brain. In A. Pellegrini (Ed.). *The future of play theory: A multidisciplinary inquiry in to the contribution of Brian Sutton-Smith* (pp. 23–44). Albany, NY: State University of New York.

Fein, G. (1987). Pretend play: Creativity and consciousness. In D. Gorlitz & J.F. Wohlwill (Eds.), *Curiosity, imagination, and play: On the development of spontaneous cognition and motivational processes* (pp. 281–304). Hillsdale, NJ: Lawrence Erlbaum.

Fine, G. (1983). *Shared fantasy: Role-playing games as social worlds.* Chicago: University of Chicago Press.

Freud, S. (1952). *A general introduction to psychoanalysis.* New York: Washington-Square.

Freud, S. (1967). *Beyond the pleasure principle.* New York: Bantam.

Geertz, C. (1972). Deep play: Notes on the Balinese cockfight. *Daedalus,* 101: 1–28.

Goffman, E. (1961) *Encounters: Two studies in the sociology of interaction.* Indianapolis: Bobbs-Merrill.

Goffman, E. (1974). *Frame analysis: An essay on the organization of experience.* New York: Harper Colophon.

Goodman, P. & Goodman, P. (1947). *Communitas: Means of livelihood and ways of life.* New York: Random House.

Groos, K. (1976). *The play of man.* New York: Arno.

Hall, G. (1917). *Youth, its education, regimen, and hygiene.* New York: Appleton.

Handelman, D. (1998). *Models and mirrors: Toward an anthropology of public events.* New York: Berghahn Books.

Hans, J. (1981). *The play of the world.* Amherst, MA: University of Massachusetts Press.

Heidegger, M. (1962). *Being and time.* New York: Harper and Row.

Henricks, T. (1999). Play as ascending meaning: Implications of a general model of play. In S. Reifel (Ed.), *Play contexts revisited: Play and Culture Studies, Vol 2* (pp. 257–277). Stamford, CT: Ablex.

Henricks, T. (2001). Play and postmodernism. In S. Reifel (Ed.) *Theory in context and out: Play and Culture Studies, Vol 3* (pp. 51–72). Westport, CT: Ablex.

Henricks, T. (2002). Huizinga's contributions to play studies: A reappraisal. In J. Roopnarine (Ed.), *Conceptual, social-cognitive, and contextual issues in the fields of play: Play and Culture Studies, Vol 4* (pp. 23–52). Westport, CT: Ablex.

Henricks, T. (2006). *Play reconsidered: Sociological perspectives on human expression.* Urbana, IL: University of Illinois.

Henricks, T. (2009). Play and the rhetorics of time: Progress, regression, and the meanings of the present. In D. Kuschner (Ed.), From children to red hatters: Diverse images and issues of play. *Play and Culture Studies* 8. New York: University Park Press.

Huizinga, J. (1955). *Homo ludens: A study of the play-element in culture.* Boston; Beacon.

James, W. (1952). *Principles of Psychology.* Chicago, IL: Encyclopedia Britannica.

Lancy, D. & Tindall, B. (Eds.). (1976). *The anthropological study of play: Problems and prospects.* Cornwall, NY: Leisure Press.

Levine, D. (1971). Introduction. In G. Simmel, *On individuality and social forms* (pp. ix–lxv). D. Levine (Ed.). Chicago, IL: University of Chicago.

Levy, J. (1978). *Play behavior.* New York: John Wiley and Sons.

Lieberman, J. (1977). *Playfulness: Its relationship to imagination and creativity.* New York: Academic Press.

Lin, S-H. & Reifel, S. (1999). Context and meanings in Taiwanese kindergarten play. In S. Reifel (Ed.), *Play contexts revisited: Play and Culture Studies, Vol 2* (pp. 151–176). Stamford, CT: Ablex.

Marx, K. (1964). *Selected writings in sociology and social philosophy.* T. Bottomore (Ed. and Trans.). New York: McGraw-Hill.

Marx, K. (1999). Economic and philosophical manuscripts. T. Bottomore (Trans.). In E. From *Marx's Concept of Man* (pp. 87–196). New York: Continuum.

McMahon, F. (1999). 'Playing with play': Germany's carnival as aesthetic nonsense. In S. Reifel (Ed.), *Play contexts revisited: Play and Culture Studies, Vol 2* (pp.177–190). Stamford, CT: Ablex.

McMahon, F. (2007). Community play at the mall. In D. Sluss & O. Jarrett (Ed.), *Investigating play in the 21st century: Play and Culture Studies, Vol 7* (pp. 233–254). New York: University Press of America.

Mead, G.H. (1964). *On social psychology.* A. Strauss (Ed.). Chicago: University of Chicago Press.

Millar, S. (1968). *The Psychology of Play.* Baltimore: Penguin.

Miller, S. (1973). Ends, means, and galumphing: Some leitmotfs of play. *American Anthropologist,* 75–98.

Opie, I., & Opie, P. (1969). *Children's games in the street and playground.* New York: Oxford University Press.

Ottenberg, S. (2005). *Playful performers: African children's masquerades.* New York: Transaction Publishers.

Pellegrini, A. (Ed.). (1995). *The future of play theory: A multidisciplinary inquiry into the contribution of Brian Sutton-Smith.* Albany, NY: State University of New York.

Piaget, J. (1962). Play, dreams, and imitation in childhood. NY: Norton.

Piaget, J. (1965). *The moral judgment of the child.* New York: Free Press.

Roopnarine, J., Johnson, J., & Hooper, F. (1994). *Children's play in diverse cultures.* Albany: State University of New York Press.

Rosenau, P. (1992). *Post-modernism and the social sciences: Insights, inroads, intrusions.* Princeton, NJ: Princeton University Press.

Sawyers, J. and Carrick, N. (2003). Symbolic play through the eyes and words of children. In D. Lytle (Ed.), *Play and education theory and practice: Play and Culture Studies, Vol 5* (pp. 159–182). Westport, CT: Praeger.

Schwartzman, H. (1978). *Transformations:The anthropology of children's play.* New York: Plenum.

Simmel, G. (1950). *The sociology of Georg Simmel.* K. Wolff (Trans. and Ed.). New York: Free Press.

Singer, J. (1992). *The house of make-believe.* Cambridge, MA: Harvard University Press.

Singer, J. (1995). Imaginative play in childhood: Precursor of subjunctive thought, daydreaming, and adult pretending games. In A. Pellegrini (Ed.). *The future of play theory: A multidisciplinary inquiry in to the contribution of Brian Sutton-Smith* (pp. 187–219). Albany, NY: State University of New York.

Spariosu, M. (1989). *Dionysus reborn: Play and the aesthetic dimension in modern philosophical and scientific discourse.* Ithaca, NY: Cornell University Press.

Stonequist, E. (1937). *The marginal man.* New York: Scribner's.

Sutton-Smith, B. (1966). Piaget on play: A critique. *Psychological Review* 73:104–110.

Sutton-Smith, B. (1977). The dialectics of play. In F. Landry and W. Oban (Eds.). *Physical activity and human well-being.* Miami, FL: Symposia Specialists.

Sutton-Smith, B. (1997). *The ambiguity of play.* Cambridge, MA: Harvard University Press.

Sutton-Smith, B. & Kelly-Byrne, D. (1984a). The idealization of play. In P. Smith (Ed.), *Play in animals and humans* (pp. 305–321). London: Basil Blackwell.

Sutton-Smith, B. & Kelly-Byrne, D. (1984b). The phenomenon of bipolarity in play theories. In T. Yawkey & A. Pellegrini (Eds.), *Child's play: Development and applied.* (pp. 29–47). Hillsdale, NJ: Laurence Erlbaum.

Sutton-Smith, B., Mechling, J., Johnson, T., & McMahon, F. (1995). *Children's folklore: a sourcebook.* New York: Garland.

Turner, V. (1969). *The ritual process: Structure and anti-structure.* Chicago: Aldine.

# Contributors

**Mira Tetkowski Berkley** is an Associate Professor and Coordinator of the Early Childhood Program at SUNY Fredonia. She has been involved in the field of early childhood care and education for over 30 years. Before working in higher education, she spent 15 years as an early childhood classroom teacher. She is an advocate for play-based experiential learning which she has recently had the opportunity to explore in Wales, UK and northern Italy.

**Thomas Henricks** is the Danieley Professor of Sociology at Elon University. His scholarship examines the organization of human experience in societies, with special focus on play. He is the author of numerous writings on play and related subjects. His most recent book is Play Reconsidered: Sociological Perspectives on Human Expression, published in 2006 by the University of Illinois Press.

**Robyn Holmes** is a Professor of Psychology at Monmouth University where she teaches courses in anthropology, child development, play and folklore and qualitative methods. Her recent research focuses on cheating at play, play at mealtime, and parental attitudes toward play. Her writings include How Young Children Perceive Race, Fieldwork with Children, and numerous chapters and articles on play.

**Nina Howe** is a Professor of Early Childhood and Elementary Education in the Department of Education, Concordia University, Montreal, Quebec, Canada and holds the Concordia University Research Chair in Early Childhood Development and Education. Her work is in the area of young children's social, cognitive, and emotional development, specifically play and curriculum. She has also worked extensively in the area of sibling relationships in early and middle childhood with a focus on pretend play, conflict, and teaching. Currently she is co-editing a book on new directions in early childhood education in Canada.

**Hui-Chin Hsu** is an Associate Professor in the Department of Child and Family Development, University of Georgia. Her research interests are in social interaction between mothers and infants and peer interaction between preschoolers. One of her recent research investigations examines the contribution of mother-infant interaction to later social understanding in preschoolers.

**Patricia Janes** is a Visiting Assistant Professor in the Department of Psychology, College of Charleston. Her research interests focus on the cognitive development of preschool and school-aged children. As a graduate student of Hui-Chin Hsu, she studied the social interactions of preschool children during pretend play. Her most recent work is on the development of mathematical strategies in early elementary children.

**Rachana Karnik** is a PhD student in the Department of Human Development and Family Studies at the University of North Carolina at Greensboro, United States. She has completed her undergraduate and master's degrees in India, at the Maharaja Sayajirao University of Baroda. Her master's thesis focused on the social construction of fatherhood in the Indian context. She has worked on various child- and adolescent-related projects in India before coming to the United States. Broadly, she is interested in theoretically driven cross-cultural and context-sensitive research. Her dissertation and current research interests focus on examining the everyday play activities of young children in India. She is also interested in parents' beliefs regarding their children's play activities.

**Sandra Chang Kredl** is a lecturer in the Department of Education at Concordia University in Monreal, Quebec, and is completing her doctorate in Curriculum Studies in the Department of Integrated Studies in Education at McGill University. Her research interests include the study of children's symbolic play, the discursive formation of childhood in literature and film, and the use of memory work with early childhood teachers. She has contributed publications in the areas of curriculum studies in early childhood education, media studies, and childhood studies.

**Kate Mahoney** is an Assistant Professor in the Department of Language, Learning, and Leadership at SUNY Fredonia where she teaches courses in educational research and teaching English as a second language (TESOL). Through her research, she evaluates policies surrounding the assessment of language minority students in public schools. Dr. Mahoney's current research addresses the validity of using achievement and language proficiency test scores for English Language Learners (ELLs), language minority program effectiveness through meta-analysis, and evaluating policies and practices concerning ELLs in Arizona and nationally.

**Gail Melson** is a Professor of Child Development and Family Studies and a member of the Center for the Human-Animal Bond at Purdue University where she conducts research on the role of animals in children's development. Dr. Melson is the author of the book, *Why the Wild Things Are: Animals in the Lives of Children* (Harvard University Press, 2001), also published in Chinese and French editions, as well as over 20 articles or book chapters related to children and animals. She received her B.A. *cum laude* from Harvard University in philosophy and M.S. and Ph.D from Michigan State University in psychology. Dr. Melson's latest research focuses on children's interactions with and understanding of robotic pets.

**Eva Nwokah** is an Associate Professor of Communications Sciences and Disorders, University of North Carolina at Greensboro. She has held faculty and clinical positions in four countries. Her research interests are in language, play, narrative skills, and social interaction in families, between mothers and infants, and child peer interaction. Her recent work has focused on humor and language play in social interaction. She has been actively involved in local adolescent parenting programs and the implementation of clinical and educational support for language and literacy intervention with high risk families.

**Michael Patte** is an Associate Professor of Education at Bloomsburg University. For ten years he worked as a public school teacher and in his interactions with children he developed an appreciation for the precious stage of life known as childhood where self-directed, spontaneous, and freely chosen play reign supreme. It is through these interactions that his interest in promoting, preserving, and protecting children's play began. Dr. Patte has shared his work on children's play through journal articles, book chapters, international and national conference presentations, and advocacy projects. Recently, Dr. Patte was awarded a Distinguished Scholars Fulbright Lecturing/Research Scholarship to study the field of Playwork at Leeds Metropolitan University in the United Kingdom in the Spring of 2010 under the direction of Dr. Fraser Brown.

**Jihyun Sung** received her doctoral degree from the Department of Child and Family Development, University of Georgia. Currently she is a Postdoctoral Research Fellow at the Department of Education and the Department of Molecular Biology, Cell Biology, and Biochemistry, Brown University. Her research focuses on the interaction between mothers and young children and the development of young children's social and cognitive development.

**Michelle Tannock** is an Assistant Professor of Early Childhood Education at the University of Nevada, Las Vegas. Her research area encompasses early childhood education with an emphasis on play behaviors, educator training, and parent involvement. She has coordinated and participated in a series of studies examining the role of rough and tumble play in early childhood settings, the form and use of kindness by young children, and inclusive early childhood programming.

**Jonathan Tudge** is a Professor in the Department of Human Development and Family Studies, University of North Carolina at Greensboro and has also been a visiting professor in Brazil and Estonia. His research examines cultural-ecological aspects of young children's development both within and across a number of different societies, particularly focusing on the years prior to and immediately following the entry to school. He has written *The everyday lives of young children: Culture, class, and child rearing in diverse societies*, published by Cambridge University Press, and has also published two co-edited volumes and over 60 journal articles and book chapters.

# Index